R E |

MW00491729

Praise for *Refraction*

"A captivating and much-needed diversion from the literary tradition that declares as heroes those who venture to the Earth's poles. In *Refraction*, Bruce Rettig vividly captures the harsh environment north of the Arctic Circle and the people who earn their living there. *Refraction* honors those workers, illuminating the grueling manual labor that goes into getting oil out of the ground and into our gas tanks, while confronting the massive corporations who profit from that labor, and who have yet to be held accountable for the massive role they've played in creating the climate crisis."
—TANJA HESTER, author of *Wallet Activism*

"*Refraction* is a journey of adventure and self-discovery. Fast paced, the book brims with tales of worker comradery and the hardships of a twelve-hour workday in brutally cold weather and dangerous working conditions. Throughout these tales, Rettig weaves a subtext of personal challenges regarding his college sweetheart, the direction of his formal education, and ultimately his ideology around big business and environmental stewardship. *Refraction* is a timely and unforgettable narrative that will leave you thinking about your own personal journey as well as your place on this rock on which we live."
—RON D'ALEANA, author of *The Madness of Being*

"Opening *Refraction* is like opening a portal to another planet, where time and characters and the omnipotence of nature plunge into the unknown with the burden-heavy pace of an arctic tugboat. Rettig's writing is exquisite and the crush of reflections into the frozen canvas of his experiences pulls you directly into this wild biographical northern adventure. "
—M.C. BEHM, author of *The Elixir of Yosemite* and *Once Upon a Quarantine*

"Feel the arctic wind slap your face and the bone-chilling tundra under your feet. Absorb the beauty of the northern lights twirling in a black Alaskan sky. This book takes a deep dive into the murky waters of big oil and our love/hate relationship with filling our gas tanks. *Refraction* is timely, informative, and unforgettable."
—LISA MICHELLE, author of *Blue Mountain, Calaveras,* and *Forest Creek*

"In *Refraction*, Rettig takes the reader on an engaging journey into a remote part of the world, where surviving the constant dangers posed by Alaska's harsh environment is interwoven with a deep appreciation of the untamed beauty of the landscape. Readers will become immersed in Rettig's experiences and internal revelations as he recounts the emotions and heartbreak with coming of age, of re-evaluating the course of his life, relationships, and perceptions of the world over time, and moving toward a deeper understanding of the human and environmental consequences of our reliance on oil."
—JENNIFER QUASHNICK, author of *Trail of Murder* and *Burning Revenge*

"Through Rettig's words, I was transported to the desolate Arctic outpost. I could feel the monotony of the industrial work, the depth of relationships, and visualize the desolate landscape. His growth as a person is nearly palpable. As he learns about the area, this line of work and life, so do readers."
—KATHRYN REED, author of *Lake Tahoe Trails for All Seasons*

REFRACTION

AN ARCTIC MEMOIR

BRUCE RETTIG

WAYFARER BOOKS
BERKSHIRE MOUNTAINS, MASS.

WAYFARER BOOKS

WWW.WAYFARERBOOKS.ORG

© 2022 TEXT BY BRUCE RETTIG

Published in 2022 by Wayfarer Books
Cover Design by Bruce Rettig
Cover Photograph © Bruce Rettig
ISBN 978-1-956368-25-3
First Edition Trade Paperback

10 9 8 7 6 5 4 3 2 1

Look for our titles in paperback, ebook, and audiobook wherever books are sold. Wholesale offerings for retailers available through Ingram.

Wayfarer Books is committed to ecological stewardship. We greatly value the natural environment and invest in environmental conservation. For each book purchased in our online store we plant one tree.

For Robbin, Conner,
Brianna, and Riley

refraction

1: deflection from a straight path undergone by a light ray or energy wave in passing obliquely from one medium into another in which its velocity is different
2: the change in the apparent position of a celestial body due to bending of the light rays emanating from it as they pass through the atmosphere; also: the correction to be applied to the apparent position of a body because of this bending
3: the action of distorting an image by viewing through a medium

CONTENTS

NIGHT PASSAGE

ON THE BOOKSHELF next to my bed sits an object resembling an upside-down mason jar, but the base is rounded, not flat, and it has a swirled lip at the open end. The glass is about one-eighth-inch thick and is surrounded by a slightly dented brass cage. It's called a passageway light, and it protects a fragile lightbulb on a ship; this particular one was once attached to the wheelhouse of a tugboat so deckhands could see when working at night. I found it in 1982, over thirty years ago, in Prudhoe Bay, Alaska, crammed in the corner of a wooden crate filled with scrap items scheduled for shipment back to Seattle on a barge filled with junk and refuse.

The light cover now collects dust in my Sierra Nevada home. I wipe it clean and grasp at the memories that haven't yet slipped away like frozen deck line sliding through my hands. It's late at night, and the scenes float in different directions, and I try to pull them together the best I can, attempting to make sense of the many drifting pieces. Experiences from the years I worked for a tugboat and barge company on the North Slope of Alaska, and time spent at sea, still invade my subconscious late at night and sometimes into my sleep. I call these occasional interludes *Tugboat Dreams.*

I worked in the Prudhoe Bay oil fields of Alaska for the money. That's what I tell people when asked why I once traveled north year after year, a spring migration to one of the most remote places on earth. The answer isn't entirely true. Yes, the paychecks were larger than what a college student would ever dream of making during a summer break. The hourly pay and union-inflated overtime wages were a motivating factor, but something more pulled at me each year, tugging me to a place so far from friends and family.

It's easy to surrender to the idea that the seasonal employment was merely for the money, but looking back, the experiences garnered were more than monetary. Maybe the motivation originated in a sense of adventure or camaraderie with fellow laborers or an opportunity to prove to myself I had the toughness and stamina to work a minimum of twelve hours a day, seven days a week, in not so ideal of conditions. Or quite possibly, the main reason relied on a yearning for something, anything, that might help me better understand my life and what direction it might take and provide a greater understanding of the world. Maybe I simply longed for an escape. For better or worse, I've always been a bit of a loner and tended to buck the status quo, so heading out by myself to some unknown place and situation made perfect sense.

When I journeyed to the camp each year, I carried no more than a duffle bag stuffed with foul weather gear and a few items to get me through the season. Like most people in their early twenties, I had a lot of questions, and the more I traveled and explored, the longer the list grew. I also bore with me the weight of prior mistakes and some bad decisions, which often haunted my judgment and reasoning. The few things I thought I knew or might have believed were put to the test during my ventures north.

I hold the passageway light in my hands and have no idea what boat it once illuminated. I'm certain, however, its beam once shimmered across a deck covered by ocean mist or a layer of ice. And over the years, numerous deckhands had spun the glass free of its mount and switched out the bulb whenever it needed replacing.

I close my eyes. The light beam dances on an ice field drifting across still waters, an expansive mirror patterned with jagged blocks.

Above the horizon is a northern sky that never truly becomes dark until late fall when the ocean begins to freeze solid. The boat is riding smooth and slow, and the smell of diesel exhaust hangs in the air. Over the hum of tugboat engines and the thumping of ice against a steel hull are the voices and laughter of old shipmates and deckhands.

SEATTLE

THE BUS SQUEALED to a stop and its doors swung open to allow a group of passengers on board. A mother and her young daughter walked up the steps and took their place a few rows back. I sat on a bench seat facing the aisle. A couple of punk rockers dressed in studded black leather strutted their way to the rear. Lastly, an old man walked carefully and deliberately down the aisle, stopped, took a few steps back, then sat next to me. I shifted to the right to make more room for the man, wondering why he couldn't have taken another seat in the half-empty bus.

"Thank you," he said. He wore Ray Charles look-alike sunglasses and appeared to stare at a point hovering somewhere above the middle of the aisle. A hearing aid protruded from his ear. He was meticulously dressed in a tan suit, the color of coffee mixed with cream, his head topped with a derby hat of the same color. He clung firmly to a polished wooden cane, and a leather satchel hung from his shoulder.

"No problem." I refocused on the open book on my lap.

The whine of the bus engine filled my ears as the vehicle lurched forward. A blur of buildings swept from one window to another, ever-changing snapshots of a foggy cityscape. Alone, and in a city I had only known for two days, I acted as though I were reading my book, but mostly thinking of what lay ahead.

I had spent my share of time as a commuter on mass transit as a kid growing up in San Francisco's East Bay area, and that mode of transportation had lost its novelty some time back. Buses were not only crammed with passengers, but also with memories of obnoxious high schoolers, panhandling homeless, and unruly drunks on their way home to their fractured families. But today felt different. Maybe because I was in the Pacific Northwest, in new surroundings. Instead of the stifling effect of memories, the bus I rode that morning in May served as a launching point for a grand adventure with no preconceptions of the future. In short, I was in my early twenties and had no idea what I was doing—and it was exhilarating.

"Are you a man or woman?"

"Excuse me?" I said to the old man sitting next to me.

"I'm sorry. I don't mean to be rude." He adjusted his dark glasses but didn't turn to look at me. "I'm approximately ninety percent blind, and I only see dark shapes during the day and a few bright lights at night. My hearing is not what it should be, either."

"Oh, I'm sorry." The thick-framed dark glasses and cane now made sense, and I felt a twinge of pity for the man.

"It's perfectly fine. I only wanted to know who I sat next to."

"I'm a guy, in my early twenties—soon to be on my way to Alaska for the summer."

"Oh, I see. And what are your plans in Alaska?"

"Summer job. I'm working at a camp at the end of the pipeline—a tugboat and barge company."

I had an earlier meeting at the Crowley Maritime office, but it was probably painfully obvious to the company rep that I didn't know where I was going or what awaited me. When he asked if I had any foul weather gear, my blank face told him I didn't know what he was talking about. He took out a pad of paper and instructed me to pick up supplies in town at the local outfitting store, and he scribbled a list of gear to get me through the season; the receptionist at the front desk would provide directions to West Marine where

I could purchase everything. After then, I needed to stop by the Inlandboatmen's Union to complete some paperwork.

"So this is a seasonal employment opportunity for you?" the man asked.

"Yeah, I'm a college student at the University of Colorado—been out there for a little over a year. I'll head back to school after a summer up north." I thought of all the classes I needed to pass before graduating, of how much of a change it had been transferring from a small rural community college in California to a large university. The first couple of semesters had been tough. I wondered if I was in search of an answer or running away from one. Maybe a thin line existed between the two.

"And what about you?" I asked, more out of politeness rather than genuine interest. "Where are you headed?"

"Oh, as usual, I have a lot on my agenda." He leaned against his cane as if the question had added an undue weight. "You see, I'm an inventor."

"An inventor?"

"Yes, an inventor." His head angled upward slightly as he talked. "I'm very good with numbers, and that talent is critical to everything I create."

From my limited experience with people who called themselves inventors, I came to realize most of these individuals seemed to be nothing more than gold seekers looking for one quick idea to create a lifetime's worth of riches.

"Have you ever invented anything that sold?"

"Oh, yes, many little things, but they all have a specific function. Even if you've never thought much about them, they all serve a purpose. Like this one." The man reached calmly into his satchel then opened his hand. In his palm resided a small plastic tube, like a straw cut in half but of heavier material, slightly flattened and slit down the middle.

"What is it?"

"Painters and other men of labor spend day after day carrying buckets with wire handles that cut into their hands. But I thought of this idea: a plastic wrap that slips onto the wire to make it easier to hold onto. And it won't hurt one's hand."

"Huh," I said, intrigued by the modest design but not hugely impressed.

"I've invented other things, fairly simple like this one, but all very functional. Sometimes the best ideas are the easiest ones to produce." He put the plastic handle wrap back into his satchel. I wondered what other items rested alongside it or ideas bounced around within the creative enclave inside the man's head. Although he couldn't see my face, I could tell he sensed my curiosity.

"Something I found very important, and what I learned long ago, is that most inventions are not complete by themselves. Many of them evolve over time, and they might even change, or combine with other creations that have an entirely different purpose. Hopefully, they all come together to create things that are useful to people."

The odd little man spoke in a simple but eloquent way, rendering clarity and truth. In his comfort and confidence, I pondered all the possibilities that lay in front of me and felt as though he might hold deeper insights. Things that strangers share are often more meaningful than they realize.

The punkers in the back of the bus turned up the volume on their boom box, and the Dead Kennedys screeched out their version of "I Fought the Law." The mother put her arm around her daughter and held her closer as a man with a marine-style haircut turned around and shouted, "Turn that shit down!"

The brakes squealed as the bus pulled over at its next stop. I looked at the street corner sign.

"This is my stop," I said, slightly disappointed that I didn't have an opportunity to spend more time talking with the man. For a moment, I thought about traveling a little farther up the line and catching a bus back to my destination, but I knew I had to keep on schedule if I wanted to pick up my supplies, and I didn't know how long it would take to complete the paperwork at the union office.

"Good luck on your journey," the man said and continued to look forward.

"Thanks," I replied. "And good luck with your inventions."
I made my way to the door. To the left of the bus, a delivery truck blasted its horn and the bus driver opened his window and craned his neck. Halfway down the steps, I turned to take one last look at the man.

"Be good to people, and great things will happen for you," he said.

That's it? I thought to myself. *That's the great message this guy is leaving me with?*

He then turned his head, looked toward me, and took off his glasses.

His eyes were a hazy white, reminding me of the heavy fog that blanketed the city. For what felt like a slight fraction of a second, it seemed as though I could see inside the man's soul, and he could see inside mine. I can never adequately describe how I felt at that moment, but I remember a cyclone of numbers filling my head, as if spinning at the speed of light.

The bus driver turned, looked at me, and said, "Gettin' off?" I stammered something in reply, then made my way to the bottom of the stairway and stepped out onto the street. I stood alone on the sidewalk as a thick billow of dark exhaust enveloped me, and the bus disappeared into the Seattle traffic.

DEADHORSE

ANCHORAGE INTERNATIONAL AIRPORT terminal, embellished with everything "Alaska," included a huge stuffed polar bear behind a wall of glass near the main walkway. A clear blue sky made it difficult to imagine a city frozen solid during subzero weather. If it hadn't been for the Alaskan decor, my layover could have been at any airport within the lower forty-eight.

Fairbanks International Airport was a lot smaller, and I spent time between flights filling out the Alaska Airlines membership form. If I logged enough miles with the airline, they would send me tiny gold ingots along with other rewards. Taking my seat on the plane and tightening my seat belt, I worried about what might happen if my duffel bag hadn't transferred. Dressed in jeans, flannel shirt, down jacket, and hiking boots, I considered the distinct possibility that I could be wearing the same attire for who knew how long.

"Another trip to Prudhoe, huh?" said the man sitting across the aisle from me.

"Yeah," I replied hesitantly. "Actually, it's my first time up there."

"Ah, a greenhorn." He grinned. "I've been working as a cook at the ARCO camp for over five years, but I still remember my first stint—I almost flew back home the very next day."

A thin smile often appeared across the faces of those who spoke of Prudhoe Bay, as if they held an inside joke shared by a select club. When I left the Inlandboatmen's Union in Seattle earlier in the week, the personnel director made a final statement as I walked out of the office. "Prudhoe Bay might not be the end of the world, but you sure as hell can see it from there."

Our metal tube with wings cruised across the sky with less than twenty passengers, a mere speck above the Alaskan terrain. The state's vastness was difficult to comprehend. The landscape looked as though someone had taken a huge knife and slashed at it in haphazard swipes. Broad areas, void of any cities or towns, pushed against towering mountain ranges. Rivers and lakes dotted the topography, glaciers feeding many of them with white streams of water. A massive mountain came into view, dwarfing the surrounding country.

Known locally by Alaskans as Denali, or "the high one," a huge mountain peak pointed upward like a giant monolith. I had read at the Anchorage airport that Denali stands as the tallest in the world from base to summit, rising over 18,000 feet to its 20,310 foot total height, and its icy north face is one of the world's highest at 14,000 feet.

"I've flown over the Rockies and past Mount Rainier in Washington, but I've never seen a mountain like that." I cupped my hand above my eyes to block the glare of the sun.

"You from Colorado?" the man asked.

"Yeah, but I'm originally from California," I replied. "I grew up in the San Francisco Bay Area, but my folks retired and moved to the Sierra foothills—a little town named Rail Road Flat."

Home. That was an abstract concept. I lived in Boulder, Colorado, for most of the year, but family and friends kept me tethered to Northern California. I now journeyed as far north as the continent would allow.

Several hours passed, the deep folds and wrinkles of land flattening as the plane continued northward. A long mountain range gave way to an expanse of frozen tundra, a conglomeration of snow, ice, and pools of water.

The Brooks Range ran east to west, like a boundary marker

before entering an arctic abyss. Past the range the land appeared flat and lifeless, void of trees or any other large foliage. Alaska's North Slope is defined as the area north of the range with two Arctic Ocean seas: the Chukchi Sea to the west of Point Barrow, and the Beaufort Sea to the east. The Beaufort Sea includes Prudhoe Bay, located over three hundred miles north of the Arctic Circle. Underneath the North Slope was an ancient seabed, the source of vast fossil fuel reserves.

"There's the pipeline." The man tapped on the window.

Below us, one of the world's largest pipeline systems zigzagged across the tundra: the Trans-Alaska Pipeline. Completed in 1977 at a cost of eight billion dollars, it was the primary artery for crude oil flowing from Prudhoe Bay to Valdez.

"Why are there angles—why isn't it straight?"

"It compensates for expansion and contraction, so it won't break because of hot and cold weather changes." The man rubbed his chin. "About seven hundred thousand barrels a day run through it, from what I hear. Of course, the oil companies don't like to share a lot of exact numbers—they're as secretive as the fuckin' government."

I knew little about the history of the pipeline, only that it existed and remained a huge economic boom for the state of Alaska. Over time, I pieced together the background of the project and learned the controversy over its construction.

Heated political debates followed the discovery of oil at Prudhoe Bay in 1968, followed by the Kuparuk River oil field in 1969. The oil crisis of 1973 caused a sharp rise in prices in the United States, and the higher costs made exploration of the Prudhoe Bay oil field economically viable. Legislation soon passed to remove legal oppositions to the project, including challenges set forth by Native Alaskans, which I learned later in greater detail. Pipeline construction took place between 1974 and 1977. According to the United States Geological Survey (USGS) the entire area of the North Slope held over fifty billion barrels of oil and natural-gas liquids, and 227 trillion cubic feet of gas. The region included the Arctic National Wildlife Refuge, a focal point of controversy. Petroleum drilling within ANWR boundaries had often attracted consideration.

As a geology major with an emphasis in Paleontology, I had

been looking for a summer internship. Paleontologists often worked in oil exploration, and my professor at CU had spent many years employed by oil companies in Saudi Arabia. I considered myself environmentally conscious, but also pragmatic about how I viewed large industry. I believed companies like Shell and Exxon most likely tried to minimize their impact on the land. They were highly successful, and therefore it made no sense for them to take undue risks that might damage their ability to extract oil. The world needed fuel, and they provided it—simple enough in my mind.

My uncle served as vice president of one of the largest maritime corporations in the world, Crowley Maritime, a company contracted by the oil companies. I inquired if there were any internship opportunities with the oil companies, and my uncle said he would look into it. When he got back to me, he said there was nothing presently available, but there were openings for laborers in the Alaska North Slope at Arctic Marine Freighters, a division of Crowley Maritime. After he told me the wage, I jumped at the opportunity to travel north.

"We're now approaching Prudhoe Bay airstrip," the pilot announced. "Please fasten your seat belts and prepare for landing. The present temperature is eighteen degrees."

The runway approached—a thin strip stretching like a scar across the frozen tundra, then an unsettling rush as we slid across the tarmac.

The airport stretched alongside the community of Deadhorse, an outpost whose buildings consisted mainly of storage units and facilities for the workers and companies that operated at the nearby Prudhoe Bay oil fields and outlying company camps. Its population fluctuated anywhere between twenty-five and three thousand residents, depending on the time of year and amount of activity in the oil fields.

The plane came to a stop and a couple of airstrip workers rolled a metal stairway to its side allowing us to debark onto the runway. A few hundred feet away stood a building not much larger than a gas station back home, resembling a roadside stop found in the middle of the Nevada desert. We disembarked the plane and walked toward the Deadhorse Airport.

A blast of frigid air swept through my jacket. An immediate chill crept into my body core, and I realized that no amount of clothing could completely fend off the new environment we had stepped into. The terrain and surrounding cluster of ramshackle structures all appeared to be faded, as if the dry arctic air had sucked all the hues and tones out of them, leaving only a hint of flat gray-brown.

The office manager at Crowley Maritime had said that a man named Joel Burckhalter would meet and drive me out to the AMF camp. The luggage was unloaded, and I was happy to see that my duffel bag had been transferred. I grabbed the handle of the three-and-a-half-foot-long bag stuffed with everything needed to get me through the next four months.

The passengers streamed into the airport waiting room, and for the first time I realized I had no idea what Joel Burckhalter looked like. Several men leaned against a wall, all appearing both tired and bored, with bags under their eyes and wind-burned slackened cheeks. One of them, a shorter dark-haired man with a mustache, wore a blue cap with a company logo—a large letter "C," and "Arctic Marine Freighters" stitched underneath it. Inside the Crowley "C" was the silhouette of a polar bear head, its mouth agape.

"Mr. Burckhalter?"

"Yeah—Rettig?"

"Yes, sir."

"Call me Joel. Truck's out front."

We walked outside onto a mixture of ice, frozen mud, and stagnant water puddles. Joel opened the driver's door and slid behind the wheel of the Chevy long-bed pickup. Most of the vehicle blended with the surrounding mud, and any surface that did not feature the local color was a faded industrial yellow. I took the passenger's seat. Above us, the arctic sun hovered in a pastel sky, reminding me of a gloomy water painting.

"When does it get dark around here?" I looked at my watch.

"October," Joel said, showing no change in facial expression.

We made our way through Deadhorse, a mix of trailers, Quonset huts, and other prefabs—a haphazard cluster of structures built of aluminum, steel, and rubber. Instead of streets, angular gravel roads jutted between structures resting on gravel pads. We passed the Prudhoe Bay Hotel, nothing more than a couple rows of travel trailers stuck together, then drove past the Prudhoe Bay General Store, another building that looked like a decent gust of wind might send it cartwheeling across the tundra.

We bounced across potholes, mud and ice splashing against the truck's undercarriage as we passed trucking camps and other heavy equipment facilities. Joel turned the heater fan to high and put on a pair of sunglasses that had been sliding back and forth across the dashboard.

"Welcome to Prudhoe Bay, Bruce. What you see is what you get."

We negotiated a turn at the outer edge of Deadhorse and drove until we reached a security gate. Passing through the checkpoint, we traveled along a packed gravel road that sat several feet higher than the tundra and stretched out into the oil fields—a vast horizon of nothingness pockmarked with drill rigs and a network of pipelines.

SUCK 'EM UPS

THE ARCTIC MARINE FREIGHTERS camp was located at the end of a two-and-a-half-mile gravel road called a "causeway" that stretched into Prudhoe Bay like a large finger pointing north. Where the causeway began, and the land ended, was a little over fifteen miles from Deadhorse. My home for the next several months resided as far north as you could travel on land, and another two and a half miles into an arctic bay. Frozen seawater surrounded both sides of the road, fractured ice uplifting onto the gravel embankments.

"Welcome home," Joel said when we reached the end of the causeway and pulled up to the AMF camp.

The camp resembled a scrapyard partially covered with snow and ice. No other location we had passed looked as rough as this one. I realized some structures were barges and on top of them rested a myriad of equipment, storage vans, and containers, like unrecognizable carcasses strewn across metal slabs. Jetting upward from barges farther down the row were radio antennas, insect-like against the dull gray sky. The camp floated, or more accurately, remained trapped in ice at the tip of the causeway.

Great. If there's an official end of the line, both physically and metaphorically, this is it.

I climbed out of the truck and grabbed my duffel bag from the back. Two small barges caught my eye. They floated in an area that had begun to thaw, creating a mini lagoon. Each barge had a row of large white hoses and a small blue shack on their deck. On their sides, stenciled white lettering designated SUCK 'EM UP NO. 1, and SUCK 'EM UP NO. 2. Joe noticed me studying the shacks.

"Another one of The Bear's experiments."

"The Bear?"

"Bill Payne. Our boss."

They certainly are hung up with bears—a stuffed one at the airport behind glass, one used in the AMF company logo, and even the boss was named after the large mammal. *Must be an icon of the north.*

We made our way up a gangplank to one of the small barges, walked across the deck, and then up another gangplank to a larger barge. Our footsteps emitted a hollow echo across the metal-framed walkway. I still couldn't understand where anyone could sleep in the monstrosity of outbuildings and equipment. A drone of a generator filled the air, as did the smell of diesel, rusting metal, and frozen seawater.

"Your room's up this catwalk—second story."

A stairway angled alongside what looked like trailers from a trailer park, stacked two high, three rows deep. From the number of doors, it looked like each one had three living quarters. At the very top corner of the conglomeration of boxes, rested one long unit, and a slightly higher smaller unit with windows on each side, allowing a full view of the camp and Prudhoe Bay.

"You're in number two, with Townsend and Ronnie. We'll have some work for you in the morning."

I opened the door and walked into my quarters. The area, approximately twenty feet long by fifteen feet wide, reminded me of the spare room in my grandmother's mobile home where I used to visit as a kid. Two bunk beds ran lengthwise along each of the walls, and a table with an ashtray stuffed with cigarette butts resided near the one and only window. A row of four closets spanned the shorter wall.

Four workers live in one room? No way.

A growing pool of water meandered across the floor. Drops splattered down from the roof, feeding the flow toward my feet. I had descended into trailer trash status. I turned the knob on the heater—lifeless.

My first year at the University of Colorado included classes held in buildings with textured sandstone walls and red-tiled roofs, their architectural design described as "Tuscan vernacular revival." As a part-time job, I bartended at nights and on weekends, having earned my "mixology" degree at the International Bartending Institute in Denver. I proudly created perfectly mixed drinks as waitresses in short black skirts served them to high-tipping customers. I had begun a serious relationship with a girl who grew up in Denver whose father was a geologist, and she and I spent time away from school exploring the Rocky Mountains and greatly enjoying each other's company. In short, life had been good back in Boulder, Colorado.

I took another look around the room. Cheap paneled walls, well-worn scuffed linoleum floor with no carpeting or rugs, and one nonfunctional wall heater—all to be shared by four coworkers after a twelve-hour workday. Outside the window was a field of ice that stretched about thirteen hundred miles to the top of the world—the North Pole. The room served as a personal torture chamber in a frozen hell.

I wasn't a novice at roughing it. My uncles had taken me hunting, fishing, and camping ever since I was old enough to walk. As a teenager, I had backpacked almost one hundred miles through the backcountry of the Trinity Alps. I skied, hiked, and biked whenever I had the chance. But standing in that room, for the first time in my life I questioned myself. I didn't see how it could possibly work. I had never been in a situation where I wanted to do nothing more than run in the opposite direction as fast as I could; serious doubts about spending one more minute there seeped into my head. *How difficult would it be to find Joel Burckhalter and have a talk with him?*

The sound of footsteps on the metal grate catwalk signaled approaching workers. The door swung open and hit the inside wall with a bang as two men walked in. One had longish dark hair and a matching beard; the other was tall, well over six feet, with blond-red hair and a half-grown beard. Both wore the same kind of Carhartt coveralls that were stuffed in my duffel bag—but theirs were dirty and worn.

"Hey," the man with the dark beard said.

"Hi." I extended my hand. "I'm Bruce."

"We heard we were getting another roommate." We shook hands. "They're really going to pack the camp this year. I'm Ken—Ken Townsend. The tall guy's Ronnie."

"How's it going?" Ronnie reached out and we shook hands. The small stream falling to the floor caught his eye. "What the heck?"

"Damn." Ken took a towel out of one of the closets and threw it on top of the water. "Everything in camp is thawing out. Someone'll have to take a look at the roof. I noticed our heater died this morning, too."

I stood before them and looked down at my duffel bag.

"The top two bunks are empty—take your choice," Ken said. "The locker at the end is empty, and you can throw your gear in there." He tapped the ashtray with his finger. "I'll smoke outside."

"No problem. I used to bartend at night—I'm used to cigarette smoke." I looked around. "Where's the men's room?"

"There is no *men's room*," Ronnie said, then smiled at Ken.

"The head's down below, under the catwalk." Ken slid open the window. He lit a cigarette, took a deep inhale, and flicked the match into the ashtray. "It's a cold walk there and back, so a lot of guys keep piss cans in their lockers."

"That's disgusting." Ronnie squinted his eyes.

Thoughts of finding Joel Burckhalter and catching the first ride out of camp began to fade. Maybe I had only been exhausted by the long trip. I could possibly ride it out for a few days and see what kind of work awaited me. I unpacked my duffel bag and stowed my gear in the locker, then set the book I had been reading on top of one of the bunks.

"Ken is an engineer," Ronnie said. "A company man—I'm a grunt."

"I guess I'm a grunt, too," I said.

"Who's your contact?"

"Contact?"

"Yeah—if you're a PA, who's your sponsor?"

"PA?"

"Yeah, 'Political Appointee.'" Ken smiled. "What's your last name?"

"Rettig."

"Ah—one of the big guys." Ken set the cigarette into the ashtray. He leaned over and took off his boots. "If you're not a full-time employee, you have to know someone to work up here."

That made sense, especially after completing all my paperwork at the union office. To gain membership into the maritime union, you had to have a job lined up. And applying for a job in the maritime trade required possession of a union card. I had wondered how one managed to negotiate that catch-22.

"C'mon, I'll show you where the head is." Ronnie opened the door and stepped out onto the catwalk. We walked to the bottom of the stairs and he pointed to one of the doors in the lower unit. "That's the head. Sea showers only, limited to every other day." He then pointed with his thumb over his shoulder. "And that's the galley. Angelo is the cook, and he serves breakfast from five a.m. to six a.m. Work begins at 6:00 am, ends at 6:00 pm. Dinner just ended, but you can probably get a sandwich."

The head was about two-thirds the length of one unit: four stalls, five sinks, and two showers. I assumed that when the camp filled up, you had to schedule your shower based on non-peak times. Everything was basic but somewhat clean, and the hum of the camp's large generator continued to reverberate throughout the camp, like the thumping of a heartbeat.

I walked out of the bathroom, and the smell of charbroiled steak still hung in the air between the modules. In the morning, I would be the new guy walking into the galley, the greenhorn without a clue. They'd probably wonder how long I'd last.

I decided to check out the upper catwalk near my quarters. The wind had picked up, and a blast of cold air hit me in the face; there was no telling how far it had swept over the seemingly endless ice field. The camp below was an entanglement of equipment, boats, storage vans, and living units. I had no idea what any of the equipment was used for, or if it was even functional. To my eyes, it appeared as a *Sanford and Son* junkyard of the north.

I walked to the other end of the stacked living modules and overlooked the small lagoon next to the gangplank. The barges with blue shacks floated in the still water, a stenciled name on each one.

Suck 'Em Up.

FIRST MORNING

THEY SAY THE KEY TO LEARNING is being a good listener, and as the years have passed, I've valued this concept a lot more than in my early twenties. Whenever mishaps have occurred throughout my life, it has mostly resulted from inattention to detail or not fully understanding or comprehending the task at hand—or sometimes, pure negligence. My first season at Arctic Marine Freighters required not only focusing on what was being told, but a second skill also surfaced: observing, then imitating the actions and procedures of more skilled and knowledgeable coworkers so as not to reveal myself as a complete idiot, or worse, an injured or dead one.

The night before my first day on the job, I did a lot of thinking as I lay quietly in what they called the "top rack" as my roommates Ken and Ronnie slept in the lower bunks. There were two objectives in my plan of attack: 1) If I was going to give this job a decent shot I needed to blend into the crew and my surroundings the best I could (a tactic still taken when in unfamiliar surroundings or situations), and 2) I needed to work my ass off.

My father had instilled a strong work ethic in me. He had spent most of his years at Alameda Naval Air Station, and he knew how to get a job completed, come hell or high water. And my mother's father had immigrated to the United States from Sweden, then worked several years in a lumber mill (sacrificing five fingers in the process) to earn enough money to purchase over three hundred acres in northern California, where he became a ranch owner. My mother's side of the family were all ranchers and farmers, and combined with my father's Navy and civil service experience, hard labor and following orders by superiors were not new concepts to me. There were a couple of challenges, however—I had absolutely no clue about seagoing vessels, heavy equipment, or living in a seasonal Arctic work camp.

Ronnie had shown me where the warm-up shack was located when I first arrived at camp. It was an overly heated unit with rows of hooks on its inside walls, and an area along the floor to pile work boots. Only nine or ten of the hooks were presently being used. I hung my new Carhartt coveralls, and placed my work gloves and Sorel boots underneath as Ronnie suggested, preventing the embarrassment of walking into the galley the next morning fully dressed in foul weather gear purchased only a few days prior. I instead entered the galley in a pair of worn jeans, faded gray hoodie, and tennis shoes.

The smell of bacon and eggs permeated the confined area, a room not much larger than a four-table coffee shop. Ken sat at one table, and another man reading a paper sat near the corner. At the end of the room was a metal counter, the kitchen behind it. A man behind the counter greeted me in a muffled Rodney Dangerfield-like voice, which belied a personality focused on the work at hand.

"Good morning," I said, wiping the sleep out of my eyes.

"Whatta ya know? I'm Angelo."

"Hey, Angelo—I'm Bruce."

"What'll it be today, Bruce—anything you want—eggs, ham, sausage, bacon, pancakes? Eggs any way you want 'em. Over easy, scrambled—whatever you want."

"How 'bout two eggs over easy, ham, and a couple slices of toast."

"Hash browns? Ya like hash browns?"

"Yeah, that sounds good."

"Hash browns sound good—you got it." He turned and walked to the stove. "Hah, what a racket."

I walked to a nearby table with coffee and juice dispensers and poured myself a hot cup o' Joe. Seattle newspapers spread across another table told old news but provided something to read while eating breakfast.

The galley door swung open, and a short man walked in. He took off his gray knitted cap revealing hair like silver and black wire, and he scratched at the side of a full, matching beard with his stubby fingers. He wore a faded Pendleton shirt, and if you were to form a picture in your mind of what a crusty old mariner might look like, this was it.

Angelo swung around with a perfectly prepared plate of breakfast and slid it across the top of the stainless-steel counter to me. "Here ya go."

"Thanks," I said, then took a seat at the table with Ken. "G'morning."

"Hey." Ken spread jam across a piece of toast with a knife. "That guy who just walked in is Jack Bourke—he'll tell you what to do."

Angelo switched his attention to Bourke, who made his way to the counter. "Jack Bourke, whatta ya know?"

"Every day's a holiday, and every meal's a banquet," Bourke bellowed.

"Hah! What a racket, what a racket," Angelo responded.

"Scrambled eggs, bacon, and toast loaded with lots of butter," Bourke said to Angelo. "Or better yet, make it a shitload of butter with a dab of toast."

Bourke strutted over to the coffee table and poured himself a hot cup, then turned and sat at the table with Ken and me.

"Morning," he said, one eye squinting behind a swirl of coffee steam.

"Good morning," I replied.

"You Rettig?"

"Yes, sir."

"I'm Jack Bourke. You can call me Jack—some call me Bourke. Either's fine, just don't call me late for dinner." He shot a wink. Twisted wrinkles at the corners of his eyes and his face framed by a bedraggled beard told a story of hard workdays, and late nights.

"More guys'll be coming into camp in a few weeks. Ken and Ronnie got up here early. I heard you guys were puttin' a swimming pool in your room."

"What?"

"The leak in your roof—we'll get it fixed."

"Scrambled eggs, bacon, toast with lots of butter—*lots* of butter!" Angelo shouted.

Bourke got his breakfast. "Thanks, Angelo," he said, then sat back down. "I'm not sure what you'll be doing yet. The Bear'll have something for you."

After breakfast, I walked with Bourke to the warm-up shack. There was something hanging on one of the walls that I hadn't noticed the night before—most likely the result of sleep deprivation. A telephone. Bourke saw me eying it as though it was a lost treasure.

"That's the only telephone in camp and it's to be used *only after work*—no other time." Bourke pointed to the phone with his cup of coffee. "During Sealift with so many in camp, it's tough to get a call out of this damn place." He reached to a shelf above the line of hooks and grabbed an orange hardhat. "Brain-bucket. Wear it around heavy equipment—or not." A long row of hardhats lined up on the shelf told me there would be many more workers in camp.

After putting on my coveralls, boots, and hardhat, we walked across *Barge 213* and crossed a wooden plank that served as walkway to the next barge, the *212*, known as the van barge. We made our way to the tool van, a container filled with almost everything needed to keep tugboats and barges afloat and diesel engines running. A space heater at the rear kept the van as warm as possible, a magnet for tired workers. It was the ultimate wrencher's paradise and a tool could be found within its confines to fix almost anything that broke. The tool van also served as one of the main gathering areas for the camp—a place for seemingly endless sea stories and mindless B.S.

"No drinking coffee on the job—or eating, either." Bourke downed the rest of his coffee and set the cup on a shelf. "We get a fifteen-minute morning break at nine, half-hour lunch at noon, and a fifteen-minute afternoon break at three—they usually have coffee, doughnuts, and other shit in the galley for the breaks." He pulled a cigarette out of his pocket and lit it, the smoke swirling out into the frigid arctic air.

"The Bear," Bourke said and stood a little straighter.

Walking across the barge was a man dressed in black Ben Davis work pants and a dark green parka with black fur around the collar. He wasn't tall, but stout and angular. He wore a white hardhat, the blue liner and ear warmer pulled tight over the top. There was a red and blue logo above the brim—the Crowley Maritime logo. I learned that "White Hat" was a designation given to upper management, since only they wore white hardhats, not orange like the workers. His mirrored glasses reflected the twisted angles and melee of equipment and structures scattered across the barge.

Following behind him was a tall man with broad shoulders and closely cropped hair. He walked deliberately, and his thin eyes gave me the impression of how a prison guard might look, with a face chiseled and wind burnt.

Bourke snuffed out his cigarette and greeted Bill Payne—"The Bear."

I walked up to him and shook his hand. "I'm Bruce Rettig."

"Lee'll show you what to do," he said with a gravelly growl, then turned and nodded to the man behind him. The Bear said nothing else directly to me for several days.

LEE

"C'MON, WE HAVE some work over on the *210*," Lee said as I followed him.

"What do the numbers on the barges mean?" I asked.

"They're the length—the *200* series are all two-hundred feet long."

We walked along a path that changed from wooden planks to packed ice and snow, then to the bare steel of whatever barge we were walking across. The path meandered between pallets of thick braided ship line, anchor chains, and drums piled high on top of white Pee Vees. I wound my way through the arctic-marine wasteland with an old worker I knew absolutely nothing about.

"I was bear hunting up in the Cascades last summer," Lee began. I noticed a thin whistle as he talked, air squeezing between his teeth.

Again with the bears.

"And I saw one of the biggest goddamn bears I had ever tracked. I'm a guide up there, you know. Well, it was daybreak, and this big-ass bear was walking up a ridge, and I could hear rocks roll out from under its footsteps and tumble off a ledge. I was with this stupid son-of-a-bitch that didn't know his rifle from his ass, but he was a friend of a friend, and paid me good money to take him up there.

He was about fifty yards behind me, and I was getting pissed off because I thought he'd lose a shot at this trophy bear."

Lee stopped walking and turned to look at me while he talked, the whistle now louder after each word. His eyebrows pointed up at the ends, giving him a devilish appearance as he talked.

"The sun broke the horizon, and a little lower on the ridge was a big buck, huge fuckin' rack with the prettiest points you'd ever seen—just perfect. All a of sudden, it kind of squats down and takes a piss—this long stream of pee. It was beautiful—that pee just a glistening in the morning sun, steam rising off the rocks as it splattered across 'em. One of those things you never forget."

Lee stepped closer to me.

"Well, I had to turn my attention back to the bear—take care of business—and it was about then that the stupid son-of-a-bitch finally caught up to me. He was sucking air, and I thought he was about to keel over. I whispered in his ear and pointed to the bear—*the bear*. And what does this stupid son-of-a-bitch end up doing? He shoots at the goddamn deer, and the biggest fuckin' bear I had seen that year goes haulin' ass over the ridge! I asked the numb-nuts what the fuck he was doing, and he said he never saw the bear. I pointed directly at the goddamn thing!"

"That's quite a story."

"Yeah—takes all kinds. I can't understand what's inside some people's heads—air, I guess. They just don't seem to listen when they need to."

I noticed Lee wasn't wearing a hardhat, and I asked him about it.

"I don't wear those fucking things," he said, then turned his head, put a finger to the side of his nose and blew a long string of snot from his nostril.

"I used to work for a lumber company. They wanted us to wear hardhats, too, but I tell you what—if a tree decides it has your name on it, no piece of plastic on your head is going to save you."

Lee's eyes told the story of a man who worked hard for a living, a person who viewed things straight up, either right, or wrong and inappropriate.

"I've sailed around the world three times—and I fucked a lot of beautiful women along the way."

I continued to listen attentively to Lee's seemingly endless stories as we worked about the barge, moving pieces of equipment from one place to another, attempting to make order out of the chaos. I had grown up in a family of storytellers. My father's tales of the old Irish neighborhood in Oakland where he grew up included a bounty of colorful "buddies"—bootlegger friends of the family, neighborhood cops who stopped by for a Friday afternoon drink, and bar fights where my grandmother had to bail my father out of jail, only to have him immediately go back to the same bar the incident had taken place only a few hours prior. These stories held me spellbound as a kid. Often told at a holiday dinner table, laughter filled the room. The farming side of my family cherished much different stories, those of rural life—hunting trips and deer so large they caused "buck fever" and froze the shooter in his or her own tracks, fish so large that my cousin once ripped off his shirt and dove off a ledge and into a frigid Sierra stream to pull out his brother's catch, and exploring northern California hills and majestic backcountry few people had ever seen.

Most of the stories became legendary in my mind, others I filed away in folders labeled "complete bullshit"—fabrications told only for the benefit of the teller and a hearty laugh at a hapless victim. I had been prey to a fictional snipe hunt, was told my grandfather attended high school at San Quentin State Prison, and raced after Santa Claus with my brother in a black '56 Corvette through the Hayward hills on Christmas Eve (we had spun out on wet payment and into an embankment with the 'Vette, and then spiraled into a field, minus a rear fender.)

There was an old saying in my family: "You can't bullshit a bullshitter." But as I listened to Lee's string of stories over the years, I became more and more convinced all of them were at least partially true. The war stories and the time he spent in the military particularly interested me because he told them in such detail, as one who had witnessed the scenes firsthand. I fact-checked many of them later, and everything seemed to fit with how he recounted them. Lee was a simple man; I found it difficult to believe he had somehow gleaned information from some other source in order to construct his many tales.

"Okay, we better get to work before The Bear gets up to the comm shack." Lee pointed upwards to the small unit at the top of camp crowned with radio antennas. "He watches everything from up there with his binoculars. If he catches you screwing around, it could be your ticket home."

We walked to a tall stack of fifty-gallon oil drums stacked six-high, pallets between each row. A variety of rusted red and blue barrels featured at least a few dents and gouges across their surfaces, and the letters "MT" scribbled across each one in yellow marking crayon.

"These are empty ones, and we'll use them for slop."

"Slop?"

"Yeah, that's the shit we'll have to pump out of the boats when we muck out the bilges. It's mostly seawater, oil, and anti-freeze. We'll move the barrels to the end of this barge so the crane can reach 'em once they fire up the heavy equipment. I don't know why they didn't park the forklifts in front of the barrels so we could use them to move all this, instead of behind the vans—now we'll have to carry them over there by hand. No one thinks at the end of the season—they only want to get the hell outta here."

"They write 'MT' on the *empty* ones—what do you write on the full ones?"

"F-U-L-L," he said, then smirked.

"That's some hefty rope." I pointed to a couple of palettes of coiled line.

"Those are boat *lines*—not rope. They'll have to be moved, too."

"You said you sailed around the world?"

"Yeah, I was on a fuel tanker in World War II, 'Nam after that, then sailed as a merchant marine. Some of the best times of my life. People bitch about bein' in Vietnam—I had a hell of a time."

"So, I'm assuming you know a lot of knots."

"Just about any a guy would ever need."

"Will you show me some of the basics?"

"Yeah, we'll pick up a couple of small lines during the break and bring them back out here. We'll start with a bowline and a couple others you'll need to learn. A guy is worthless if he can't tie a good knot." He took a deep breath. "There's one basic rule that every *real* knot follows."

"What's that?"

"You have to be able to untie it. If you can't untie what you've done, you're screwed."

Lee showed me some basic line work that day and continued to provide me valuable instruction that first season at Prudhoe Bay. He supplied what I needed to be a worthy laborer and coworker. There were many of us greenhorns in camp, and whoever wanted to master the tools of the trade only had to work on Lee's crew for a while; he was always willing to share anything he had learned during a life of sailing, lumbering, construction, game guiding, and hell-raising.

I would continue to learn from Lee over the years. I don't know if he ever fully knew everything I took away from our working relationship. The things that define a person range from strong to subtle—from the way one judges or not judges another person, to the way one simply ties a knot.

LIFELINE

THE OUTSIDE WORLD—limited connection with friends, family, and loved ones. It usually took at least two weeks to get a message to or from its destination. Receiving mail or hearing a voice from outside the camp helped immensely in maintaining one's sanity.

The warm-up shack usually had a line of guys waiting outside to use the one phone after work. A lot of things pass through a person's mind during a twelve-hour day, and by the time 6:00 pm rolled around, a lot of workers were eager to talk to someone at home. Normally no major complaints surfaced about how long a person took; we had plenty of hours to burn.

The best time to use the phone was after dinner, when many of the workers were watching movies in a unit set up as a makeshift theater. I tried to plan my weekly calls accordingly. That one phone remained the only real-time connection to the outside world, messages traveling along thousands of miles of copper wiring from one of the farthest northern camps.

I waited patiently in line, a wad of Copenhagen in my lip, a book in my hand. I learned the foul routine of chewing tobacco when attending a community college in the California foothills, compliments of a schoolmate who was a turkey rancher's son. The habit resurfaced after a few days at Prudhoe. I had asked Joel Burckhalter to buy me a roll of ten tins on his next daily run into Deadhorse.

As tobacco helped pass the time during the working hours, reading books served as a mental anchor when off the clock. It was a big mistake only bringing two books to camp, the frightening reality that at some point I'd complete reading both of them. I first read Hunter S. Thompson's "The Great Shark Hunt," then a collection of Steinbeck stories. The camp possibly had the largest collection of Louis L'Amour and Zane Grey on the North Slope, but not much else.

The door swung open and the only one in front of me in line was Jack Bourke.

Bourke disappeared behind the door, and I studied the view of Prudhoe Bay. As much as it held a certain "sameness," it appeared slightly different each day. The pools of water were getting larger and reflected the sky like a pattern of shimmering mirrors. The sun maintained its circular path above us, the sky never getting darker as the hours blended within each other with nothing to separate them—one continuous span of time.

The surreal surroundings created a blank canvass for which many thoughts layered themselves on top of each other and provided time to drift to faraway places. Sometimes these were positive experiences, and other times they felt like mentally dangerous areas.

Bourke walked out of the warm-up shack with a grin on his face.

"That was quick," I said. "You talk to your wife?"

"Yeah—she was with her boyfriend." He laughed, then limped off toward the movie room.

I scratched my head, then took my turn in front of the phone and closed the door. It was a dial phone, a simple black box connected to spans of wires and airwaves crossing several states and into my girlfriend's condo in Boulder, Colorado.

I completed the eleven circular motions of the dial with my finger. The phone rang. It was a Friday, and I knew Chris expected my call and she picked up after two rings.

"Hey, it's me," I said.

"Hiii," she said in a voice that was both warm and longing. Even over the thousands of miles, I felt as though she were next to me. I could see her blonde-brown hair, feel her soft skin, and enjoy that beautiful smile. "How are you?"

"Good," I said. "Same shit, different day. How are things down there?"

"Good. The summer classes are going well—I miss you."

"Miss you, too."

"So what's it like up there—are the guys you work with okay?"

I laughed. "Well, I don't know if any of them are what you would consider *okay*, but we're all in the same boat together—no pun intended."

We talked about what classes we were going to take during the fall and how we were both looking forward to skiing together once the winter snow fell. I told her I hated thinking about snow and ice right then, but I would surely have my skis tuned and waxed by ski season.

So much of me missed her, but as the days went by, a growing part of me seemed to feel as though the camp was where I needed to be at that point in my life. It was as if I were searching for something, a compass to guide me along a pre-determined course. Whatever that direction was, I felt it possibly buried somewhere under the piles of rusting machinery and wooden planks, residing deep within the hulls of one of those ice-battered barges, waiting to be uncovered.

"We'll be together soon," I said. "Hey, there's quite a line for the phone tonight—you know I've never been very good at talking on the phone. I mostly wanted to hear your voice."

"It's good to hear your voice, too—look forward to your next call. Miss you so much."

"Yep—I miss you, too. Hey, if you have a chance, can you send me a book or two? I need some reading material."

"Any requests?"

"Anything besides Louis L'Amour and Zane Grey—apparently, a lot of people above the Arctic Circle enjoy westerns. And I really enjoy your letters, too."

"I sent one a couple of days ago. You should get it soon."

"Thanks. Next Friday?"

"Next Friday. Love you."

"Bye—love you, too." I hung up the receiver and held onto her voice, trying my best to keep it tucked away in my head. I realized I could slowly become a prisoner of my own volition. The distance was daunting and time away changes everything for better or worse. Adverse conditions can bring people together, and at other times drive them apart. I clung to the hope we would be closer upon my return, avoiding a phone call like Bourke's.

I walked out of the warmup shack, and the next person in line took his place in front of the telephone.

NEVER-ENDING DAY

I THOUGHT I HAD DONE my fair share of snow shoveling, having lived in Colorado. I soon achieved a higher education in the fine art of snow removal as our crew worked to uncover every barge, tugboat, forklift, and any other piece of equipment covered by winter snowdrift.

The AMF camp had filled with workers, an odd mixture of company employees and college students like myself, the latter trying to make good money before heading back to school. Even a full-time teacher worked at the camp during his summer break. Others were laborers who drifted from one project to the next, like Lee, who worked the summers so he could take large spans of time off during the fall and winter to hunt. Everyone had a connection with either Crowley Maritime or one of the oil companies—it was the only way to hold a job at AMF if you weren't a company man. The company workers were professionals: engineers like Ken, electricians, welders, or crane operators.

"Time for a muck break," one of my coworkers, Jeff Selenjus said as he took out a tin of chewing tobacco.

"I don't know why you guys chew that shit," Lee said.

"Helps get us through the day," Jeff said.

Mike Tompkins and Jeff Selenjus were friends and attended Washington State University in Pullman. They, along with Lee and I, had been assigned to dig out a large mound of snow between the units and open a walkway—days spent in a world of snow and frozen metal.

"It's not like the work is grueling," Mike said. "It's more the psychological mind-fuck of putting in long, monotonous hours and not going crazy by doing the same exact thing day after day."

"All I've written on my time sheets for the last three weeks is 'shovel snow,'" I said. "Twelve hours a day, seven days a week."

Many co-workers went to their rooms during the morning and afternoon breaks to smoke a couple of pipe-loads and ease the grind. I did my best to limit drugs other than tobacco and caffeine, and AMF was supposedly a dry camp, void of alcohol or controlled substances.

My thinking was that I had already exceeded my lifetime limit of cannabis when I attended Columbia Junior College for a few years in the Sierra foothills. My roommate at the time had grower friends, and our rented cabin housed over three hundred young sprouts carefully planted in plastic Dixie cups, meticulously maintained and watered. In short, I was trying my best to leave experiences of pot growing and smoking where I thought it belonged—in the past.

"Hey Lee, what's the story with those little barges with the blue huts on them?" I asked. "The ones that say, 'Suck 'Em Up.'"

"Oh, those were one of The Bear's ideas. When all the transport barges with oil rigs and other stuff get up here during Sealift, they're offloaded at the end of the causeway—at West Dock. We'll probably all be working on pump crews, filling up the hulls of the barges with water to sink 'em."

"Sink the barges?" Mike asked, then spit a stream of tobacco juice that left a brown stain on the pile of snow.

"Yeah, when they get into dock to offload," Lee said. "When they unloaded the first barge at West Dock, it cracked near the middle—the weight of the module they tried to unload was too heavy. Now they sink the barges to the bottom, then unload them. The Suck 'Em Up's were used to suck out the water when the barges went back out to sea, but this year we're getting a bunch of shiny new submersible pumps."

I had a tough time visualizing the entire offloading process and assumed seeing it in progress provided better understanding. I only heard bits and pieces about Sealift, which took place near the end of the season, and from what I understood, it resulted in a lot of working hours—more than our usual twelve-hour days.

Lee took a pocket watch from his coveralls. "Looks like coffee break in another seventeen minutes."

"That's a cool watch, Lee," I said.

He handed me the piece. "Ten bucks—you can get one at most any variety store in Seattle."

It was the only thing the crew could rely on for a sense of time. There really wasn't a *night*, only one continuous day, the delineation of time marked only by a cheap ten-dollar pocket watch.

"I overheard Bourke say that a load of paint was coming in by truck tomorrow. That means they'll probably want us to work on the boats soon." Lee put the watch back in his pocket. "I saw Lance working on a couple of grinders in the tool shack the other day."

"Grinders?" I asked.

"Yeah, they'll want us to get all the rust and crud off the boats before we prime and paint all of 'em. That'll be our next big project, and it'll probably burn up the better part of a month."

"Hey Lee, tell us an industrial accident story," Jeff said.

Mike burst out laughing, a speck of tobacco flying out of his mouth. "Yeah, c'mon Lee—let's hear a story."

"Did I ever tell you guys about the time I worked on that high-rise in Seattle?"

"You worked in construction, too?" I asked.

"Oh yeah, I was on crews that built dams, buildings—all kinds of stuff." Lee stabbed his shovel into a mound of snow and leaned his hand over the top of the handle.

"I worked on one of those huge towers in the middle of town when it was nothing more than steel framing. We were up there having lunch one day—had to watch your step and pay attention to what you were doing. No one was going to watch out for you. You were on your own, especially at lunch. Well, I don't know what this one poor son of a bitch was thinking, but he was eating a sandwich and talking with us, then stood up and began walking around. Sure enough, he walked right off the goddamn girder and fell over thirty stories to the street below. The entire way down we could hear him yell 'son of a biiiiiiiiitch...'"

"No way," Jeff said.

"Yep, the whole way down. Then splat, he hit the pavement—his sandwich landed right next to him."

We all laughed after Lee's colorful narration, not at the unfortunate and untimely death of this poor fellow. Who knew how many crews Lee had worked with and how many times he told similar stories—tales of his time at sea, working on vast construction projects, or hunting down large game.

We picked up our shovels and resumed our quest to reduce the large mound of snow blocking the walkway between the units. The hours interwove into one long continuous day interrupted by meals, coffee breaks, and short periods of sleep, the sun maintaining its tight orbit above us. With the last of the snow removed, we used axes to break remaining winter ice from the decks of the barges.

My time sheets, filled with scratched pencil marks, told a story of tedious hours and the monotony of snow and ice removal. They did not, however, record Lee's stories, or the camaraderie developing among our crew.

UNCOMFORTABLY NUMB

I CLIMBED DOWN FROM the top rack, staggered toward my locker, then slapped the back of my hands on top of the small Formica table in the corner of our room. The action was another morning routine and the only way I could get my hands to wake up. Once they did, it felt like thousands of ants ran across them; it took several minutes before I could curl my fingers and make a fist.

Our crew had completed a full month of digging pieces of buried equipment out of snow and ice, only to have that task followed by another month of chipping, scraping, and grinding the rust from the hulls of every dry-docked tugboat. There were eleven of these vessels in the Arctic Marine Freighters fleet during my first season, and they all required thorough prepping with electric grinders before we primed and painted.

Every boat featured the same colors: black hull and bulwark, buff main housing, white wheelhouse, and red exhaust stacks that identified Crowley Maritime tugboats and the company once known as "Red Stack Tugs." The hulls required black epoxy-based maritime paint applied with a roller, the toxic fumes causing heads to spin. Thin facemasks were basically worthless, resulting in a lot of glazed eyes amongst workers. But the prep work remained the toughest physical challenge.

"Hands numb?" Ken asked as he buttoned his work shirt.

"Yeah, takes a while for them to warm up."

"Carpel tunnel syndrome." Ken lit a cigarette. "Lying on your back and grinding the hull of a boat for ten to twelve hours a day will do that to 'em. A lot of the guys who work in the Seattle boatyards have scars on their wrists where they've had surgery."

"I try to take breaks and rest them for a few minutes." I pulled a sweatshirt out of my locker.

"Yeah—but they need *days* of rest, not minutes." Ken slid the window open a few inches, blew out a wisp of smoke, and looked out at the frozen sea. "Another beautiful day on the Beaufort. I'm headed down to the galley. Want this closed?"

"No, I'll get it when I leave," I replied.

The door slammed shut, and his steps faded down the catwalk between the living units.

I looked out at the thawing bay, the arctic air spilling through the open window and filling the room as our small wall heater kicked on. The feeling slowly crept back into my hands. It was a hell of a way to wake up, but another day in camp had begun. The breeze felt soothing as it drifted across my face. I took a deep breath. Outside, the generator continued its relentless drone as it had since the first day of camp, and the faint smell of diesel exhaust tainted the air.

I walked outside as the sound of workers' footsteps clanged against the metal catwalk that encircled the living quarters like a constricting snake. When I got downstairs and walked into the head a couple of other workers nodded to me, then continued a discussion about one of their roommates.

"Before he even gets out of bed I can hear the bong gurgling—then the smoke drifts up to my bunk."

"Is it good pot?"

"The best."

"Don't bitch—breath it in."

After finishing morning duties in the head, I walked into a

crowded galley with Angelo cranking out food faster than ever. His bull cook, a young kid who looked like he was still in his teens, appeared frazzled as he tried keeping up with the frantic pace. The bull cook's duties included assisting the chief cook, disposing of garbage, cleaning rooms, and basically, any menial shit-work. "I feel like butter spread too thin over too much toast," the bull cook mumbled.

Angelo remained unfazed and greeted each hungry crewmember with the same jolly greeting, "Hah, whatta ya know?," and the next person in line replying, "Whatta ya know, Angelo…"

I sat to have a cup of coffee with Lee, and a worker who arrived at camp a few days prior joined us. Josip Gvozdic from Croatia, more commonly referred to as "Big G" or simply "G," was an imposing presence, about the same height as my roommate Ronnie. Like Ronnie, G had also played basketball at a high level.

"Good morning, gentlemen," he said in his low voice, then took a sip of coffee.

G spoke clear English; however, a bit broken and sometimes jumbled.

"Hey, G," Lee said. "The Bear told Bourke he wants the two of us to finish moving all those barrels to the edge of the 210. They keep moving us from job to job and *nothing* gets finished—they've moved me around so much, my corners are wearin' round. Anyway, he wants us to get the forklifts fired up and straighten up all that shit."

"Sure—no problem in doing that."

Lee and G were two of the bigger guys in camp, both physically and in the general hierarchy of the crew. Lee was the most experienced of all the workers, and G worked the winters for ARCO and Exxon, so he knew his stuff and how to negotiate the system. Lee and G's duties seldomly included grinding and painting the boats—work of lower-level grunts like myself.

Lee looked at the headline on the several-days-old *Seattle Times* on the table. "I see here that your Russian friends are having a pissin' match with the Poles."

"I talk to Croation friends only—and only occasionally."

"As tough as it is over there, I bet a lot of them wish they worked up here like you," I said.

"When talking to friends, I tell nothing about my work. I especially never tell how much money I make."

"Really?"

"Never." G looked into my eyes. "They would never believe me."

I felt naïve about world affairs. My mind remained numbed by the media and no matter how many newspapers I read, or television news stories I watched, it was nothing like the knowledge held by people who had lived under extreme or stifling conditions. More than ever, I wanted to travel and witness firsthand what life was like outside of the United States. Sailing on a boat as a merchant marine could provide that ticket.

I sat in the galley and listened to G talk about life in Croatia and how lucky we were to be living in the United States. Years later, I learned he had worked his way up the ladder of the leading oil company in Russia and the world's largest publicly traded petroleum company. The paths of power and those who lead or follow it, ebb and flow.

I opened and closed my hands. The ants had retreated and wouldn't return until the next morning; ready for another day of work.

SWAN

ANOTHER CREWMEMBER arrived in camp one day: Bill Swan. Swan sat in the galley drinking a cup of coffee as everyone else ate their dinner. Dressed in black leather, he wore a pair of welder glasses with round dark magenta lenses. His hair stood on end, not spiked but jutting upward in a variety of angles proclaiming, "I don't give a fuck how I look," which could have been a perfect example of a Bill Swan statement. He wore a studded belt and matching wristband that flashed back to Johnny Rotten. Exposed metal shined from the tips of his steel-toe boots, the covering leather worn and ripped in jagged chunks.

He was a skinny, pale, Seattle punk-rocker who somehow made his way to the Arctic, and I could not for the life of me understand where he was coming from or feel any sense of common ground—other than our ages. I loathed punk music, and anyone dressed as a punk rocker only annoyed me. My musical tastes remained firmly grounded in rock, blues, and jazz, with a dab of reggae and classical mixed in for flavor. Any other music, especially country or punk, did not make the list. At the same time, I maintained a strong curiosity about how others viewed the world, and Swan's vantage point was definitely different as he looked out of those dark welder's glasses.

The buzz about Swan was that he was highly intelligent and had majored in chemistry at the University of Washington. He had a distinct dislike for anything conventional or mainstream and his quirky personality could come off as a bit intimidating. He could mentally shred most anyone to pieces in a conversation or debate, but in physical conflicts he proclaimed himself as "king of the wimps." With all his eccentricity, and my resistance to "punkdom," we struck up a conversation on music.

"So, you're from Caleeefornia, huh?" Swan asked.

"Yeah. I'm attending college in Colorado but am originally from the San Francisco Bay Area."

"My band played a couple of gigs down in S.F."

"*Your* band?"

"Yeah, I manage a band in Seattle. Or did. Maybe still do."

"A lot of punk music—especially the guitar licks—just sound like old beach music to me—bad beach music with a ton of distortion."

"Exactly—it's pure shit. I love it." Swan took a pouch of tobacco from his leather jacket along with a pack of rolling papers. "My band experiments with sound frequencies and how they can affect the audience. They once played a set that actually caused some people to climax." One of Swan's eyebrows pointed upwards in a v-shape from behind the dark glasses.

"Really?" I said, trying to visualize the concerts Swan attended.

"*Really.* No shit." He rolled a crooked cigarette and stuck it in his shirt pocket. "What kind of music are you inclined to listen to?"

"Up here, Pink Floyd has been a good fit."

"The Floyd is great—at least the original work. The new album has too many recycled riffs. How 'bout books—whataya read?"

"I was a little short on reading material when I got up here. My girlfriend just sent me Stephen King's latest novel."

"I hate Stephen King—he scares the hell out of me!" The unlit cigarette bobbed up and down as he spoke. "Ever read *The Illuminatus! Trilogy*?"

"What's that?"

"*The Illuminatus! Trilogy* is comprised of three books written by Robert Shea and Robert Anton Wilson. They'll twist your gray matter—I'm finishing the third one right now. I won't tell you a thing about 'em—you have to experience it yourself if you're up to the challenge. Come by the *Prudhoe* tomorrow and I'll give you the first book to pique your interest."

Apparently, Swan always captained the tugboat, *Prudhoe Bay*. Considered his boat to captain, The Bear left him alone to do most anything he wanted with it. The *Prudhoe Bay* was much like Swan himself—a bit unusual and out of the norm—and a sister boat to the *Mop King*, another small, flat-bottom, twin-screw boat with a ramp at the bow that could be raised or lowered as needed. A utility crane on the foredeck jutted forward, ahead of a thin wheelhouse. Swan worked on the *Prudhoe's* engines himself, kept the crane in operation, and maintained everything else to keep the vessel operating smoothly, as it was a much-needed workhorse for AMF. For this, he gained the respect of the camp engineers and The Bear himself.

"And once you get a taste of *Illuminatus!*, I'll feed you some Pynchon," Swan smirked.

In the coming seasons, Swan provided more "absolute, unequivocal must-reads" along with some personal poems, writings, and notes. In the bleak surroundings, it felt amazingly enlightening to get a glimpse of how things appeared through the eyes of Swan—and it didn't require a pair of dark welder's glasses.

As a bi-product, I somehow developed a taste for loud, overamplified punk music resonating across a frozen wasteland two hundred and fifty miles above the Arctic Circle.

BOATS IN THE WATER

ONCE THE ICE BROKE UP around camp, there was a change in tempo to the seemingly endless days, and time seemed to move a little faster. Our crane mechanic had the Manitowoc 10000 crane ready to go, and its engine fired up one morning with a blast of diesel smoke swirling into the sky. It was one of the largest mobile cranes built and the weight of its tracks caused unsettling creaks and pops as it crept across the wooden decks of *Barge 210*.

"Bob Edwards is the best crane operator," Lee said. "A union guy will be in camp later in the season, but Bob's better. Some of the other guys who come up here are dangerous as hell."

Bob had a moderate temperament, a perfect personality for operating heavy equipment. His official title was "oiler," which meant he kept the heavy equipment maintained and running smooth. But since he knew the crane so well, everything within its massive metallic shell and towering boom, he was the Zen artist of crane operators. He respected the equipment and cared about the people working underneath it. Communication between operator and longshoremen relied on hand signals and eye contact. You could tell what Bob was thinking through these basic gestures and the look in his eyes.

The Bear was eager to get the boats in the water. Once they were afloat, the moneymaking days of the operation swung into effect. It also marked the approaching of Sealift, when a fleet of seagoing tugboats and barges sailed into Prudhoe Bay with equipment for the oil fields, including towering drill modules.

"Sealift is the reason we're up here," Lee said as we walked to the end of *Barge 210* to meet the rest of the crew. "Most every piece of equipment in the oilfields got here by sea—some was shipped by truck, along the Haul Road, but most was brought up here during previous Sealifts."

"When do they arrive?" I asked.

"Depends on the ice floe. They usually get held up around Point Barrow, but once it clears out, they haul ass to Prudhoe. There'll be anywhere from fifteen to thirty barges and it'll look like a city coming over the horizon. One morning you'll wake up, and there it'll be."

We met up with Mike, Jeff, Ronnie, and Big G who were at the end of the barge. The Bear and Jack Bourke were across the deck watching the approaching crane.

"We need to tie tethers on the boats," Lee shouted above the roar of the crane. "The Bear wants us to do the *Yuba* first then work our way down the line."

Two of the crew grabbed coiled lengths of line and climbed up a shaky ladder to the deck of the *Yuba*. Lee's knot-tying lessons came in handy as they tied one end of the line to the boat's H-bitts, then threw the rest of the line down to the barge.

Bob walked the Manitowoc down the surface of the barge, the large cat tracks creating a high-pitched squeak as it approached the first boat, then stopped. Lee hand-signaled to Bob, his finger pointing downward and circling. The crane ball and hook lowered, the whine of cable accompanying its descent as Lee and G reached out to it.

"There's a reason it's called a 'headache ball,'" Lee shouted as he grabbed the hook.

"That's why I wear hardhat." G picked up a large shackle and we connected four straps to it—braided cables with loops at each end. G lifted the shackle and straps onto the hook of the headache ball and the safety latch clicked shut. Once attached, Lee pointed a finger upward with a circular motion and Bob raised the cables.

Lee pointed his thumb down and the crane boom lowered over the *Yuba*. He then raised a fist and it stopped. Waving his hand to the left, the boom swung in that direction until he again made a clenched fist. Once centered directly over the *Yuba*, the cables descended and a couple of crew members shackled the straps to eyelets along the tugboat's bulwark.

Lee made a circular hand signal above his head and the hook slowly raised. The crew on the *Yuba's* deck guided the four cables clear of any obstructions as the cables tightened. They then climbed down and carried the ladder away from the boat.

"I need four guys to man those lines." Lee pointed to the four tether lines hanging from the *Yuba*. Ronnie, Mike, Jeff, and I walked over and grabbed each one.

"Everyone ready?" Lee looked at each of us. "Up we go." He made a thumbs-up signal above this head.

Bob revved the engine of the crane and the cables strained against the weight of the tugboat as the crane boom rose higher. The screeching noise of metal against wood signaled the boat's release from the wood pilings, and she hung there, suspended a few inches in the air. I held the line tight to keep the vessel from spinning.

"Don't pull too hard," Lee shouted. "Keep it straight."

Near the crane stood The Bear. He said nothing to us, but it was clear he would provide orders if needed. He occasionally shouted instructions to Bob, who nodded his head in confirmation.

The crane boom swung toward a section of open water alongside the barge and the crane crept a few feet closer to the edge, its huge tracks rolling across the deck. The Bear walked over to the *Yuba*. As she hung near the edge of the barge, he put a hand on her hull to help us steady it, and once it was clear of the edge, he nodded.

Lee lifted an arm over his head and made the circular signal.

Slowly, the boat descended over the side of the barge. The rear of the crane rose a few inches, the weight of the boat challenging the downward force of the crane's rear counterweight. Then, all at once, the four cable straps slackened. I looked over the edge of the barge and saw the *Yuba* afloat, surrounded by circling ice floe.

"That's number one," Lee said. "A couple of you guys jump down there and disconnect 'er. The rest of you come with me and G and we'll get straps on the next one."

The next boat in line was the *Meridian*, and I took special care when I attached the final strap to an eyelet, careful not to scratch the paint job I worked on for most of the month of July.

The process repeated, boat after boat, until at last, the entire fleet was in the water. After almost two months of shoveling snow off them, chipping, scraping and grinding their rusted hulls, decks, and wheelhouses, painting every square inch of their metal shells, they finally entered the sea. It was their home, and they would soon sail across the bay and beyond.

I went over to a daypack I'd stashed near a stack of pallets and took out my camera. Prior to declaring geology as my major, I had been a Fine Arts major and even tried to break into architecture. I still clung to the notion I had some creative talent.

My only concern in taking photos during the working hours was The Bear. I had a couple of conversations with him in the galley, but they were limited to him asking how I liked the camp, me saying "great," and his deep, guttural laugh as a reply. When I began taking photos of the boats entering the water, he gazed over at me and I froze for a few seconds. He nodded his head in approval and I continued to capture as many images as possible, then set the camera back down and got to work.

At the end of the day, a centipede-like line of workers waited to use the telephone, stretching down the edge of *Barge 213* like every day prior. The camp seemed different, however. There was a heightened buzz and the pressure of being so far away from home subsided slightly—at least for a brief period. The mood had changed.

The boats were in the water.

LATE SHOW

I'M THE ONLY ONE awake at our home in Tahoe. My wife and two daughters are asleep in their beds and I'm in my son's room, the glare of the laptop filling the space. He moved out of the house a year ago to attend college, but everything inside the room he no longer occupies makes me feel close to him: the books he read while living at home, his high school graduation cap, academic awards, the cross-country trophies and medals. A few remaining band and movie posters left behind hang on the walls. Mr. Green, Mr. Black, and my favorite, Mr. Pink (Steve Buscemi), and all the rest of the boys from "Reservoir Dogs," peer at me through dark sunglasses. A window is partially open and the cooling air is a welcome respite after another record-setting day of summer heat. The empty room is a perfect place for late-night writing and watching a video from what feels like a former life.

It's difficult to comprehend that a snippet of time I spent working at the north slope of Alaska can be found on a streaming video titled, HD Historic Stock Footage, *Alaska Oil Reserves—Journey to Prudhoe Bay*. The weight of the words, "Historic Stock Footage," sinks into my realization of passing time like an anchor descending into frigid waters. I click the play arrow and the video opens with a cheesy image of scratchy film leader and a number countdown. An advertisement regarding college financing pops up and I quickly click the white X in the corner, forcing it to disappear. Although I've worked in advertising and marketing for over twenty-five years, pop-up ads annoy me as much as anyone else—maybe more so.

I turn my attention to the video stream. I've watched it several times over the past few months but seem to notice something new each time while viewing it; another thought or feeling forms in my mind like rust across aging metal. The footage was transferred from film taken in 1975 and produced by the Atlantic Richfield Company, then later converted to this free watermarked video stream, and also made available for purchase as a downloadable high-definition digital file.

Trumpets signal the beginning of the video, and bold green capital letters fade in. The title, JOURNEY TO PRUDHOE, is superimposed over an aerial shot of tugboats and barges stuck in a sea of dense icepack. It's difficult to determine where the ice ends and the sky begins; any hint of color has been washed away, the images appearing ghostlike across the computer screen. The narrator's strong, authoritative voice is overlaid on a bed of background music composed with a large horn section. The scene cuts from the tugboats and barges to a sweeping shot of caribou herds running across a vast stretch of tundra, and the music transitions to a composition featuring a full string section. The scene reminds me of one of those old Disney wildlife documentaries we used to watch when we were kids.

"Once this vast land belonged to the wild animals. Today, there's still room for the caribou to graze peacefully in a largely unspoiled environment..." The narrator's voice drones on, describing the seemingly symbiotic relationship between man and the wilderness. The scene moves to shots of an oil field camp—roughnecks working on drill rigs as the history of oil expansion is chronicled. According to the video, man's survival depends on tapping into the ten billion gallons of oil trapped in a natural reservoir beneath the arctic tundra.

The video transitions to tugboats and barges sailing from Houston, Texas. Their decks are loaded with oil field equipment, and they journey through the Panama Canal and up the west coast of the United States. I imagine them sailing past whales, dolphins, and other sea life, the huge boat propellers churning through the water. They arrive at a special facility in Puget Sound, Washington. "In view of snow-clad mountains... a huge industrial complex is being constructed for transportation to Prudhoe Bay," the narrator announces.

At the Tacoma-Seattle facility, oil-processing facilities were built as independent interlocking sections called "modules." I'm reminded of the Lego building blocks my son had as a kid, and how they snapped together to create something larger, but the singular pieces of this complex could be as high as nine stories tall and weigh fourteen-hundred tons, and the something larger will cover thousands of acres. The individual modules serve as sections of flow stations, gas injection plants, or fuel processing systems. One oil field compressor plant might consist of over forty of these modular units. The equipment is protected from the harsh northern environment by insulated steel-encased walls, most of which are painted a dull olive drab, not the colorful yellow, blue, or red of my son's old Lego pieces.

Scenes of welders, construction workers, and crane operators, sweep across the screen like actors, in front of an industrial backdrop of steel girders, stacks of pipe, and heavy equipment. Diesel exhaust billows from the stacks of towering cranes, drifting over the panorama of "snow-clad mountains."

The process of loading equipment onboard the seagoing barges took almost a month. Over 100,000 tons of cargo packed tightly aboard the vessels included modules, housing units, earth-moving equipment, trucks, crawlers, and miscellaneous crates filled with instruments and tools. The narrator talks of the "rugged crews" that man the flotilla of tugboats, and a shot of the bow of one of the barges comes to view; I hit the video pause button. Floating on the waters of Puget Sound is *Barge 213*, with its rows of living units that would become the Arctic Marine Freighter's camp—the place I called home for at least four months out of each year, from 1982 to 1985.

I had heard stories of how and when the AMF camp had been established, but it isn't until thirty-two years later that I'm watching the images of the living units moving north along with the huge shipment of equipment for the oil fields. Every year since 1968, thousands of tons of supplies, production modules, and equipment had been transported by sea from west coast ports of the United States to the Prudhoe Bay oil fields on the north slope of Alaska. 1975 was the year *Barge 213* and the AMF camp arrived.

The volume of cargo moved that season was the largest peacetime sealift in U.S. history. It required twenty-three tugs and fortyseven barges to deliver supplies, equipment, and modules; a total of 160,000 tons of cargo valued at $500 million was to be delivered. Crowley Maritime, the parent company of AMF, was the prime contractor, but several other tugboat companies were subcontracted to complete the endeavor. The modules on ten of the barges were the top-priority cargo, as they were needed to complete the flow stations and processing plants at the oil field. These modules would bring the pipeline to life.

The fleet departed the Seattle area on July 5th to journey over 4,000 miles across the open sea. They navigated in heavy fog through the Bering Straits toward Point Barrow, 180 miles west of Prudhoe Bay. But as predictions had forecast, the ice did not recede in early August as it had in past years, creating a frustrating waiting game as the twenty-three tugs and barges gathered together and waited between Port Clarence and Wainwright. Day after day and week after week, unrelenting storms and heavy drift ice kept them in a virtual gridlock in the frigid waters, with ice damage a constant concern.

The days of waiting turned into days of frustration for the 184 crewmembers aboard the seagoing tugs. On August 28th, a decision was made to single up (one barge per tug), and the ten barges with priority cargo would make a desperate dash around Point Barrow if a safe passage opened up. On September 2nd, an ice patrol plane spotted a small gap. The next day, four tugs and barges rounded Barrow and squeezed their way through heavy pack ice.

It took two days for the tugs to navigate the 165 miles of ice-choked waters, and the first one arrived in Prudhoe Bay on September 4th. The temperature was twenty degrees with heavy snowfall. After refueling, the four tugs returned to Point Barrow to assist the next group of boats and barges. With two tugs pulling and pushing each barge, the second group made it to Prudhoe Bay on September 7th.

The video continues and shows oil field activity in Prudhoe. Hundreds of miles of gravel roads were constructed and cement and steel pilings were sunk into the tundra to support the arriving modules. A vast industrial complex would soon be pieced together.

"... the men of Prudhoe Bay are heirs to a tradition of arctic exploration begun in the last century by Ousland and Kagge ... searching for oil may seem less romantic than racing to the pole by dogsled, but the potential for mankind is no less impressive." I pick up a glass of filtered water and take a swallow as I struggle to digest the narrator's statement. The *potential for mankind* meant a dependence on oil, a commodity whose cost would fluctuate widely over the years due to several factors, but mostly because of a struggle for power, and endless political maneuverings. Oil production would affect world trade, politics, and most importantly, the environment, due to global warming. Consumption would be deemed a "necessity" as the seemingly unconscious reliance continued to grow. These thoughts flow through me like the dark crude bursting from deep inside the earth, into an entanglement of endless pipeline.

The video continues with a view of Point Barrow. "From an Eskimo village, Barrow has grown into a prosperous community. Many of its natives are employed in Prudhoe Bay..." the narrator states—another reminder that this video was produced by the ARCO public relations team.

In late August, as some of the boats and barges made their way from Barrow to Prudhoe, an unexpected storm engulfed the remainder of the fleet that were trapped in ice at Wainwright. The force of the storm-blown ice sank one of the barges, but a rescue operation was able to save the cargo and salvage the barge.

Finally, a break in weather in September allowed ten more of the barges to travel the final 180 miles to Prudhoe—among them, *Barge 213*. Fifteen others, stalled in the ice and loaded with smaller supplies, turned south toward land in order to unload for overland transportation. The video shows an aerial view of West Dock stretching out into the Beaufort Sea. *Barge 213* is docked at the end, a lonely outpost in the wide expanse of arctic desolation.

It's late, and I feel the weight of a long workday pulling me back to bed. I'll return another night to watch the remainder of the video, and I turn off the computer and look out of the open window. I wonder how my son is doing—what he's experiencing and learning now that he's on his own.

Silhouettes of pine trees etch the starry night sky. The high Sierra air is laden with a thick pine fragrance, a result of another day of high temperatures. We're in the third year of the worst drought in recorded history in California. I take a long, deep breath of mountain air and hope that the next few winters will wash away my concerns of global warming and what the future holds for a changing environment. But I know it won't—or shouldn't. Like the tugboat dreams that await me in my sleep, these thoughts are here to stay.

RETURNING FROM R&R

THE PLANE TRAVELING BACK to Prudhoe Bay had been a lot quieter than the one that took us home for "Rest and relaxation" (R&R), a one-week break afforded to the crew before Sealift. Most everyone slept, read a book, or stared out a window. It was a sharp contrast to the excessive drinking, boisterous chatter, and shrill hooting during the flight home to a week of freedom. "When we got off the plane in Seattle," one engineer reflected, "my wife said it was easy to tell which guys were from the North Slope. They were worn-down and dirty—long hair, unshaven, and three sheets to the wind."

The landscape transformed as we traveled north, from towering peaks to the flat frozen tundra we had escaped only a week before. Every minute we traveled across the sky took us farther from our homes and the memories of R&R grew more distant, fading into the shallow fissures and ravines, scarring the permafrost below. Seeing my family and girlfriend had been a welcome respite from the two months of twelve-hour workdays, but returning home for such a short duration only confirmed everything we were missing. The crew got a taste of a summer lost, of warm days spent with friends, spouses, families, or girlfriends. It was also a reminder it was more than our labor we were being paid for at Arctic Marine Freighters;

it was also compensation for living at the outskirts of an arctic oil field, cut off from the outside world for months at a time, the sun circling over us in its twenty-four-hour vigil, robbing us of starry summer nights.

Things change when you're away from home for long periods of time. People's lives naturally evolve with new experiences and interactions, but camp entrapped us in a time warp—routines confined to interactions bound within the confines of seven barges and eleven tugboats anchored off a thin spit of land jetting due north toward the Beaufort Sea. The earth's rotation has a slower surface speed above the Arctic Circle and sucked us into its languid gyration, both physically and mentally. There was no television, no radio reception, and the only source of outside news was the several-days-old editions of *Seattle Times* scattered about the galley like forgotten castaways. Even though the days never ended in the "land of the midnight sun," we remained enshrouded in darkness from the outside world.

We landed at Deadhorse Airport, drove through the Prudhoe Bay oilfields, and found ourselves back at the AMF Camp. The feeling of familiarity and a weird tinge of acknowledging this was now home—at least for several more months—sank in. I walked up the gangplank and onto the metal stairway leading to my living quarters. The drone of the generator still filled the air as it had before we left. I slammed the door to muffle the sound. Ken was sitting at the desk having a smoke.

"Welcome back." He took a drag of his cigarette.

"Thanks." I dropped my duffel bag at the corner of the room.

"How was the time off?"

"Not long enough."

"Never is."

I climbed to the top rack and pulled a blanket over myself. I dreamt a lot when I was in camp. Scenes from the workday blended into periods of sleep because of a heavy dose of overwork and fatigue. The boundaries between waking hours and sleep broke down, creating a weird semiconscious state further enhanced by lucid dreams where I often woke up not knowing if I had actually completed a job or not.

Some of the work crew worked as deckhands aboard the boats. I soon learned a Merchant Mariner's Document, known as a Z-card and issued by the United States Coast Guard, is mandatory for sailing aboard a marine vessel. Many of the younger workers in camp, including myself, wanted to work on the boats and rack up some boat-time but we didn't have our Z-cards. Without one, there was no way they could assign me to a boat. Although I felt anxiety over not knowing what to do as a deckhand, an even stronger yearning to work at sea replaced it. With no chance of boat-duty my first season, a very depressing feeling hit me whenever I looked at the fleet tied next to camp.

If you weren't serving as a deckhand on a boat, you were somewhere on the dock or barges working long hours as a longshoreman. A longshoreman's duties included working under the crane (referred to as "slinging pallets") and operating a forklift. Forklift duty required keen attention to the work on hand, and kept my mind off a yearning to sail.

The camp had miraculously transformed over months of organizing and took on a semi-orderly appearance—well-stocked equipment vans, barge decks free of clutter, and freshly painted tugboats tied and docked alongside each other. I knew the location and usage for most all the equipment.

After a morning shift, I stood at the edge of *Barge 212* with Lee, Jeff, and Mike. The air, heavy and frigid, clung to our clothing— each sentence spoken between us, punctuated by a puff of steamy breath. A stretch of ice floe drifted across the bay as Lee broke into another one of his stories.

"I was lookin' out over the water like this during the Battle of the Coral Sea—on the deck of the USS *Neosho*, what they called an "oiler" back then—a fuel tanker supportin' the rest of the fleet. I was only eighteen and didn't know my ass from a hole in the ground."

Lee continued to look across the bay as if he could still see the battle of the Coral Sea hovering somewhere above the surface of the water like a never-ending mirage. "Japanese dive-bombers started droppin' their shit on us, a wave of black specks floating through the air. When the bombs came in, you knew you were safe as long as their shapes were long—you knew you were seeing the sides of 'em and they'd miss the ship and land to the port or starboard and fall into the sea."

"Well, I watched this one son-of-a-bitch come in and it looked like a perfect, fucking circle. It got larger and larger, and I knew we were in deep shit." Lee turned and looked down the side of *Barge 213*. "When I woke up, I was lying on my back about thirty feet down the deck."

"What the hell?" Jeff said.

"Yeah, I could tell it was almost thirty feet because when I looked back, my shoes were still there on the deck where I'd been standing. The blast blew me completely out of my shoes. It was the damnedest thing. We took seven direct hits and a suicide dive by one of their fuckin' bombers. The bastards really let us have it. Guys were screamin' and jumpin' in the water, fires breaking out, and some of the crew was on fire—all hell broke loose, pure chaos. But the ship stayed halfway afloat for four days. Some guys jumped into rafts, others clung onto the sinking ship—but most, like me, floated with life jackets waitin' for someone to come along and pick us up."

"Holy crap—were there sharks in the water?" I asked.

"A shitload of 'em. A few guys got ate up, others just drifted off—never found. We'd been hit on May 7, 1942—I'll always remember that date. Four fucking days later, the uss *Henley* came along and plucked a bunch of us out of the water. We stood on the deck of the Henley and watched the Neosho finally sink the rest of the way down. A day later, the uss *Helm* picked up four more of our guys who'd drifted a few miles out, and it was the last of 'em. About a hundred, out of nearly three-hundred, had survived—the rest were gone."

The four of us continued to stare out at the sea in silence.

I questioned Lee's stories many times that first season, wondering if the colorful tales were true, or if he was merely a skilled storyteller with an enormous imagination. But I wanted to them to be true, and I tried my best not to challenge their authenticity for fear of breaking the spell of something that captured my imagination and carried it out of the confines of the camp. I, along with many others, listened attentively to each one and never questioned them aloud.

Lee took out his pocket watch. "C'mon, it's break time."

I watched as other workers streamed toward the galley for coffee and one of Angelo's afternoon snacks. They laughed and joked or talked about their latest job duties as they made their way across the decks of the barges. Reflections of tugboats glittered off the water in spiraling patterns of white, buff, black, and red.

Our crew was together, and the camp was alive, the generator maintaining the constant heartbeat of the camp, the smell of diesel fumes, rusting metal, and saltwater hanging thick in the air. R&R was a mere memory, and the last months at camp would undoubtedly be the toughest. I still questioned many things, including my ability to ride out my season to the end, and how those last days would feel. Besides the money, why the hell was I up there? I pondered the possibilities of what I might learn along the way, the benefits the experience could yield, but most of all, what the future held.

SEALIFT

LEE HAD DESCRIBED it accurately. The stark view of a dark gray ocean blending into a light gray sky outside my window had changed. What looked like a city—tiny buildings on the horizon of the Beaufort Sea—drifted toward West Dock. I grabbed my camera out of my locker and stuck it in my daypack.

After breakfast in the galley and several cups of coffee, workers gathered outside the warmup shack and assembled into groups. "You're with Lee," Bourke said to me, "and G, Salenjus, Tompkins, and a Seattle longshoreman. You guys'll head out on the *Prudhoe* with Swan. Grab a life vest, hardhat, and stick with your crew."

"Okay, let's get everything on board and head out," Lee said.

"Finally." Jeff grabbed a tin of Copenhagen out of his pocket. "We're gettin' out of camp for a while."

Longshoremen, white-hats, and other company workers had arrived for Sealift, stuffing the AMF camp. Every bunk in camp was full and the line to the telephone longer than ever. We hopped aboard the *Prudhoe Bay* with Swan as captain.

"Let's load 'er up, boys." Swan leaned over the wheelhouse railing. "We don't want to keep the flotilla waiting." Dressed in his usual black jeans and steel-toed boots, a blue sweatshirt had replaced his

73

black leather jacket and it looked as though he might have spent the prior night aboard the *Prudhoe* getting her ready. As he finished his morning smoke, he wiped mist from the wheelhouse windows.

I jumped down to the deck of the *Prudhoe* along with Jeff and the longshoreman. G, Lee, and Mike lowered down white plastic buckets full of tools. The longshoreman counted everything as it came on board, taking a mental inventory of everything we'd need for the day. With everything accounted for, Swan walked into the wheelhouse where the music of "Throbbing Gristle" poured out the open door. He fired up the *Prudhoe's* twin engines and exhaust billowed into the air, joining the sound of distorted industrial punk music.

We tossed the lines and pulled away from *Barge 213*. From high atop the camp, inside the comm shack, The Bear peered down with a pair of binoculars as we sailed toward the fleet of Sealift boats and barges.

It felt good to be on the bay, bouncing across the tops of waves, the camp growing smaller in view from the *Prudhoe's* stern. There was a sense of freedom and a feeling of going somewhere, not merely across the bay toward a fleet of boats and barges, but to new experiences and a break from the monotony of camp. Somewhere in the expanse of the Arctic Ocean, I could piece together the feelings I had about the camp, going back to college, my girlfriend, and life in general. Being at sea might help me get a grip on the thoughts rattling inside my head, or maybe silence them.

Lee sat on the bulwark railing near the stern as we made our way across the bay. His short-cropped white hair bent slightly in the wind, his eyes squinting from glare reflecting off the surface of the water. He had sailed around the world three times, guided hunting parties in the Washington Cascades, served in two wars, worked as a laborer, and witnessed seemingly countless men take their last breaths. He looked tired and worn, but had a broad smile on his face, and the wrinkles at the corners of his eyes told the story of a man who lived a rough but adventurous life. I pulled the camera out of my daypack and shot a quick photo before he could realize I was taking it. The image of him sitting on the bulwark at the stern of the *Prudhoe Bay* with the sea behind him is the first image to come to mind whenever I think of him today. It provides me a sense of peace, and the acceptance that we may only realize true life fulfillment in a few brief moments, maybe even seconds, but it remains all-encompassing.

As the flat-bottomed tug slapped the surface of the water, we approached the fleet of twenty-two barges and tugboats that had completed their journey north. Each of the barges had at least one drill rig or module towering upward from its deck, all of them many stories tall.

My only experience sailing had been as a kid in the San Francisco Bay. My brother owned a wooden sailboat named *Tipsy*. In the springtime, he would take me with him down to the Alameda Estuary where the boat was dry-docked and we would scrape, sand, then repaint the entire hull. Once seaworthy, we'd sail it along the shores of Alameda, then into the San Francisco Bay. Our father worked at Alameda Naval Air Station, and as we sailed by, my brother always said, "Wave to dad." *Tipsy*, a small boat, got tossed around by whitecaps on the bay, and I loved it. The scenery was spectacular—rolling hills to the north and east, the towering buildings of San Francisco to the west, and at the entrance to the ocean, the Golden Gate Bridge. I daydreamed of what it was like on the open sea with no land in sight and a boat capable of negotiating large rolling ocean swells.

I stood at the starboard side of the *Prudhoe* as we approached a towboat named *Guardsman*, one of a special line of vessels designed specifically for heavy seas and towing large cargo. A deckhand waved at us as we sailed by, and I wondered what it was like to tow two barges, bow to stern, with structures the size of buildings on their decks, across thousands of miles of ocean covered in ice. I wanted to be that deckhand, waving at a dayboat packed with laborers.

The lure of the sea is the wind and salty mist slapping you in the face as you negotiate one wave after another. It's the primordial attraction to the ocean, a world where our species once lived, then evolved from. But it's the little things that drew me in more than anything, churning through my soul like wave-tossed flotsam: the loading of supplies on deck early in the morning and the laughter of crew members; the casting off of lines and pulling away from a dock or barge; the whine of twin turbines atop high-revving Detroit Diesel engines; the deck rolling under my feet; a smell of burnt coffee; and if you're on the *Prudhoe Bay* with Swan as captain, the electronic reverberation of "Throbbing Gristle" spilling out of the wheelhouse.

As we sped past the *Guardsman*, I made a vow to make an appointment at the Coast Guard station in Alameda when I got back to the San Francisco Bay Area. Acquiring a Merchant Mariner's document would be a priority when returning to the lower forty-eight, and I promised myself to follow through with this newly forged commitment.

Lee stood, his legs negotiating the rise and fall of the deck as the *Prudhoe* crested the oncoming waves. Seawater splashed over the side of the boat, spraying us with the salty lifeblood of the Arctic Ocean.

Lee grinned. "There's nothing like being at sea."

POWER OF OIL

THE BARGES THAT ARRIVED during Sealift were huge, much larger than the ones in the AMF fleet. Instead of names beginning with 100's or 200's, these began with 400's—well over a football field long. When we sailed alongside the first one, we craned our necks to the towering oil field equipment sitting on their decks. Packed tight, "drill modules" looked like large buildings void of windows, their steel walls painted olive drab.

The floating city made me feel small. I could not fathom the amount of money put into getting all the barges and rigs to such a remote destination. As a teenager, and later during community college, I had worked at a couple of Shell service stations, a Mobil gas station, and two Goodyear shops. I serviced cars and performed my share of oil changes, and I couldn't estimate how many gallons of gasoline I had pumped. The oil companies were enormous, but I never fully understood how much power they actually yielded. As the mini-city floated around us, I realized for the first time the true dominance of the oil companies; they could go anywhere in the world and do anything they wanted.

The Prudhoe Bay oil field in total area remains the largest in North America with a lifespan stretching as far as 2075. Major players have included BP/ARCO, Conoco Phillips, and Exxon. In 1988 the Trans-Alaska Pipeline delivered twenty-five percent of all U.S. oil production. In 1989 two million barrels of oil per day flowed down the 800-mile pipeline south to Valdez—it's estimated that about 547,000 barrels per day still flow today, although it fluctuates. The Kuparuk River oil field, about 130 miles east of Prudhoe Bay, is the second-largest oil field in North America by area, producing approximately 230,000 barrels per day. The state of Alaska received a record $900 million for the Prudhoe Bay oil lease. It's difficult to calculate the exact profit that the oil companies have made over the years, but they continue to pay taxes to the state, its major source of revenue.

I had never thought much about who called the shots in decisions affecting our world and always believed government officials were ultimately in charge of most anything global in scope. The more I saw during my time in Prudhoe, the more I realized who controlled everything. I maintained a *question authority* attitude, but I was making excellent money working for a maritime company whose clients included several large oil companies. Proud of the work we completed, I wasn't in any position to bite the hand that generously fed us. At family dinners, my uncle often discussed politics with my brother, who previously taught U.S History. "Big industry runs everything—and always will," my uncle stated. My brother simply nodded his head in agreement. It made me wonder if society lost its way quite a while back. What were the consequences if big industry carelessly freewheeled along an unbridled and self-indulgent path?

"It's supposed to be a big ass secret what's inside those things," Mike said, looking up at a module. "They're locked up tight. The oil companies don't want anyone besides their own crews to see what's inside."

"For security," Big G said. The tall Croation adjusted his hardhat and looked toward the modules. "They have technical equipment inside—handling oil is tricky thing. ARCO and Exxon spend lot of money on them. Don't fuck with anything when working on barge."

G had been inside a lot of drill rigs when he worked for the oil companies in the winter. In fact, he said most of the winter months were spent working inside; the subzero winter temperatures made it impossible to leave the confines of a drill module or other shelter. During frequent whiteouts, you had to make sure to count your steps and keep a keen sense of direction if you went outside for any length of time. It was easy to get lost in the Arctic during months of complete darkness and blinding snow, and swept away by a winter blast.

"Hey boys, is this where you want me to tie 'er up?" Swan shouted down from the wheelhouse and pointed toward the middle of the barge.

"Yeah—anywhere on the leeward side, so it's not so damn choppy," Lee called back to Swan.

We approached the side of the barge, a flat metal wall with white markings showing how much depth the vessel was drawing. Next to the marker were a series of footholds and handholds. The *Prudhoe Bay* bounced higher in the waves as we approached the side of the barge.

"It should be a little calmer once Swan gets closer," Lee said. "One of you guys'll have to scramble up there so we can get a line up there."

"I'll do it." The longshoreman picked up a coil of thin line, wrapped it around his shoulder, and made his way to the side of the *Prudhoe*.

We came in contact with the barge and I reached for the wheelhouse hand railing, the jolt nearly knocking me to the deck. Swan revved the engines to a higher rpm and the tug powered up tight against the barge.

The longshoreman put one foot on the bulwark, and another into the foothold. With a quick hop, he grabbed onto a handhold and climbed to the top of the barge. Once on top, he tossed one end of the line down where it landed at our feet. G had already grabbed the eye of a large deck line and he tied the thin line around it. The longshoreman hauled up the large line, then dropped it around a cleat on the barge. G pulled the slack out, then made a couple of wraps around one of the H-bitts on the *Prudhoe's* bow.

Swan gunned the engine and used the bow line for leverage, swinging the stern in so the tug was now parallel with the barge and as tight as possible. The longshoreman then tossed the thin line down again. Another deck line was pulled to the top of the barge, and a stern line tied fast.

"Okay, let's get topside and pop the lids," Lee said.

That's when the adrenaline kicked in. One after another, we climbed up the side of the barge and onto its deck. We tossed the line down again, and Swan tied on a plastic bucket and Jeff hoisted it up. The bucket contained ratchets, sockets, a couple of large wrenches, and a pry bar. After all the buckets of tools were on deck, we turned to the longshoreman. "Okay," he said, "let's open all the hatches. We need to break up into crews of two."

"I'll begin this side with Lee," G said. "We work toward stern. Tompkins, Selenjus—you work toward bow."

"Okay, I'll make my way down the other side and take this guy with me." The longshoreman pointed to me. "Grab two ratchets and sockets, and a pry bar—that's all we'll need." He held out his hand. "Name's Rick."

"Bruce," I replied.

The longshoremen were rowdy and cocky as hell in the galley the previous night. Rick was lower key and more introspective as he kept track of the equipment and double-checked everything. We made our way across the wood-covered deck and wound our way through the maze of equipment to the other side of the barge.

"You ever done this before?" he asked.

"Nope," I replied.

"No problem. It isn't brain surgery—just be careful and pay attention. I worked on a couple of these barges in Seattle, and it was hot outside when we buttoned down these hatches. Up here with the lower temperature there'll be a huge vacuum when we pop the lids. When they head back down south, they'll gain pressure and tend to blow out." He grabbed a wrench. "It can be dangerous if you're not careful—they can take your head off. That's why you leave one or two nuts halfway on when you first break the seal—in case the cover blows into the air."

"Did all these barges come up from Seattle?"

"Most of 'em came out of Texas, maybe Galveston, then a couple out of San Diego and Seattle." He began loosening the first bolt. I followed his lead and began on the ones closest to me.

"Put 'em in the bucket so they don't get kicked overboard. We'll put them back in the holes once the hatches are off. That's what the *Never Seez* is for. Brush each of the bolts with "sneeze" to keep them from rusting in the holes." The second bolt was frozen tight, so he leveraged the wrench with the sole of his boot to break it free. "They'll air out for a while, then the inspectors will crawl down inside and check them out."

"Inspectors?"

"Yeah, they go down to make sure there's no structural damage. These things get really beat up from the ice. If there's anything screwed up, the welders make repairs. But first, the inspectors need to make sure the air quality is okay—they use gauges to check the oxygen levels and sometimes there're pockets of 'dead air.'"

With all the bolts removed except for two, Rick loosened both of them about halfway. "Okay, watch yourself—I'm going to pry it up."

He stuck the pry bar under the lip of the hatch and worked it under as best he could. He then used his foot to apply pressure on the other end and the hatch lifted slightly and there was a thin whistle before it slammed shut again, and the pry bar clattered across the deck.

"A sucker," he said. "That's good. The one thing you never want to do is try to pry it open with your hands—it can easily cut your fingers clean off."

He re-positioned the pry bar under the hatch and applied pressure. This time he seemed to have a better angle, and the lid rose about an inch. A huge vacuum sound whistled through the gap, and dirt and debris sucked down into the blackness of the barge. The longshoreman fought against the pressure with the pry bar.

"Take a wrench and stick it in between," he said. "Be careful and don't put it too far in—don't let it drop."

I stuck the wrench into the crack and the longshoreman released his hold on the pry bar, and the lid clamped down tight. The vacuum continued to whistle for about ten minutes, like a huge lung sucking in air after having held its breath for the long journey north. I had a chew and Rick smoked a cigarette. As we waited, the rush of air abated, and Rick grabbed his wrench and took off the other two bolts. We pulled the hatch cover off and I looked down toward the black void of the barge's hull.

"Go ahead, take a look," Rick said. "Just don't drop in—the fall would kill you."

I lay on the deck and craned my neck into the opening. The hull of the barge appeared skeletal, with large beams supporting its massive shell. I imagined the men who constructed her, welding the framework of the main structure, then slowly encasing it in sheets of three-quarter-inch steel plate—the arc welder twinkling along the seams, the light flashing across the tall walls of metal. They would have followed the plans my uncle had drawn himself, or another team of engineers had designed and he had approved. The idea was to keep the design of these vessels simple, but big; the scale and number of barges in the fleet was daunting. It took hundreds of cranes and forklifts to build these barges, all burning diesel fuel. The completed barges then transported equipment north to drill for more fossil fuel. The cycle continued on and on. My head spun at the thought of the corporate progression of supply and demand, and the amount of money exchanged between so many entities.

In my teenage years working part time at the Shell station, the manager had recited all the required duties during my first night shift. "This is where we stock all the oil." He pointed to a wall of shelves lined with oil cans. "Always make sure these shelves are full—always. There are more boxes in the storeroom. And they need to look clean." He took a can off the shelf, pulled a shop rag from his back pocket, and wiped the surface clean of fingerprints and oily residue. "And make sure the labels are straight, and the correct cans are on the correct shelves, just like you see it now. When you sell one to a customer, write it down." He pointed to a clipboard hanging on a wire clip on the shelf. Rows of oil containers sat on the shelf, meticulously organized by color and the weight of oil: Shell

X-100 in red cans (30 weight), Shell x-200 in white cans (10w-30), and Shell Plus (10w-40), in white cans with gold lettering.

I lowered my head farther into the manhole and peered into the interior of the barge and contemplated its massiveness. All the nothingness—a dark void with pockets of "dead air" supporting all the towering drill rigs above, equipment that would soon pierce through frozen tundra and deep into the earth to suck out a precious blackness.

Red, white, and gold cans. Keep them clean, and the labels straight.

I shouted as loud as I could into the void, my voice echoing off the cold steel walls.

PUMP CREW

SWAN LIT A HAND-ROLLED CIGARETTE, flicked the match over the side of the *Prudhoe Bay*, then climbed down from the wheelhouse and onto the deck. Taking his place behind the crane controls, he pulled back on one lever and the boom rose upward. Tugging another handle, the boom extension stretched outward.

"Works like a charm." Swan patted the side of the controls with an open hand. "I turned some wrenches on 'er yesterday when we got back from opening hatches—a little tweaking late last night, and she works just dandy." He lowered the boom back into its cradle, then stepped away from the controls and crossed his arms. "Two seasons prior, I painted the extension pink," he said, the crooked cigarette bouncing between his lips. "It strongly resembled a large canine penis when it extended."

"No way," I said.

"Unequivocally true story. The first time I demonstrated the new look, there were several oil company bigwigs, and The Bear, standing at the end of West Dock. They didn't appear as amused as I was. The Bear made me re-paint it. It took five coats of buff to cover the pink."

Under Lee's direction, the crew loaded the pump equipment

on board both the *Prudhoe Bay* and *Mop King*. The gear included submersible pumps, ten-foot lengths of white flexible twelve-inch hoses, coils of longer blue hoses, and several bundles of yellow straps. Once everything was aboard the boats, we sailed from camp to a Sealift barge. I thought about the morning rituals of some crew members getting stoned at the beginning of each workday. Hopefully, everyone kept their head screwed on tight. Swan definitely refrained from getting high—synapses inside his brain continued to operate like rapid machine-gun fire.

The module and equipment offloading procedure involved pushing a barge tight against the steel wall at West Dock, and pumping seawater into the barge so it sank and rested on the bottom of the sea floor for stabilization—a process deemed necessary after the first season of attempting to unload one of the large modules. Its massive weight, partially distributed onto the dock during unloading, and the counterweight of the other cargo near the stern, had resulted in a see-saw effect and the vessel fractured mid-deck.

Jeff, Mike, and I climbed to the *Prudhoe's* wheelhouse. Swan gulped coffee and steered closer to the barge then reached up and turned off a barking radio filled with boat chatter. "Shut up, will ya," he snapped, then turned to us.

"Once I get alongside the barge, you three gentlemen will need to attach flex hoses to each of the submersibles along with a couple of straps, then we'll set the hoses into each manhole. The *Mop King* and Lee's crew will work the port side."

Challenged by a strong northerly, the *Prudhoe* bounced along the stern side of the barge like a cork. I looked at the crane boom swaying to the rhythm of the ocean like a conductor's baton.

"The sea's kinda rough today," I said.

"An accurate observation," Swan confirmed sharply. "Once we tie up at the first location, I'm going to leave the wheelhouse to operate the crane. If we slam against the side too much, we might have to make some adjustments—snappy decisions will be required." Thin lines formed across Swan's forehead paralleling the top of his welder's glasses. "So when you're on the barge deck, keep an eye on both me, and the lines. Okay—do things."

"Do things" was Swan's signal that it was time to get to work, and you damn well better know what to do. If not, you could ask—but of course that would result in sharp, sarcastic, but detailed instructions that might piss you off for a while, but at least you'd be clear about the task at hand. Watching him work around camp, then how he captained a boat, it quickly became clear that he was more than a unique intellectual in the guise of a cocky punk rocker. He had a knack for decisiveness and finding the best solution (if there was one) for most any given job.

Four large submersible pumps sat on the deck of the *Prudhoe*. Each one was about three and a half feet tall and a foot and a half wide, cylindrical, and looked like miniature aircraft engines; a large hole on top and a grated opening at the bottom.

"These new submersibles are a lot more powerful than using the old 'Suck 'em Ups,'" Swan said. "And hopefully more reliable and faster. Let's attempt to set the first one, shall we? That is, if the *Prudhoe* remains in the proper position. Selenjus, I want you on deck with me and I'll teach you how to operate the crane so you can take over if I need to hop up to the wheelhouse. Rettig—you and Tompkins find your way to the top of the barge, tie up the *Prudhoe*, then guide the hoses. All-righty then?"

"Sounds good," I said, and we went back down onto the deck.

We carefully lowered one submersible on its side and attached a strap, then connected a length of hose and wrapped a second strap around it so it would properly lift along with the pump and avoid crimping. We then connected the two straps together with a shackle. Once properly rigged, Swan eased the *Prudhoe* to the side of the barge.

"Easeee," we heard Swan say in a loud voice from the wheelhouse. He then craned his neck out the doorway and yelled, "Tompkins, Rettig—topside—immediately if not sooner."

We stepped onto the bulwark, then to the side of the barge. It was about a ten to fifteen-foot climb with narrow depressions serving as foot and handholds. As we made our way up, I stopped and looked down at the *Prudhoe* banging against the side of the barge. It was the same climb up as when we opened the hatches, but dif-

87

ferent weather conditions. White frothy seawater churned between the two vessels and seawater spiraled into the air. In what had been an attempt to find a summer internship in geology, I instead clung to the side of a barge with arctic water swirling underneath me.

I never considered the possibility of falling, but in the back of my head I knew one misstep would result in a plummet down a steel wall to the frigid water below, followed by a tugboat-against-barge body-crushing. It's not a pretty image, which is the reason I pushed it out of my mind as we negotiated each hand and foothold. Sometimes I think about all the instances when something could have gone wrong; one slip in a split-second of time could have changed or ended my life, and in turn, negated my future family. It's too large and complex to consider all the outcomes—positive and negative in one's life—and how and when they could have veered off in a different direction. It's easy to cling to moments that are key turning points, the few seconds that help define or influence a life.

Keep climbing. Diesel exhaust swept past my face. Swan looked up from the wheelhouse and smiled. I tightened my grip as I made my way to the top and reached for the handrail, then pulled myself onto the deck.

It had taken the crew several days to open all the hatches of the Sealift barges, and at each of the openings were chalk marks with the inspector's initials and the date of inspection. We tied up the *Prudhoe* with bow and stern lines, then threw down a line to connect to the pump strap and pulled it tight after the connection. Swan took his place behind the controls of the crane, Jeff by his side. The first pump swung precariously back and forth as it raised higher in the air. We grabbed onto the strap and dropped the open end of it over a cleat, added a longer blue flex hose, and wrestled it into the open manhole. I gave a signal to lower the crane cable, and the pump slowly descended into the water and the strap tightened.

"Beautiful," Swan shouted up to us. "With any luck, the pump won't slap against the side too much, but it looks like it's moving with the barge—helluva deal."

We made our way down the side of the barge setting each of the pumps, then watched as another tug towed in a small float with a generator on top of its deck. We positioned one gen-set on each side of the barge and ran electrical lines to the pumps. Once connected, we fired up the generators and puffs of diesel smoke signaled we were in business. Turning on each pump caused the flex tubes to tighten, and seawater roared into the confines of the barge.

"Definitely a learn-as-you-go kind of operation," Mike said to me.

I laughed. "Yeah, not much of a training course for this stuff."

I had found two small pamphlets in my quarters back at camp. One was titled, *Guides to Safety*, and the other was *Hypothermia and Cold Water Survival*. No one actually suggested we read the guides, and most likely few of the crew did. I used one as a bookmark when I was deep into Hunter S. Thompson's *The Great Shark Hunt*.

I still have copies of these booklets and they measure four inches by five inches, and both are sixteen pages long—some of the pages are blank. The booklet on hypothermia begins with this opening paragraph: "Each year a number of Crowley employees experience the cold of arctic water. Due to the fact that this hazard is our constant companion, this pamphlet has been produced to give you some basic information that could mean your life." *Constant companion? Could mean your life?* Apparently these two booklets—less than thirty-two thin pages—held everything we needed to know in terms of safety.

Regarding the dangers of hypothermia, Lee's advice seemed the most valuable: "Whatever you do, don't fall in the fuckin' water..."

Making it through the first season at camp was more than putting in the days and racking up payroll hours. It wasn't enough to blend into camp and gain acceptance by fellow workers in order to shirk the "Greenhorn" label. It relied more on figuring out how to "Do things," whether it was a simple task, or protecting your life. No room for doubt.

Keep climbing.

INTO THE FIELDS

A CASCADE OF SPARKS FILLED the camera's viewfinder, and I squinted at the sudden brightness. Derald Anderson, the camp welder, burned through the last of the footings that had secured a module to the barge. A white haze and the smell of burning metal drifted between the cargo and dissolved into the surrounding fog. I walked to the end of the barge and made my way across the dock to photograph the module offloading.

The pump crew had done their job, and the barge rested solidly on the bottom of the bay at West Dock. Located at the end of the causeway within walking distance of the AMF camp, West Dock functioned as the Sealift offloading location. A long metal wall served as the dock face and prevented the gravel staging area from dissolving into the bay.

After unloading a barge, the crew would switch the submersibles around to pump seawater out of the vessels. When they floated high enough in the water, a couple of tugs towed them back into the bay to make room for incoming barges. The cycle of docking, sinking, offloading, and raising the barges continued nonstop, the crew free to work as many hours as they wanted. When Sealift began, I cut my sleeping hours down to four a day and eventually worked three days straight, which meant eight hours of regular pay plus sixteen overtime hours per day that paid time and a half. With the amount of caffeine in my system, I struggled to steady my camera.

Two low-slung, tractor-like pieces of machinery with wide tracks positioned themselves under the module. They reminded me of the snowcats that groomed the ski slopes back in Colorado, but one of these pieces of heavy equipment was almost twice as large and lacked a driver's compartment on top. Instead, the drivers were located low to the ground, between the two wide tracks. Where the compartment was normally located was a large pneumatic lift, strong enough to elevate one end of a module, while another tractor lifted the other end. The two drivers communicated back and forth to each other via headset radios.

The pneumatic lifts in the center of each vehicle rose, and the structure slowly lifted several inches from the surface of the barge. The machinery crept the module off the barge and onto the staging area.

A line of building-like configurations lumbered down the causeway and made their way toward the Prudhoe Bay oil field, as would all the other cargo. Some modules served as pump stations, designed to manage the flow of oil, and keep it moving through a network of pipes feeding the Trans-Alaska Pipeline. Sections of drill rigs made their way toward the oil field for reassembly. Every day, semi-trucks arrived one after another to transport sections of pipeline.

Each year, more drilling equipment and pump houses would travel across the sea from Texas and other states to this northern destination. The oilfield continued to grow, miles of pipeline spreading across the tundra-like tentacles, sucking the crude from deep inside the earth. The oil would make the 800-mile journey down the main pipeline to Valdez, then loaded into the hulls of supertankers and transported to various locations around the United States, and some of it, overseas to other countries. As I continued my life at college, and pumped gas into my Datsun pickup to go camping or skiing somewhere in the Rockies, the fuel could very well have come from Prudhoe Bay.

I put a wad of tobacco in my mouth and pushed everything I had seen out of my mind. My thoughts shifted to going home. Sealift provided a lot of work hours but had wound down and I needed to get back to school. I thought of seeing my girlfriend again, free of the camp and crew I had lived and worked with every day for over three months, and the incessant clatter of heavy equipment and diesel engines.

SHORT TIMER

THE CAMP SLOWLY EMPTIED. The longshoremen headed out and other workers planned their voyages home. Joel Burckhalter made daily excursions to the Deadhorse airport in the company Suburban, and every day after work the line to the telephone shortened.

"Hey, short-timer—you're down to days now," Ken said, then took a sip of coffee.

Several of the same crew members from the first day at camp sat in the galley having breakfast. I tried to remember when I had met everyone; it seemed like years had passed.

"Yeah, getting close." I stretched my hands and rubbed my palms. I had gotten used to the numbness at the beginning of the season and wondered how long until they felt normal again. "I need to get back to school before the first semester begins."

"Ah, Colorado," Ken smiled. "Nice country. Mountains—no more of the tundra and ice we've all come to enjoy."

"I'm down to hours," Ronnie said. His eyes had dark circles under them, and his smile lacked the same energy as earlier in the season. "I have a wife to get home to—a real-life."

"Lucky guy." Ken nodded his head. "I hear we might've landed a side job—supposed to bring some equipment out to an oil rig on some island. The camp'll keep running for a while. Pull the boats out of the water—dry-dock and winterize 'em. I'll stick around until the water freezes up. The Bear feels better when everything's frozen solid and nothing's going to break loose."

As much as I was aching to get back home, a part of me wanted to stay until freeze-up and experience the first sunset after four months of continuous light. I finished my breakfast and said thanks to Angelo for all the meals he had served.

I walked outside and stood at the edge of the 213. The noise of the generator continued its relentless roar as it had since the first day I arrived. Except for the drone of the generator, the camp was quieter, as if resting after the onslaught of Sealift. Tugboats rested alongside a row of barges, a web of lines tethering them to the camp. Their glittery silhouettes shimmered across the water, the sun swinging lower in the sky with each passing day.

In four months, I had made as much money as many people make in an entire year. I wondered if they would consider hiring me again next year. The Bear made all rehire decisions, and I hadn't spoken more than a couple sentences to him all season. But I knew he had been overlooking the entire operation and kept an eye on all the workers. A weird feeling of being watched happened several times over the course of the season. Whenever I felt it, and turned in the source's direction, all I would see was the backside of The Bear as he walked away, or the outline of his figure high above the camp in the com-shack, holding a pair of binoculars.

"What's goin' on'?" Jeff said from behind me.

"Nothing—what's up?" I said.

"We're going to seal-up another barge—Swan's taking us out."

"I'll grab my pack and camera and meet you at the *Prudhoe*."

After grabbing my gear from my quarters, I hopped aboard the *Prudhoe* and we sailed out to an empty barge. The wind had died down and the sea reflected a calm flatness. We pulled alongside a barge drained of seawater by the pump crew, and it rode high and light it the water. We climbed up the side and onto the deck, and when I turned back to the *Prudhoe*, Swan waved. The tug spun around, and he gunned the engines.

"Where the hell's he going?" I asked.

"He'll be back later—they need him to make some other runs." Mike walked over to a plastic bucket filled with socket wrenches and Never-Seez. Over the past week, most of the barges had been sealed before they made the trip south and this one remained one of the last. Each bolt needed to be coated with the thick Never-Seez compound and all the hatches tightened down for the trip back home.

"We have plenty of time—let's kick back for a while."

"But first, we need an attitude adjustment." Jeff took out a pipe and packed it tight. He lit it, cheeks expanding, then handed it to me.

"What the hell—I'm a short-timer now." I took a long hit from the pipe and handed it to Mike.

"That's the spirit," he said and grinned. "We made it through the season—time to get back home."

The pipe made another round, then we walked to the side of the barge and sat on the edge, our boots dangling over the water far below. It was completely quiet except for the faint sound of slow-rolling waves lapping against the barge. I couldn't remember how long it had been since my ears were completely void of the sound of heavy machinery and diesel engines.

"Okay, I can't be *that* high," I said and pointed to a massive ice floe on the horizon. It appeared to hover several hundred feet in the air, blue sky underneath the long stretch of whiteness. "What the hell am I seeing?"

"Refraction."

"What?"

"Swan said it's called 'refraction.'" Mike took a tin of Copenhagen from the pocket of his coveralls. "It's kind of a mirage at sea, an optical illusion. Of course he had a more scientific explanation, about the bending of light and how your eyes see it through the atmosphere, like looking through some kind of lens—weird distortion shit caused by something called 'thermal inversion.' But what the hell do I know—everything up here looks weird to me."

I learned later the phenomenon was also called a "Fata Morgana," a mirage seen in a narrow band above the horizon. It's the Italian name for the Arthurian sorceress Morgan le Fay, from a belief that these mirages, often seen in the Strait of Messina, were castles in the air or false land created by her witchcraft to lure sailors to their death. Fata Morgana mirages distort distant objects, sometimes making them completely unrecognizable, and they're especially prevalent in polar regions and deserts.

We sat in silence and watched the huge ice field continue to float above the arctic horizon, then turn into what appeared to be a towering wall of ice. I didn't fully realize it at the time, but I had seen and experienced more than I could have imagined possible in a remote frozen wasteland over two hundred and fifty miles north of the Arctic Circle. I had no idea what the future held, but the experiences during that personal odyssey would expose me to situations and events that formed how I viewed the world for the rest of my life.

I had come to believe in Lee's adventurous tales as unwaveringly as I had bought into the idea of migrating north to Alaska every year. Arctic Marine Freighters was my summer home that first season, and for three years after.

MONEY TALKS

I WAS IN MY EARLY TWENTIES and attended the University of Colorado in Boulder for eight months out of the year. The other four months I traveled and held a summer job in Alaska, making enough money my first season to shop around for a new four-wheel-drive truck. Almost every first-timer who worked in Prudhoe Bay bought a new car when they returned home, and I followed that trend when I walked onto the car lot with a buddy of mine and began looking at the latest lineup of Datsun 4x4 pickups. We both wore dark sunglasses, shorts, and sandals. A Marlboro cigarette dangled from my friend's mouth, burning down close to the filter and his overgrown mustache. I wore a Doobie Brothers jersey t-shirt, and my hair hung well below my shoulders.

"Can I help you guys?" A car salesperson walked up to us and held out his hand. He appeared not much older than either my friend or I.

I shook his hand, and my friend said, "Yeah, he's interested in taking one of your trucks for a test drive."

"Sure—you interested in a used vehicle?" The salesperson looked down at my sandals.

"New." My friend plucked the cigarette from his mouth and flicked it into the street.

"Okay, sounds good." The salesperson rubbed his chin and looked toward the main office. "How 'bout we sit down and get you pre-approved—we have some great low-interest loans. How's your credit?"

"I'm paying cash." I smiled.

Driving off the lot in a brand new four-wheel drive, free of future payments, gave me a sense of accomplishment and validated all the days spent at Prudhoe Bay the prior summer. The long hours, hard work, and never-ending arctic daylight dissipated within the scent of the "new car smell." I asked the salesperson to leave the sticker cost on the windshield, and it remained there when I drove it home to show my girlfriend, Chris.

Since it wasn't a full-size truck, it got fairly good gas mileage, but that really wasn't much of a concern. Gasoline hovered around $1.19 the summer of '82. The gas shortages and energy crisis of the '70s were a distant memory thanks primarily to the Alaska Pipeline. America was now less reliant on foreign oil and a halt to decreasing consumption was underway. With Ronald Reagan elected president, the "Reagan Revolution" enveloped the country in a promise of economic growth through conservatism.

Later in the fall, I added a camper shell to the truck so my girlfriend and I could take it camping into the Rocky Mountains under the golden hue of aspen trees. During the snowy Colorado winter, it was the perfect vehicle to get us to the ski resorts. When a new year began, it was time to make plans for the following summer.

"I sent a letter to the Crowley office in Seattle last week—asked if they would hire me back next season."

"What about your application to the Mountain Research Station?" She asked. "It's only a few hours out of Boulder."

"Didn't get it—the rejection letter came in the mail, yesterday. It's okay. I'll make some great money up north."

The Mountain Research Station was a University of Colorado facility devoted to the study of mountain ecosystems. Undergrads could help facilitate research in biology, geography, and geology.

Their primary goal was to study patterns and processes of biotic and physical systems in mountains, and how environmental changes influence these patterns and processes. I was a geology major, and the MRS would have been an excellent opportunity, but they rejected my application.

"Oh." Chris was quiet for too long, and I could tell that she was mulling everything over. She looked out the window at the Rocky Mountains in the distance.

Chris and I met the first year I transferred to the University of Colorado. She was smart, pretty, and we laughed a lot. She was open with her thoughts and feelings, and offered a sense of balance to my life, a counterweight to my tendency to partake in the college party scene a little more than normal.

I worked a couple of midweek bartending shifts at the local Elks Club, and on weekends poured drinks at the Boulder Theater, a music venue modeled after The Roxie in Los Angeles. I often attended after-hours parties, then eventually stumbled my way back to the condo as the sun rose the following day. Drinking to the point of blackout had become a common occurrence, and with a family history of alcoholism, I knew I was walking a slippery slope. As a bartender, I had tasted every alcohol in stock (need to know your product) and Dewar's scotch and water became my drink of choice.

Time Magazine had proclaimed Boulder as the "Cocaine Capital," and the title was not undeserved. I often received a bindle or two as tips, and there was more than ample blow at every after-party attended. Drowning the cocaine high with enough alcohol to get to sleep and waking up with morning nosebleeds was a common occurrence. Scotch and cocaine is a powerful mixture.

Chris worried about me but was patient. Her commitment and devotion to her studies provided an example to follow. I had to work hard in order to graduate, and she set a tempo to focus on that goal, providing a diversion to the weekend binges. I might not have made it through college without her.

The need to escape the Boulder party scene and clean out both my system and head before beginning a new semester became another motivation for heading north each summer. I also realized I had developed what one of my Prudhoe Bay bunkmates referred to as "itchy feet." College expanded my mind with a rigorous class schedule, but working at the North Slope offered life lessons. And through those lessons, an entirely new gamut and level of questions presented themselves. With the structure of formal education ripped free, my mind opened-up to new thoughts and ideas during the long, monotonous days in remote nothingness. Learning about myself in an environment so different from where I lived the rest of the year, I welcomed the change.

"What do you think about spending the summer in California, with my brother and his family?" I asked Chris. "They have an extra room. And you could take summer classes at Ohlone—it's a community college a couple of miles from their house and offers a lot of classes."

"Let me think it over."

"We could drive out there the day after school ends, then spend a couple weeks together before I head up north. I'll probably get a week of R&R in early July and we'll be together then. And I can ask to get back home a few weeks before the first semester begins—we can bum around California for a while before going back to school."

As I made these plans, images of the camp at Prudhoe flashed inside my head; boats sitting dry-docked on top of barges all winter long in the frozen wasteland. The generator, silenced when the last man left camp, now waited to come back to life when we returned. Most of all, I imagined being at sea and possibly landing a job as a deckhand on one of the boats.

"I can sail this year now that I have my Z-Card."

"Your what?"

"Z-Card—a merchant mariner license. When I got back last season, I went over to Alameda and the Coast Guard station issued it to me. You need a Z-Card if you want to sail. It's monotonous as hell around camp and I really want to get on a boat."

"Isn't that dangerous? From what I understand, it can be very rough living on those boats. Is that really what you want to do?"

"The fishing boats are dicey—the tugboats aren't bad."

I had absolutely no idea what it was like to live on a tugboat. I had sailed on my brother's sailboat in the San Francisco Bay, and remembered the freedom and sense of adventure that it offered. But my experience with boats remained limited to scraping and grinding their hulls, then repainting them. I did, however, learn how to tie up a barge when it sailed into dock, and Lee had taught me basic knots and showed me the finer points of sailor's ropework. There had been plenty of things to learn during the first season, and a lot of hours to master a few.

"It's difficult when you're away for so long," she said.

"I know, and I really miss you. But this is a great summer job— I need to refill my bank account with some cash after buying the truck. This next season I can stash a lot away in my bank account. By the time I'm out of school, I'll have a good savings stored up."

"Everything's not about money."

No, it's not. It's about adventure and trying to find out who you are, or what you want to be. It's about *not* knowing, more than knowing. It's about raising your arms high over your head as you descend from the top of the Big Dipper roller coaster in Santa Cruz. It's about trying to figure things out, and burying both past and current mistakes as deep as possible under the gravel causeway of West Dock.

"No. You're right. It's not all about money."

I thought of my fellow crew members, and if they were the same decisions. I wondered which ones would return, and others who wouldn't. If the paths we take truly dictated our lives, I wondered why some decisions were so much clearer than others. In my heart, I knew I would be back in Prudhoe Bay the day I walked down the gangplank of *Barge 213* after the first season.

STATE OF FLUX

THE MILITARY DUFFEL BAG, stuffed with everything needed for another summer at the North Slope, rested at my feet as I waited to check-in at the San Francisco International Airport. With the "US" stamped in black ink across its worn green surface, I thought of my father carrying the bag aboard an aircraft carrier during World War II. The thought provided a certain comfort but also an overriding feeling of escapism—of running away for the next four months.

In addition to limiting drug and alcohol use, the trip north also filtered tension derived from recent world news. As television reports swelled with stories of increasing pressures of the Cold War, I would escape to my summer home over two hundred and fifty miles above the Arctic Circle, receiving only snippets from days-old newspapers of events happening in the outside world. I prayed that the political climate did not worsen, and the situation might be better upon my return.

An executive order ending price controls on domestic oil had marked Ronald Reagan's first act as president. He now focused on two primary goals: tax reforms and increased military spending with "Peace through strength," the rallying cry. Scrapping all arms reduction talks with the Soviet Union, the president argued that the only way to end the Cold War was to win it. With the deployment of Pershing II medium-range ballistic missiles and cruise missiles in Western Europe, tensions between the U.S. and Soviet Union brought the world closer to the possibility of nuclear annihilation than ever before.

The infamous "Doomsday Clock" took three clicks toward midnight as the United States nuclear stance toward Russia toughened. The symbolic clock represents a countdown to possible global catastrophe, maintained since 1947 by members of the Science and Security Board of the *Bulletin of the Atomic Scientists.*

I had attended protests at the University of Colorado, detesting the actions of the administration, but my paycheck came from a company providing oil field support. Was I now a tiny cog in the corporate and political machine? I constantly assured myself that I worked for a maritime company, *not* an oil company.

I grabbed the handle of the duffel bag and moved farther up the check-in line, my mind racing with thoughts of what to expect upon arrival at West Dock. Any ideas of familiarity with the camp and knowing what to expect had quickly vanished after a phone call to the Arctic Marine Freighter's office a few weeks prior.

The letter I received from AMF back in March confirmed my summer employment with the company, and it requested I call two weeks prior to check-in. I had assumed they wanted to confirm travel arrangements and my arrival date, but the call provided some additional news. The prior fall, the boats and barges had ripped free of their moorings during an arctic blast and drifted over one hundred miles east, toward Canada. A makeshift crew rounded them up like the devil after lost souls, then ditched them on a thin spit of land named Barter Island before the sea froze solid. The fleet remained trapped there throughout the winter until our crews and the spring thaw could release them. Only a couple of tugboats and barges remained at West Dock including the 213, which was a stroke of luck since all the living units rested upon its deck. I thought back to the prior season and the way The Bear kept changing our work duties, switching us from one job to another. Everything changes— a constant state of flux.

It was my turn in line at the SFO check-in counter. I nodded to the attendant and set the duffel bag on the scale. She squinted her eyes as I handed her my ticket.

"That's a large bag. What do ya' have in there?"

"Enough to get me through a summer in Alaska—too big?

"No, it's fine. Alaska—*that* sounds fun." The attendant typed on the keyboard to look up my reservation on the IBM then finished checking me in.

I gave Chris and my brother one last hug, then made my way to the departure gate. I hoped the duffel bag would make it and not get lost somewhere along the way. My father had carried the bag when he was in the Navy during World War II, the fight against Germany and its allies. One of the main factors of Germany's eventual collapse was a lack of oil, and its inability to power its huge war machine. That same duffel bag was now traveling to the largest oil field in North America.

In a few years, they would elect President Reagan to serve a second term. The oil supply pendulum was swinging from "crisis" to "glut." With the fifty-five mile per hour speed limit raised to sixty-five, oil consumption would begin its steady increase toward record high levels. Maybe the world is ever-changing, but the impact of oil has been consistent for quite some time.

I boarded the plane and took my designated seat next to a window. I clicked the belt tight as the whine of the engines reverberated throughout the compartment. Outside, exhaust from burning jet fuel distorted the lines along the surface of the tarmac—thin waves of alternating yellow and white.

KEEPING SANE

THE '83 ARCTIC MARINE freighter's camp, or what remained of it, looked even bleaker than expected. Only a couple of barges and tugboats remained frozen fast next to West Dock—an obscure, helter-skelter outpost at the end of nowhere. Jammed into the side of the gravel causeway, the barges rested at crooked angles, a spiderweb of lines stretching haphazardly across their decks. Before last year's freeze-up, a frantic crew desperately hung onto this small section of camp as an autumn storm swept the rest of the fleet out of Prudhoe Bay and over one hundred miles east into the Beaufort Sea.

The gangplank rested against the causeway embankment, embedded in a stretch of ice like a prehistoric fossil. *Barge 213* and the living quarters awaited our skeleton crew's arrival, and we found a ladder on its deck that would serve as a makeshift gangplank until the actual one thawed free of its frozen resting place.

Jack Bourke opened the generator room door and after a half-hour onslaught of cussing and clattering of tools, the machinery sputtered for a few seconds then roared to life. The smell of diesel exhaust once again drifted along the breeze, and electricity pumped through the network of wires sprawled throughout camp. The crew carried provisions into the galley, then unpacked their baggage in assigned living quarters.

Four boats had been built to join the AMF fleet; two of them were at West Dock, one had drifted off with the rest of the camp, and the last one would be sailing from Seattle during Sealift. The four newer boats, referred to as "Point Boats," included the *Point Barrow, Point Oliktok, Point Thompson,* and *Point Milne.* Built specifically for AMF, two 2,110 horsepower Caterpillar V-12 diesel engines powered the boats. Two additional Caterpillar auxiliary diesel engines supplied electricity. The tugs held 60,000 gallons of fuel oil, 650 gallons of lube oil, and 4,000 gallons of potable water. Towing winches held 1,900 feet of one-and-three-quarter inch wire cable, and 450 feet of six-inch soft line on an emergency towing hawser.

Designed as low draft vessels, the Point Boats rode high on the water surface, and the twin diesels offered ample towing and pushing power. Built to handle the Arctic, I very much wanted to sail upon one of their decks when they broke loose of their frozen prison. Until then, the crew surrendered to the invisible and impenetrable walls of camp. Daily routines of shoveling snow, organizing and repairing equipment, and general camp maintenance kicked in full swing. Work routines, long forgotten during the school year, reestablished themselves. The monotony of camp and persistence of seemingly endless hours presented themselves once again.

The prior year I learned a term that held more relevance as each season wore on. The "Prudhoe Stare" was best described as an affliction that drifted throughout the AMF camp as we made our way past mid-season. Workers who had been at camp too long, and whose mental state had slightly slipped, stared off into the distance at some object invisible to anyone else but themselves (several steps beyond the "pining-for-girlfriend-missing-family-must-have-sex-need-a-fucking-beer" stage.) The gaze sometimes drifted toward the north, across the vast expanse of ice. Or maybe southeast, following the causeway then over the tundra to the far distant Brooks Range. Other times, the focal point simply fell upon a rusting weld mark along a barge deck, a jagged path running between one's work boots. In more advanced stages, the eyes did not focus on anything at all, the fixation fading somewhere into the overcast sky above Prudhoe Bay. I speak from experience.

I had learned a lot from the first year at camp and felt well-prepared to avoid contracting a case of the "Prudhoe Stare" affliction my second season. I felt mentally stronger than the previous year—a lack of drugs and alcohol also helped.

Items packed into my duffel bag included things to help endure the long days of isolation. In addition to camera gear, three books resided within the bag: Steinbeck's *Grapes of Wrath*, Stephen King's large collection of short stories, *Different Seasons*, and Ken Kesey's *One Flew Over the Cuckoos Nest* (admittedly, this last one not the wisest choice for pushing slipping sanity out of mind). I also jammed ten cassettes into the overstuffed duffel bag, then carried my brick-sized Sony Walkman aboard the plane inside the pocket of my goose down jacket. The repertoire of music included Bob Marley, Peter Tosh, the Stones, Floyd, Zeppelin, Dylan, the Dead, Jimmy Buffet, Willy Nelson, and Lou Reed.

I discovered something the prior season in one of the storage vans that also helped prevent a serious bout of spiraling arctic depression. When I walked into the van, a sweet smoke aroma emanated from a crudely constructed wooden box. I later learned that Derald Anderson and one of the other welders had built a fish smoker, and I realized there must be fish to catch after ice breakup. Upon request, my father had shipped me my fishing rod, reel, and an assortment of lures that season, and I brought all of it along with me for this second year. My father had also bought me a new Canon AE1 as a Christmas gift, providing me a much-needed high quality camera—another tool to help maintain a healthy creative mind.

As prepared as I felt the second season, stories of workers "losing it" pulled me into a sea of murky doubt. It was a constant reminder that much of the heavy lifting at the AMF camp was mental, not only physical. I walked into the galley a little earlier than usual one morning, placed my order with Angelo, and grabbed a cup of coffee.

"Morning." I nodded to The Bear and Bourke. They both nodded back.

"It's gonna to be a long season." Bourke said to The Bear. "Gettin' the rest of camp back to Prudhoe after ice break-up—we'll need to hustle to get up to speed. Guys'll be tired come July and August. Some might get a little wackier than usual."

"Remember Dan Mclean?" The Bear took a sip of coffee.

"Yeah." Bourke smiled. "We had to get him on the plane early that season."

"I'll never forget that. I walked outside my quarters and he was on top of one of the containers, howlin' at the moon. Of course there was no moon." The Bear turned and smirked. "That guy was loony as hell—really went off the deep end."

I wondered if The Bear was talking figuratively, or if Dan McLean, whoever he was, had actually tilted his head skyward and howled at the top of his lungs. An image of Lon Chaney on top of a storage container popped into my head. The scene became even more bizarre given the sun's twenty-four-hour circle directly above camp. I thought of the quarters next to mine, and the windows covered with black spray paint. When I inquired about it, Lee told me the constant daylight had nearly driven a co-worker insane a couple of years back. "One night, the crazy fuck spray-painted all the windows black."

"And there was Wayne Sanders the year after that," Bourke continued. "We were finally able to catch him—he was runnin' down the causeway to god knows where—said he needed to water his lawn. Shipped *him* home early, too."

"Not everyone makes it through the season." The Bear stood up and dumped his dirty dishes into a gray plastic tub near the door.

The camp had changed a lot, but so had I. I felt more confident and knew fairly well what to expect. Another year of college had exposed me to many new thoughts, and I had the tools to negotiate the moments that make up a dull day. But Bourke was right—it *was* going to be a long season. Once again I was in a position of questioning whether I could make it through not only the first days, but the entire summer.

Group isolation from a larger populace creates some interesting consequences, including a distorted sense of time. People who spent long periods living underground without daylight often experienced a syndrome termed, "time-shifting." A sociologist once reported a feeling of slowing time as he conducted research on the subject in 1993. The researcher, Maurizio Montalbini, spent 366 days in an underground cavern near Pesaro in Italy, a cave designed with NASA to simulate space missions. When he emerged, he remained convinced only 219 days had passed. His sleep-wake cycles had almost doubled in length. For reasons unclear, researchers have found people eventually adjust to a forty-eight-hour cycle when in total darkness—thirty-six hours of activity followed by twelve hours of sleep. People who spend over four months in total daylight feel a similar shift.

The need to endure long work hours and even longer days in order to minimize the "Prudhoe Stare," haunted me along with the rest of the crew. My camera, books, music, and fishing pole served as talismans. Much like the sparkling new Point Boats were well-stocked with fuel, oil, and water to operate smoothly, the collection I carried to my northern home prepared me for the season ahead. I constantly reassured myself I had planned well for the long haul, and the chance to sail aboard a boat opened up the possibility of another new journey.

When The Bear walked out of the galley, I grabbed my cup of coffee and caught up to him before he made his way up the catwalk. He turned to me as I approached.

"I went to the Coast Guard office after last season and got my Z-Card." I looked him in the eye. "I can sail on a boat this year—if a position opens up."

The Bear turned his head and gazed out over the frozen sea. His face appeared as though he was considering what I had said, the words dissipating into the dark realm of gut-reasoning and instinctual decision-making.

"We'll see."

I waited for more, but he only offered those two words.

The day was overcast; the camp enveloped in a dull light. A grey hue covered the two new Point Boats tied to the side of the 213, drifts of snow piled against their bull rails. A gust blew across the ice and a faint whistle swept along the catwalk as we both peered into the sky and watched a seagull struggle against the oncoming wind. Its wings bent awkwardly for a moment as it hung in the air before it relented to the strength of the incoming squall. It turned to ride with the current and quickly became a small disappearing speck about the frozen horizon.

"Crazy bird—that guy really had to fight to find his way." The Bear squinted his eyes. "Helluva place up here, huh?"

SPLICING LINE

THE GALLEY WAS QUIET during the fifteen-minute afternoon break. The scaled-down crew included a couple of engineers and a few grunts brought in to shovel snow off the decks of the barges and clean up after the chaos of the prior season. It felt like camp was only an appendage of its total self, the larger core lost somewhere near the Canadian border at some diminutive stretch of land named Barter Island.

Several of the laborers went to their quarters to get high as I sat with Lee and a couple of others in the galley, reading and swapping old editions of the *Seattle Times*, gulping coffee. We devoured any news, even old, as long as it didn't pull one too deep into the abyss of spiraling world affairs. I focused on a story about a recent nuclear test out in the Nevada desert, the second one that May. They detonated the first bomb, named Crowdie, in a shaft. The other, named Mini Jade, discharged in a tunnel. I pondered the differences between a shaft and a tunnel, but thankful that at least both explosions were underground. Of course, the nearby populations that relied on the groundwater for the next few thousand years probably weren't too happy.

A month prior, they exploded a 150-kiloton bomb in the same area, a joint effort by the United States and England. The bomb wasn't the only thing triggered by the test—over 70,000 people linked arms to form a human chain between three nuclear weapons centers in Berkshire, England. The anti-nuclear demonstration stretched for fourteen miles. Three days later, China performed a nuclear test at Lop Nor, a test site built with Soviet help in 1959.

The coffee suddenly tasted sour. I stood from the table, walked to the sink, and tossed the black sludge down the drain.

"Whatta ya know—coffee too strong?" chimed Angelo, the lead cook. He continued to stock shelves with recently delivered provisions.

"I think my stomach's too *weak*."

Angelo smiled and lifted a can of Libby's corn to the top shelf. "Need to be careful—that stuff'll dissolve the pipeworks."

"Mine or the galley's?"

"Both."

I tried to extinguish thoughts of increasing bomb tests, but additional concerns continued to flare. Nevada was next to California, where I was born and my family lived—and my girlfriend, Chris, was spending the summer. Nevada's neighbor to the east was Colorado, where I attended college. Even though the tests were underground and supposedly no airborne radiation detected, it still wasn't comforting having them so close to the people I loved. I thought of Chris sitting in the passenger's seat as we drove to California, before I left for Prudhoe. Our route across Nevada had been only a few hundred miles north of the vast military test area. The combination of the Tonopah Test Range, the Nellis Air Force Range, and the Nevada Test Site was 5,470 square miles, one of the largest unpopulated areas in the United States.

My thoughts on nuclear power previously lived in the same realm as oil production—a needed evil that provided the country with energy, and a necessary technology that kept everything moving and functional. Properly regulated and managed, it made sense. Nuclear bombs, however, were a totally different beast, and I wondered why the test area was under the jurisdiction of the United

States Department of Energy. From what I understood, they performed tests to see if limited nuclear attacks against enemy forces were feasible. What did bombing our enemies have to do with the DOE? The complexities of nuclear advancement filled me with a need to learn—to understand what rabbit hole we were going down.

Lee stood from the table and approached me, freeing me of thoughts of charred sedimentary rock and radiated sagebrush.

"There's new ship line in a bunch of crates next to the tool van," Lee said. "The Bear wants us to get it ready. We'll most likely need every bit of it to tie up the rest of the camp when we get it back—whenever the hell that is."

I welcomed a break from the bleakness of the news headlines, and I'd also had my fill of shoveling snow for a while. Working with boat lines was a welcome respite, and I had finally mastered some basic knots during the first season. Thanks to Lee's patience, I learned how to quickly tie a bowline, square knot, sheepshank, and a trucker's hitch. The chance to learn some new ropework and listen to Lee was the perfect tonic for the early-season blues.

"I'll show you how to splice line. We'll get Bowman and Masiel to help."

Jim Bowman, a UC Berkley student, bunked with Lee along with David Masiel. Dave graduated from UC Davis, and when not working, he was often in his room writing. It didn't surprise me when twenty years later he published a novel with Random House, *2182 Kilohertz*, the setting and characters loosely based on the AMF camp.

We walked across *Barge 212* toward the tool van and stopped in front of several large wooden crates. Drifting snow had smothered storage containers and equipment before winter hit, and sub-zero temperatures froze everything to the decks. Like an archaeologist in search of ancient fossils, there was no telling what one might find during a spring thaw.

"How 'bout a couple of you guys grab some shovels from the equipment van so we can clear away the snow." Lee leaned over and put a hand on a crate. "We'll need a pry-bar, too."

"Rettig and I'll get them," Dave said.

We each grabbed a couple of shovels and a pry bar from the

equipment van. On the way back, we talked about some of the news stories we had read during the break.

"Yeah, they detonated another nuclear bomb out in Nevada—makes two this month."

Dave grabbed a tin out of the top pocket of his coveralls and grabbed three finger-fulls of tobacco. "We're going to blow up this entire planet someday." He jammed the wad behind his lip. Lee walked over to us, and I could tell by the way his eyes narrowed we were about to be treated with another "Lee story."

"I've seen a nuclear explosion—full fuckin' mushroom cloud."

"Really—when was that?" Dave asked.

Jim walked closer and our tight semi-circle focused on Lee as he embarked on another engrossing tale.

"1946. Bikini Atoll. I was on board a cruiser. It was the first atomic testing since we dropped the bomb on Nagasaki in '45. They called it the 'Crossroads Test.' They exploded two of 'em at Marshall Islands, and I watched the second one go off. They dropped the first one from a B-52 and it exploded above the test area—kind of a dud and didn't land where they wanted. The one we were at, they detonated under water. It pushed a mushroom cloud into the air that covered most of the sky. Somethin' I sure as hell'll never forget."

"Jesus, Lee—how close were you?" Jim's eyes widened, as though he were envisioning what Lee had witnessed.

"Oh, maybe five to ten miles. Damn close, that's for sure. Close enough to get soaked with ocean spray when it made its way to us. I always laugh when they show those guys wearing sunglasses right before the explosion. Hell, only officers wore sunglasses. Us enlisted men had nothin' for our eyes. We all wore t-shirts—it was hotter than a well-digger's ass out there. Some guys were even bare-foot, wearin' shorts."

"Did you at least look away when it detonated?" Dave asked as he cleared snow off the crate.

"There's no looking away from something you might see only once in a lifetime." Lee gazed down at his work boots for a few seconds, then turned back to us and continued the story. "Several of our ships were circled around the blast area, and after the explosion settled down a bit, we sailed toward the center toward any of the test fleet that was still there and not destroyed. Well, it was our job to check 'em out. We also took some time to wash off all the mist from our ship."

"Aren't you concerned about all the radiation you were exposed to?" Dave asked and set down the shovel. "That water had to have been highly radioactive."

"Shit, I feel fuckin' great." Lee stood a little taller and puffed out his chest. "The government sent me a goddamn book—thicker than the Seattle phonebook. It lists how much radiation I received, measured in radons or some damn thing, and gives exposure information. If I can fit it in my bag, I'll bring it up here next time and show you guys."

Lee jammed the pry bar under the crate lid. A couple of nails made a screeching noise before it popped open.

"Hell, I'm almost as strong as I've ever been—hard work keeps a guy healthy."

I remembered viewing film footage of a nuclear test in the Nevada desert. Soldiers played cards, smoked cigarettes, or took naps only minutes before the detonation. Later, they hunched down in foxholes as a plane flew high overhead. When the bomb went off, the blast blew dust and sand across the desert floor and into their faces. They then rose out of their shelters and walked directly toward the mushroom cloud. It was difficult to put the thought of Lee's radiation exposure out of my head. He quickly diverted our attention to the line work.

"All right, we gotta get workin' before The Bear sees us shootin' the shit. Go ahead and take the first length of line out of the crate and leaf it out across the deck."

Dave, Jim, and I removed a section of line from the crate and pulled it in a straight path for about thirty feet toward the bow of the barge, then looped it back the other way. We continued this progression to create an elongated squiggle of line across the deck as Lee walked to the tool van.

"Can you believe that shit?" Jim kicked at the line on the deck. "He's lucky to still be alive."

"I wonder how many of his crewmates are already dead," Dave said.

Lee came back from the tool van holding what appeared to be a foot-long wooden spike along with a metal spike, and a mallet with a rubber head.

"Okay, let me show you how to do this." He said to me. "This is called a fid." He held the wooden tool out to us. One end was about the same circumference as the larger end of a baseball bat, and it tapered down to a point.

"And this is a marlinespike. A marlinspike is used when you need to splice wire cable." He held the metal spike out with his other hand. It was about the same length as the fid. "You can either splice two ends of line together to make a longer one, or do what we need to do with these—make eye splices in 'em."

Lee grabbed the end of the line and bent it back on itself to form a loop. Three independent strands at the end of the line were bound by a thin string to keep them from unwinding. He took out his knife and cut the string then separated the strands. At the section where the loop was to be formed, he stuck the fid into the line, and hammered it with the mallet to create a space. Beginning with one strand from the bitter end, he tucked from left to right, the lay of the line being opened by the wooden fid for each tuck. He pushed the other two strands into the line, but from right to left, then gave each succeeding strand an additional tuck to create a taper to the splice. Lastly, he cut away any dangling ends and completed the eye splice.

"It should taper into itself, nice and smooth. It's a lot cleaner than making a knot for a loop, and it's a hell of a lot stronger. Whenever you tie a knot, it weakens the line by nearly half its strength. That's important to remember. A lot of guys forget or are hurryin' around too much to do it right. It's better to take the time and make a splice, so the line works as one piece—not against itself."

We examined the newly formed loop and the pattern of intertwined strands. When the line experienced stress—a load of a 300-ton barge pulling against it—the strain would keep all the strands together, the individual pieces tightening into each other.

"And that's how you make an eye splice." Lee wiped his sleeve across his nose. "I'll show you another good one to know—it's called a back splice, and it's used on thinner line to keep the ends from fraying."

Lee picked up a piece of half-inch line and unfurled three individual strands from the end. Without the use of the fid, his large, work-worn hands were amazingly nimble as he opened and tucked the line back into itself in a series of successions without forming a loop. He tossed the finished line onto the deck and rolled it back and forth under the sole of his boot to complete a smooth taper.

"With poly line, you can burn the ends or tape 'em, but again, that's the easy way." Lee picked up the finished line. "Poly's strong, but doesn't hold a knot as well, and it's a bitch to splice. This manila line is best."

"In one of the vans I saw a line that was ball-shaped at the end—what's that used for?" I asked.

"That's a monkey's fist," Lee said. "You attach it to the eye of a larger line and heave it to another boat at a distance, then they can pull the larger line over. I'll show you how to make one of those later—and also how to tie whipping to the end of a line."

I knew I was learning an ancient art from a modern master, and I remained forever grateful to Lee for sharing this knowledge. Working with the lines not only connected me to a group of craftworkers that spanned thousands of generations, but it also provided a primal sense of using one's hands for the basic need of survival.

Archaeologists have uncovered artifacts of cordage and various ropework dating back to over 300,000 years. Some historians claim humans tied knots several millennia before the discovery of fire. Primitive cultures used ropes and knots to form snares, nets, and traps for capturing food. The construction of shelters, weapons, and the capability to move and pull heavy loads all required sturdy ropework. They also used ropes and knots in sacrificial offerings, and occasionally, to strangle an enemy.

Early ropes required twisting by hand or braiding, but eventually, mechanical methods by the "ropewalk method" in Europe took over. The machine, called a rope jack, consisted of three hooks and swivels that spun together to put a twist in a strand. The rope-making craft later fell under the protection of a ropemakers' guild (the predecessor of modern unions). Master craft workers taught apprentice rope makers their skills, but unlike Lee's training, they kept trade knowledge a secret.

The first printed books about knot tying and ship lines were the formal seamanship manuals of the late 1700s and early 1800s. Tarred hemp was the preferred fiber for marine use from pre-colonial times to the 1940s, but manila and sisal were sometimes used. Polypropylene, or "poly line" that Lee had mentioned, is most often used today—a material produced with hydrocarbons. We pulled more line out of the crates.

In the desolation of Prudhoe Bay, Alaska, we were splicing line, chewing tobacco, and listening to Lee's endless collection of stories. Over 3,700 miles south, in the middle of the Nevada Desert under a summer haze, the military was splitting atoms. Bombs measured in megatons shook the sparsely populated land, the resulting radiation penetrating the earth and seeping down into the water table. Less than ten miles away from the AMF camp, in the Prudhoe Bay oilfield, massive drill bits bore into the earth. Their tungsten carbide rolling cutters ripped through 300-million-year-old rock, piercing stratigraphic traps filled with hydrocarbons. Billions of gallons of crude pumped through the oilfield's veins, down the 800-mile stretch of winding pipeline to the Port of Valdez, and into awaiting supertankers.

I completed my first eye-splice, and Lee's words hung in the frigid arctic air like the crystallized fog of early morning: there's no looking away from something you might see only once in a lifetime.

HOMELANDS

TIGHTLY PACKED ON my bookshelf, directly below the tugboat passageway light, are books about Native American history and culture. I'm sitting cross-legged, scanning the titles and remembering the stories each one holds. Several include our local tribe, the Washoe Tribe of Nevada and California, known for their exquisite basketry—individual strands of willow, redbud, and bracken fern carefully woven together in colorful geometric designs.

Many of the books on the shelf do not accurately depict Native American people. They don't come close to telling a complete story—written history is often a distortion of a larger truth. But together, even with their imperfections and inaccuracies, the stories and people portrayed in the books are like strands within the Washoe basketry, woven together to create an even larger sense of complexity.

I presently work for many Native American tribes across the United States. My job is to help them tell their stories in their own words and communicate the intricacies of their culture to visitors from around the world. As I flew home from a Tribal Tourism Conference a few years ago, a passenger next to me asked why I was so interested in indigenous cultures—why I enjoyed working for the

tribes. "They were here first," I said. It was an off-the-cuff and dis-
ingenuous answer. In my search for a quick reply, I often grasp at
the first thing that enters my mind. I explained it was much more
than that. Their respect for nature, a keener awareness of the connection between human and natural worlds, a direct and unfiltered
way of negotiating challenges, and an overall resiliency to seemingly
insurmountable obstacles, are only a few of the many things that
align with my beliefs.

I take a book off the shelf titled, *500 Nations* by Alvin M. Josephy
Jr. and turn to a section on Alaska natives. Scanning the pages and
descriptions of the Inuit of Alaska takes me back to a time I learned
of their culture firsthand when working at the North Slope. The experience forever changed the way I interpret human relations—and
perceptions of history.

The name "Eskimo," given to these people by neighboring Ab-
naki Indians, means "eaters of raw flesh." They are culturally and lin-
guistically distinct from Native Americans of the lower forty-eight
states, and are now commonly known as Inuit, but prefer Iñupiat
(The Real People), and their language is Inupiaq. At the time of contact in 1741, the various indigenous nations of Alaska controlled all
of Alaska's 586,400 square miles—the Iñupiat in the Northeast and
the Arctic, the Dene (Athapascan) in the vast Interior, the Yu'pik
in the Yukon-Kuskokwim Delta, the Unangan (Aleut) in the Aleu-
tian Islands, the Sugpiaq in Kodiak and the Gulf of Alaska, and the
Tlingit and Haida in Southeast Alaska.

Their homelands stretch 12,000 miles—from parts of Siberia,
along the Alaskan coast, across Canada, and onto Greenland. It's
one of the most forbidding and desolate expanses on earth. Widely
dispersed throughout this area, the total Iñupiat population is only
around 60,000. Between 25,000 and 35,000 reside in Alaska.

I pull another book from the shelf. It's a photographic history
of American Indians as documented by Edward C. Curtis. Curtis
dedicated his life documenting native people through the lens of
his camera, and his images are beautiful renditions of a way of life
that has long passed. Unfortunately, he often paid natives to pose

in staged scenes, wearing historically inaccurate clothes and costumes to tell his story. Again, history is most often defined by the individual who documents it. I find it best to focus on the faces and look into the eyes of the people he photographed.

I turn to pages with images of the Iñupiat and try to imagine their thoughts. How did they perceive the arrival of European explorers, hunters, trappers, and settlers? What did they think of this man with the large box camera in front of them, telling them how to stand, what to wear?

The story of the Iñupiat and how they fought encroachment into their lands began in the early 1900s and increased during the mid-twentieth century after the discovery of Alaska's oil assets. In 1932, the United States Navy, and later private corporations, developed a petroleum reserve in the north. The Iñupiat would fight the exploration for oil, but another threat loomed from the United States government, who now managed their lands.

In 1958, the Atomic Energy Commission (AEC) requested some 1600 square miles of territory near an Iñupiat village at Point Hope, on the western edge of Alaska. The AEC planned to create a man-made deep-water port for unloading coal shipped by boat from the north coast of the state, then loaded onto trains for transport to the lower forty-eight states. The plan also served as an experiment to see how large alterations of geographic terrain might be possible.

The construction of this artificial port relied on the detonation of a series of atomic bombs. These bombs, strategically placed to create a keyhole-shaped crater, would fill up with seawater. The combined power of the explosions would be over three hundred times more powerful than the bomb dropped at Hiroshima. This endeavor, named "Project Chariot," originated under the umbrella of Operation Plowshare, a larger research project created to find peaceful uses for nuclear explosives. The bizarre Dr. Strangeloveian "Atoms for Peace" frenzy gained momentum.

Edward Teller, a Hungarian-born American theoretical physicist and "the father of the hydrogen bomb," traveled throughout America's newest state and promoted the harbor as an important economic development. Alaskan political leaders, newspaper editors, the state university's president, and even church groups all rallied in support of the massive detonations.

Residents of the Point Hope Iñupiat village had an entirely different view, however. Aware of the experiments at Bikini Atoll, they feared the project would destroy their lands and lives in much the same way as the islanders. Opposition from the tiny village and a handful of conservationists drew attention as three scientists engaged in environmental studies under an AEC contract.

The scientists commissioned by the AEC were to provide environmental studies to prove that the project would pose no harm to the Iñupiat village. Their studies, however, concluded radioactive contamination from the proposed blast could adversely affect the health and safety of local people with livelihoods based on hunting animals. They promptly fired the three scientists.

Records also noted that radiation from worldwide fallout was already moving with unusual efficiency up the food chain in the Arctic, from lichen to caribou (which fed on lichen), to the indigenous people of Alaska. Within five days of aboveground tests in Nevada, radioactive particles swirled above Inuit lands, trapped in the northern skies by currents and the earth's rotation.

In 1962, facing increased public uneasiness over environmental risks and potential disruption of indigenous livelihood, the AEC "held in abeyance" Project Chariot, although never formally canceling the project.

Although detonations never occurred at Point Hope, the wonder boys at AEC concocted a new plan nearly as ill-conceived as the first one. In August 1962, they transported radioactive material from a nuclear explosion at the Nevada Test Site to the Chariot site. Released into the air and waterways, the goal was to estimate the effect of radioactive ejecta landing on tundra plants, and subsequently washed down and carried away by rains. According to some reports, AEC researchers had turned the project into a study on the economic impacts of nuclear fallout on communities, "to measure the size of a bomb necessary to render a population dependent" after local food sources have become too dangerous to eat because of extreme levels of radiation.

Over thirty years later, a University of Alaska researcher discovered in archival documents the possibility of a disposal site for radioactive material at the Chariot site. State officials immediately traveled to the suspected site and found low levels of radioactivity at a depth of two feet in a burial mound. Outraged residents of the Iñupiat village of Point Hope demanded the removal of the contaminated soil. The government extracted and disposed the last remnants of this experiment, but the local Iñupiat claim that more contamination remains.

In the villages of Barrow, Point Hope, and Kaktovik from 1971 to 1994, the cancer rate increased by 33%.

Because of their experience with Project Chariot, native people organized themselves to protect their lands. Local villages and groups throughout the state filed claims for land not yet ceded to the government. Congress reviewed the situation in 1968, about the same time as oil discovery on the North Slope. Oil companies wanted to pipe the oil via the port of Valdez, and negotiations were soon underway to settle Inuit and other native claims.

The result was the 1971 Alaska Native Claims Settlement Act (ANCSA), which created twelve regional for-profit corporations throughout the state. These corporations had title to surface and mineral rights of some forty-four million acres. In addition, native people would receive $962.5 million in compensation for the 335 million acres of the state they no longer claimed. All Alaskans with at least one-quarter native blood would receive settlement money managed by regional and village corporations.

The ANSCA agreement helped pave the way for the construction of the Alaska pipeline and acculturation of the Iñupiat into modern society.

Most of the faces of the Iñupiat people in the Edward C. Curtis book are smiling. They look happy, proud, and naturally comfortable in their surroundings. In an environment most would consider extreme, they know it only as their home. I flip the page and a photograph depicts a group of whale hunters launching a boat made of wood and skin into the awaiting ocean. On the opposite page, a group of children huddle together wrapped in caribou fur. They look warm and their faces reflect a sense of confidence and optimism. Everything I admire about native culture—respect for the land, the power of connectivity and balance, and resiliency—remains juxtaposed against the hardships these people have endured.

Once again, it's late and I need to rest my mind. I close the book, the images of past Iñupiat people tucked within its pages, forever frozen within the sepia-tone photographs. My mind drifts to the shores of Barter Island, where our boats grounded ashore over thirty years ago, and the village of Kaktovik.

THE BLUE GOOSE AND THE BARTER ISLAND SOCIAL CLUB

JACK BOURKE SAT DOWN next to me as I finished eating my supper—the last bites of fresh Alaskan cod and a dwindling pile of steamed rice. Most of the galley had emptied out and the rush of mealtime had long ended.

"The Bear wants to send some guys out to Barter Island—get things ready before ice breakup, then haulin' everything back here to West Dock. You're on the crew. Pack your shit and travel light—we're flyin' out tomorrow morning."

Several questions ran through my head, but I caught myself before asking. From my experience with Bourke, I learned not to inquire about too many things. If he knew something he thought you needed to hear, he told you—if not, there was no need to discuss. He wasn't big on idle talk, especially if an answer was standing right in front of you.

I thought back to last season when we were grinding and sanding the boat hulls. A co-worker who hadn't kept an eye on the time of day worked through lunch and realized his need for a meal. He approached Bourke and asked, "Hey, Jack—what if a fella got busy and worked through his lunch break?" Bourke rubbed his beard and thought over the question for a few seconds, then replied, "Well, I image a fella'd get hungry." The coworker stomped off and Bourke turned to me and said, "I don't know what he wanted me to say—hell, I'd get hungry if I missed lunch." Yes, Bourke wasted no words and lived under the belief that there were indeed stupid questions. Everyone on the crew dealt with mind-numbing day-to-day operations on their own terms, and I learned to respect the varying ways some did or didn't communicate.

"Sounds good," I said. "I'll be ready."

"It'll be you, me, Marinkovich, Anderson, and Cubby. In a few days, Robert Rothman and Casey the cook will fly out—in the meantime, it'll be the five of us. We'll be out of communication for god knows how long, so do whatever you need to do before we ship out."

The quickly assembled crew was a sound group. I got along well with Bourke and enjoyed his quirky personality. Steve Marinkovich was a college student like me. He attended the University of Washington, and although I hadn't worked with him on any projects, he was a hard worker and seemed easy to get along with. Tim Payne was The Bear's son, so of course the crew called him "Cub Bear," or "Cubby." He was also a college student and attended Seattle University. Derald Anderson was the camp welder and a member of the Boilermakers Union, which meant he was an experienced tradesperson.

The Iñupiat village of Kaktovik resided on Barter Island, and I felt fortunate to be chosen as a member of the first crew of the summer to travel out there. The Bear called all the shots, so I assumed I must have been doing a good enough job for him to send me.

I gobbled down the remaining rice and went to the warmup shack to call Chris and my parents. I told them I'd be out of touch for a while, and if I could get a letter out to them, I would. We cut the conversations short so I could pack, but I felt as though I should have spent more time talking with them and would probably regret it later.

We crammed all our gear into a small twin-turboprop the next morning, and the pilots fired up the engines. The plane rumbled down the gravel airstrip of Deadhorse and quickly lifted into the air.

Sunlight reflected off jagged sections of ice below, a patchwork of porcelain-colored surfaces that stretched across the landscape. We bounced along the wind currents high above the frozen expanse of the Beaufort Sea and made our way east, down the coastline toward the border of Canada. I felt incredibly small and vulnerable in the plane, but more exhilarated than I could ever remember. It was one of many times on the slope when it was best not to think too much, rather sit back and meld into the experience.

"There're the boats." Bourke pressed a finger against the window. A tight cluster of tugboats and barges on the leeward side of the island came into view. I made out the colors of the boats—black hulls, buff quarters, white wheelhouses, and of course, red stacks. The barges looked like black dominoes, marked with cranes, fork-lifts, and storage vans instead of white-circled indentations. The island itself was only about four miles long, and two miles across at its widest point.

The plane dipped to the left and an outpost came into view. On the right was a ramshackle village, and to the left was a very thin stretch of land with an airstrip, several buildings, and a couple of Quonset huts. Nearby were two large objects shaped like drive-in theater screens, and next to them, what looked like half of a giant white golf ball.

"What's that down there, next to the airstrip?" I pointed.

"Bunch of Air Force shit," Bourke said.

The pilot maneuvered the plane toward the airstrip, the ground speeding by faster outside my window with the runway quickly approaching. The plane slammed down hard and skipped across the gravel, the wing flaps flipping straight up, plowing through the air. As the brakes slowed our progress, the plane vibrated across the washboard surface and came to a stop in front of a small hanger. We climbed out of the plane along with the pilots.

"Thanks for the ride," Steve said to the co-pilot. He pointed at the screen structures about a half-mile behind the hanger. "Radars?"

"Yeah, it's part of the DEW Line station."

"What's a DEW Line?" I asked.

"Stands for 'Distant Early Warning.' There's one about every fifty miles along the coast, from the Aleutians to Greenland. They're Air Force tracking stations—make sure Russian bombers loaded with nukes don't sneak over."

A sign on one of the Quonset huts read, "Barter Island Social Club." The hut blended into the surrounding terrain; in fact, it looked as though everything at Barter Island was varying degrees of gray. It almost made our camp at West Dock a shade more colorful in comparison—but only a shade. I often felt as though we were somehow walking around in an old movie, a fictional world void of color. Maybe that's the reason I took so many black and white photos.

"Well, gentlemen, I think we deserve a drink," Bourke said with an elfish grin. "They're supposed to set us up with a ride out to camp—may as well whet our whistle while we wait."

The Barter Island Social Club was part of the Air Force tracking camp on Barter Island. Basically, it was a bar in the middle of the Arctic, and the only customers were civilians who worked at the installation along with visiting Air Force staff. We ordered a drink from the only other person in the bar—the bartender. In another room was an office, and another man sat at a desk talking into a radio transmitter. The bar was dark—a welcome respite from the twenty-four-hour daylight, and it took several minutes for my eyes to adjust. There were only a couple of muted lights above the bar. A fluorescent light emblazoned with a Budweiser logo along its cover hung above a pool table in the corner.

"Welcome, gentlemen." The bartender said as we took our places at the bar. "Make yourselves comfortable. What can I get you?"

I ordered a double Dewar's and water. The alcohol burned my throat as it went down and hit the bottom of my stomach with a numbing heat. I stood and walked around the bar, gulping my drink as I viewed old photos hanging on the walls. Most were images of fighter jets along with a few bombers and pilot portraits mixed in.

The U.S. Air Force had controlled Barter Island since 1951, and they extended the runway in 1953 to support the Distant Early Warning Line Radar station. The Barter Island station controlled a section of the line aptly named the BAR sector, and it included a series of surveillance radar stations along the North Slope and stations in the Canadian Yukon and Northwest Territories.

There were nine manned stations, four of them classified as "auxiliary" sites and five "intermediate" stations. The auxiliary stations were like the primary site at Barter Island, and the intermediate sites had fewer personnel. The stations included high-powered search radars that fed antennas with a range of about 160 miles. Most of the outposts had a twenty-five-man module building for personnel and an airstrip—although the length and quality of the airstrips varied, making frequent landings a bit of an adventure. Civilian contract workers who signed eighteen-month contracts were on staff at each of the sites, but Air Force military personnel also visited frequently.

"These are great photos." I lifted my glass and pointed at one of the images constrained within a thin black frame. "What kind of plane is this?"

"Russian fighter—one of our pilots took that shot," the bartender replied as Bourke ordered another shot and a beer. "They were playing cat and mouse up there."

"A Russian plane was in our air space?"

"Yeah, or close to it. They test our pilots to see how close or deep into our area before being chased away. It's all a game—happens a lot."

As much nothingness as there was in the Arctic, there were many things we didn't see. I had heard of submarines cruising below the ice cap—both U.S. and Russian. For skies that appeared so void of anything, they had their share of aircraft roaming high above us. There were many contrasting features on the north slope—from tiny Iñupiat whaling villages on remote gravel islands only five miles long, to F-16s playing cat and mouse with Russian MiGs over 50,000 feet overhead and traveling at over one-thousand miles per hour.

I sat back down on a barstool and ordered another scotch and water. A feeling of melancholy swept over me as I talked with Tim, wishing I had spent more time talking with Chris on the phone before we left West Dock. Tim was a good listener, and we exchanged stories about our girlfriends and agreed that they must have been the most patient women in the world as we finished a second round of drinks.

We eventually slipped out of the Barter Island Social Club, squinting at the sun overhead. I felt like a mole. I knew I should have sipped the first drink and called it quits, but it was most likely my only chance for a taste of alcohol for who knew how long. Light-headedness overtook me as I walked outside into the bizarre realm at the top of the world. We walked over to get our gear as the pilots serviced the plane.

"Hey, check this out." The co-pilot signaled us to follow him.

All I wanted was to find a place to sleep, although I had no idea where that place might be. We walked for about a hundred yards on the tundra until we came to a large, dark object. It was a thick, curved arc, about the length of a long-bed pickup truck. Black-colored strands, like hanging moss, dripped from an ivory arch.

"What the hell is that?" I asked.

"The jawbone of a whale," the pilot replied. "That's the whaling village." He pointed across a stretch of land toward Kaktovik, less than a mile away.

The island had long been a place of trade, as indicated by its English name, Barter Island. But in Inupiaq, the language of the Iñupiat, Qaaktugvik meant "Place to net fish," later changed to the English spelling, Kaktovik. Caribou, sheep, muskoxen, bears, birds, seals, and whales provided subsistence hunting for the Iñupiat, and held spiritual and sacred importance. Remnants of old village sites and hunting camps dotted the island, along with both ancient whale bones and those taken in recent years. The meat and "maktak" (whale skin with blubber) of bowhead whales provided a large and necessary food source for the village.

I took a few photos of the giant jawbone, then walked over to get a closer look. It was difficult to fathom that it was only a portion of the mammal. I reached up and touched the sinewy material hanging from it. It had a texture similar to beef jerky, and I tried to imagine it as a whole, living being, maneuvering its massive body through arctic waters, negotiating drifting ice floes and ever-shifting currents.

Its life's energy had since passed onto the villagers and possibly their descendants. I hoped for an opportunity to meet some of them.

"We need to get out to the boats," Bourke said as he walked up from behind us.

"Did they set us up with a truck?" Tim asked.

"Not exactly." Bourke grinned. "Follow me, boys."

We walked back to the plane. Next to it was a vehicle that only the military could have designed. It had tracks like a tank, and the box-shaped cab featured side windows, much like portholes. Two large headlights protruding from what served as a stumpy hood made the vehicle appear bug-like. Dark Air Force blue paint covered the vehicle.

"Let's fuel 'er up and hit trail." Bourke directed us to a couple of fifty-gallon drums of fuel. He then crawled into the vehicle and stuck his head out of a hatch on the roof. The fuel cap was near the top, and Tim and Steve took a length of hose and filled the tank as Bourke directed.

"I'm naming 'er the 'Blue Goose,'" Bourke shouted from out of the top hatch.

We piled into the vehicle and Bourke instructed Derald to take the controls since he drank the least amount of alcohol. Derald turned the key, pushed a start button, and the engine roared to life. The only thing that separated the motor from the inside of the passenger's compartment was a sheet metal cowling that rattled so hard I wondered if it would hold together.

"Christ, this thing is loud," Steve shouted above the roar.

"It shakes like a son-of-a-bitch," Bourke responded.

The driver's compartment had two levers: one for forward and reverse and the other for left and right. Derald revved the engine, pulled back on one lever, and we lurched our way down the airstrip and onto a dirt road leading to a thin reach where our camp resided. We held onto anything we could to keep from bouncing around and getting overly beat up as every ravine and pothole shook us violently back and forth. It was then I was thankful we had partaken of a few rounds of alcohol back at the Barter Island Social Club. My mother used to say, "God protects babies and drunks." I assumed we were covered.

"Do you know where we're going?" Derald shouted to Bourke.

"Yeah—to hell, if we don't change our ways."

We laughed and hooted our way down a thin spit of land surrounded by the Arctic Ocean, crawling closer toward our lost fleet of tugboats and barges.

BREAKING CAMP

OUR BOOTS SLID BACKWARD a few inches with each step we took while ascending the drift. The embankment was an arcing veil of surface ice stretching from the Blue Goose to the closest vessel of the fleet, *Barge 218*. After cresting the slippery entrance to camp, we snaked our way over several smaller snowdrifts then squeezed between the tightly packed equipment strewn across the deck of the barge. We finally climbed down to one of the new Point Boats, the *Point Oliktok*, wedged between the rest of the tugboats, barges, ice, and snow. Bourke fired up the *Oliktok's* generator, and the heater pumped air into the living quarters, warming our bodies.

Three trips back to the airstrip to gather additional supplies provided plenty of time for heads to clear after our visit to the Barter Island Social Club. Exhaustion replaced the comfort of double Scotch and waters as we worked over eighteen hours carving a stairway into the drift, packing-down a trail the rest of the way through camp, then carrying provisions along the newly cleared path to the *Oliktok* where we would eat and sleep the first couple of days.

Two local Iñupiat villagers had spent an entire winter at the camp to ensure everything remained secure. With their combined watches completed several weeks prior, it was now our shift, and we checked each vessel and took an inventory of winter damage. The tugboat *Lassen* appeared to be where the caretakers had spent a lot of their time. It made sense, as she was a riverboat and had the tallest wheelhouse in the fleet and could serve as an adequate watchtower. When pushing a barge down a river, good visibility was critical, and the *Lassen* provided it. Dry-docked on top of the barge provided even more height, allowing the men to keep watch over the entire fleet and hundreds of miles in all directions, barring inclement weather.

"Jesus, look at this place." Steve kicked at some bones that were lying on the deck of the wheelhouse.

We walked around the captain's chair, pushing aside bones and pieces of fur with the toes of our boots, remnants tossed to the deck after a meal. I wondered what other food had sustained the men during the long winter, void of sunlight. I assumed whale meat had been a menu item. Three mugs sat on the control council. Black sludge sat at the bottom of one. The other two didn't appear as though they ever held any coffee.

"What the fuck kind of bones are these?" Steve kneeled to get a closer look.

"Probably caribou," Bourke said. "Fuckin' 'skimos made a mess of this place. I wonder how much we paid 'em to sit on their asses all winter. They already get a boatload of government money every year and don't give a shit about nothin'." Bourke hobbled over to the stack of bones. "Hell, they give 'em brand new snowmobiles, and the fuckers just leave 'em out on the tundra when they run out of gas." Bourke lit a cigarette and blew the smoke across the wheelhouse.

Bourke's words about the Iñupiat rolled in the pit of my stomach. I had heard similar comments many times before and said nothing, overly cautious to avoid what I thought an unwinnable argument. I regret not speaking up in every one of these instances.

There was much controversy by non-natives over the Alaska Native Claims Settlement Act, where natives became heavily involved in the legislative process during the largest land claims settlement in United States history. In exchange for abolishing larger native claims, the government distributed approximately one-ninth of the state's land, plus nine hundred and sixty-two million dollars, to over two hundred newly formed Alaska Native village corporations. The federal treasury and oil revenue sharing provided these monies. Instead of considering it as fair compensation, many non-native Alaskans termed it "Eskimo Welfare."

"Check it out." Steve pointed toward the coastline.

A couple of three-wheelers cruised along the shoreline. They stopped about a quarter mile away and appeared to look toward the fleet before turning and heading off in the other direction. I wondered if we would ever talk with the locals.

On our way out to the fleet, we had passed what appeared to be an old whaling encampment. A group of wind-bleached wooden piers angled upward from the beach. Embedded in the gravel shoal, they resembled the framework of a crude structure. The camp appeared to be old, most likely built many generations before three-wheelers or oil companies roamed the Arctic.

"This place is a fuckin' mess." Steve pulled out a tin of chewing tobacco, took a dip, and handed it to me.

I took a couple of fingers-full of tobacco as my mind drifted to a world prior the exposure of oil companies and the whaling community of Kaktovic; before the words "Alaska Native Claims Settlement Act" had any meaning, either positive or negative. I thought of the ancient whaling camp, of how the Iñupiat had survived sub-zero weather, life-threatening seas, drifting ice, and centuries of struggling for survival. The delicate balance of subsistence had changed forever. Acculturation drastically changed the lives of these people and dictated what the future held for them. Oil wouldn't be around forever. I pondered the larger implications of these radical changes at the top of the world, and what it meant for all of us when the oil ran dry.

"Hey, Rettig, stop daydreamin'—get to work." Steve kicked the caribou bones into a pile where they crisscrossed each other like a child's stack of pick-up sticks.

THE DYNAMICS
OF STEEL AND ICE

DARK VUARNET SUNGLASSES sheltered my eyes from the flat glare of frozen sea, a tabletop of ice stretching south to the mainland, holding our camp captive. After a morning snowstorm swept by, a gray sky held the temperature to the low thirties.

We referred to the cove on the leeward side of Barter Island with our fleet as "the lagoon." The shoreline, although low and flat, acted as a barrier to buckling ice and provided shelter from northerly squalls and drifting snow. One of the pilots of the plane who flew us to the island said the Iñupiat had over one hundred names for ice. I found that difficult to accept until gazing out at the ever-evolving sheets of frozen water as the hours drifted into days.

The frozen terrain constantly changed, and like the prior season, would soon crack and fracture over the next few weeks because of warming temperatures. Wind and tidal currents push and pull individual pieces during ice break-up, the pressures uniquely affecting each one. Breaking away from landmasses, the wind-driven pack ice travels in a clockwise circulation along the Beaufort Sea. This massive drift of sea ice, referred to as the Beaufort Gyre, could circulate around the Arctic for several years. I came to understand why the Iñupiat had so many names for something we simply referred to as "ice."

I shifted my thoughts to the how this frozen world dictated our work schedule. The first few days at Barter Island had been like the same grind work at West Dock, back in Prudhoe Bay. The initial goals included uncovering all the boats, barges, and equipment so they would be free of ice and snow. Shovel, ax, and sledgehammer helped accomplish this task. By the second day, we had cleared enough of the decks to make it possible to pop all the hatches on the barges. Once opened, they could air out and be safe for the Coast Guard inspectors to enter the hulls.

I watched Steve as he negotiated his way up another arcing snowdrift that made a convenient path to the bow of *Barge 218*. He carried a couple of buckets, two flat-nosed shovels, and a coil of line. He jumped across a narrow gap between the ice and barge and onto the deck.

"Bourke wants us to muck out one of the barges." He dropped everything, then pulled out a tin of Copenhagen and stuck a wad of tobacco behind his lip.

The crew had developed their own jargon, and "muck" meant several things depending on the usage. Regarding a tugboat or barge, "muck it out," meant to clean the bottom of a hull. "Muck it up," on the other hand, meant to cram as much chewing tobacco as possible behind your lower lip. The singular usage, "a muck," was the actual chewing tobacco wad—as in, "let's have *a* muck."

Mucking out a barge involved entering the interior of the vessel with a couple of ten-gallon plastic buckets and shovels. It wasn't one of my favorite tasks, and climbing down the steel ladder into the bowels of a barge always reminded me of what it must be like to enter catacombs deep within the earth. It was one of the few places in camp where I felt uneasy. Walking into a pocket void of air seemed like a very unsettling way to meet one's demise.

A common chemical reaction takes place within the cavernous interior of a barge. Iron, water, and oxygen, creates hydrated iron oxide, better known as rust. When metal rusts, it eats up oxygen. In a confined or closed space (like the inside of a sealed barge), areas void of air often form. The worst thing about encountering a dead spot is the fact that you would never know you had entered it.

Much like carbon monoxide poising, victims never realize they've succumbed to the danger until it's too late.

"Don't the Coast Guard guys need to check it out first?" I peered into the manhole. "This one's only been open less than a day."

"Bourke said 'get 'er done.' He wants it cleaned out before those guys get out here. They need to check for hull damage."

Motor sounds interrupted the conversation, and a couple of Iñupiat on three-wheelers sped down the shoreline near camp. They wore heavy parkas, rifles slung on their backs.

"Man, they didn't even slow down." I thought of raising my hand to wave as they went by, but they didn't show any intention of visiting our camp.

"For Christ's sake—they don't seem very friendly." Steve spit a stream of tobacco juice over the side of the barge where it splattered on the ice below. "They should stop and come over."

"Maybe they're afraid to."

"Let's get to work." Steve walked closer to the manhole.

He descended the metal ladder first. I tied the line onto the buckets and shovels and carefully lowered them down into the barge. Then it was my turn to climb down. I lowered myself into the manhole, swung my foot to one of the ladder rungs, then reached out and grabbed a handhold. The bright light of the arctic day dimmed as I made my way down into the darkness of the barge.

We began a cycle of shoveling rust and silt into piles, then loading it into the buckets and taking turns pulling the muck to the top deck. As the morning progressed, our topics of discussion ran the gamut of girlfriends, skiing, college parties, past girlfriends, and just about anything else that kept our minds off where we were and what we were doing. Deep into another twelve-hour workday, I pulled out my pocket watch and checked the time.

"Fifteen minutes 'till lunch."

"I'm going by our room, then'll meet you at the *Oliktok*."

"Sounds good." I kept shoveling as Steve ascended the ladder.

The sound of footsteps echoed for a few seconds as he made his way across the top deck. I picked up one of the buckets, turned it upside down, then sat down. Enjoying one last chew of tobacco before lunch, I stared into the darkness of the hull—the lack of light and sound.

The totality of the void felt as though it was something tangible, as if it held its own undeterminable weight and mass. I felt as though I could reach out and touch it, hold on to the complete nothingness, and feel the complexity of everything it lacked. Somewhere in that void, there was indeed *something*. I called into the black steel entombment: "Hello!"

Complete silence. Had I heard my voice?

"Shit," I mumbled and stood up. *This is way too fucking early in the season to let my mind spiral off.*

I climbed the ladder out of the belly of the barge, squinting as I crawled out of the manhole. A deep breath of frigid air and the moan of the camp generator helped ground my consciousness. I made my way to the bow of the barge. The expanse of frozen sea stretched to the shoreline in the same shade of gray as the sky above. I thought of putting together a warm lunch in the galley as I leapt toward the snowdrift with the packed trail to the *Point Oliktok*.

My foot fell short of the lip.

I attempted to reach out with both hands—too late—I was already hurtling down into the chasm between the ice and barge.

My downward progress stopped abruptly at the bottom, where the ice and steel hull of the barge met. The snowdrift, having formed against the bow but now separated by several feet, arced downward like the bottom of a large bowl, mirroring the curvature of the bow.

I reached down and felt my legs, ankles, and feet.

No need to panic. Nothing broken.

I assessed the situation: stuck between a layer of ice compressed against an island on one side, and wedged against a two-hundred-foot-long barge on the other. The bottom of the crevice was only about a half-foot wide where my boots were bent, toes up. The barge could pop free of the ice at any moment, shift, and crush me in a split second.

They say your life flashes before your eyes near the moment of death, but I'm not sure this is completely true. I didn't think of how I wouldn't see any of my friends and loved ones again—childhood memories didn't pass by like film highlights. I'll bet that given time to think it over, the same thing went through the minds of most people faced with the possibility of their demise as was going through mine at that moment: *I need to get the hell out of here as fast as possible—no time for life reruns!*

My boots slid against the ice with each step I attempted—zero traction.

I could feel the cold steel against my back. My breath quickened and puffs of steam spiraled from my mouth and nose. My heart pounded against the can of chewing tobacco in my top coverall pocket.

I yelled out a few times but knew Steve was back in our room getting high or had already made his way to the *Oliktok* for lunch. My voice sounded frantic and flat in the confines of the compacted space, like a babbling car sales commercial on a mono radio.

"Fuck!"

Trying to turn my body, it wedged in tighter.

A dangerous situation was quickly getting worse. I had never experienced claustrophobia, but I also had never found myself pinned between a barge and a wall of ice either.

I jerked my shoulders back and forth and could finally spin my body around.

Deep breath.

My back was now to the ice and boots against the bow. My biggest fear was slipping farther down into the narrowing gap between the ice and barge and becoming permanently stuck. I did not want to be found that way. I also realized I was excerpting too much strength in my struggle to claw my way out. A calmer, more concentrated effort would probably yield better results.

Pushing against the bow of the barge with both hands and feet in equal pressure, and pressing my back against the frozen wall, I slowly slid my way up the surface of the curved ice. I thought of how fast I slid down, compared to how slow I was inching my way upward—gravity's a bitch on a slippery slope of metal and ice.

Approaching the top, I made my move. Pushing as hard as I could with both feet, I crested the lip of the frozen drift, and spun around on my stomach.

Did the Iñupiat have a name for being crushed by steel and ice?

I rested for a few seconds until my cheek became numb from lying on the drift, and I lifted my head.

The lagoon stretched to the gravel shoreline about one-hundred yards away. In a few weeks, the glistening sheets of ice would be nothing more than fractured chunks drifting aimlessly along the spiraling Beaufort Gyre of the Arctic Ocean, each one dependent on ever-shifting winds and tides.

COMMON GROUND

I SAT ON TOP OF AN H-bitt near the stern of *Barge 218*, the toes of my boots resting against frozen ship line, a motif of whiplash curves swirled across a canvass of rusted metal. The weight of the camera and zoom lens pulled on the strap around my neck. Over-brewed "tugboat coffee" warmed my throat with its warm bitterness during the late afternoon break.

Fifty miles to the south, the purplish-blue peaks of the Brooks Range angled upward, glimmering in the crystalline northern sky. The hum of two camp generators hung in the air—one on the tug *Point Oliktok*, and the other, a recently fired-up gen on the longshoreman's barge.

I blew across the surface of the brew, creating a spiraling wisp of steam. Thoughts of uncovering a life path had been a goal since the first season of summer employment with Arctic Marine Freighters. Now, in my second season, I sat at the end of a barge on a remote arctic island near the Canadian border, the quest still unfulfilled. In fact, I was more confused than ever.

As a geology major, my emphasis had been paleontology. Studying ancient fossil life provides a view of past ecologies, and also the locations of vast reserves of oil lying under layers of rock and shale. Oil companies hire good paleontologists. But plans of finding an internship with an oil company had changed, due to two factors. One, I now worked for a maritime company, and two, I had talked to my academic advisor and changed my major to Fine Arts. I had already completed several art classes, and although I didn't know what an art degree could yield, I always seemed to fall back to the creative process, even in high school.

When first running this decision by Chris, I braced myself for a negative reaction. Her father worked as a geologist in Denver. She initially questioned my judgment but knew how much I enjoyed my art classes and the instructors, and as always, supported any effort that helped my chances of graduating soon. Now, sitting near the top of the world, near the shore of an obscure gravel shoal, confusion and second-guessing settled in as quickly as an early morning squall.

I held the camera carefully and took off the lens cap.

After crawling out of the chasm yesterday, I had taken a long walk to clear my head. An old whaling village sat along the shoreline about a half-mile away. Dry wood posts protruded from the sand and gravel in different directions. With a lack of trees on the island, the timbers must have drifted in from the sea or transported by boat. Near the corner of the structure sat a couple of empty fifty-gallon drums with faded insignias across their rusted carcasses. A couple of wooden ship planks rested closer to the waterline. I wanted to go back there with my camera to capture images of the gray posts, the rough textures of aging wood melding into the soft tonality of the encroaching fog bank.

The weather had once again changed as I sat at the end of the barge, and the sky wasn't as overcast, making it easier to search for distant objects through the telephoto lens. I looked through the camera's viewfinder at the Brooks Range.

Click.

The shutter opened and closed, preserving an image for when I returned to the lower forty-eight, and had the film developed. I took one more shot but needed to conserve. I only had eight film rolls stuffed in my duffle bag, and they needed to last until R&R, maybe longer.

Steve and Tim walked up from behind me as I put the lens

cap back on. Steve held a cup of coffee, steam swirling around his stubbled face. I noticed his hair was wilder, curls jetting outward in different directions. Tim wore a fur-lined cap that made his head appear slightly larger than normal. We all had crazy cave dweller appearances, a result of long workdays and lack of a functioning shower.

"Check this out." Steve pointed with his cup.

About a quarter mile down the island, a dark figure moved along the shoreline.

"It looks like he's headed this way, gentlemen." Tim cupped his hand over his eyes. "This might finally be an opportunity to meet one of our neighbors."

I followed Steve and Tim across the barge. We made our way over the frozen path that led to the island and followed the coastline toward the figure. He appeared to be about the same age as us, early twenties, and wore a jean jacket and hoodie, faded jeans rolled up near the bottom of the legs, and well-worn hunting boots. He walked tentatively closer, maintaining an invisible barrier. I waved my hand, and he echoed the greeting.

"Hey, how's it going?" Steve asked.

"Heeeey," the Iñupiat replied in a long nasally greeting. He had smooth, dark skin, his face framed by jet-black hair.

"I'm Steve." Steve extended his hand and the Iñupiat moved in closer. He seemed to relax a bit, and they shook hands. "And this is Bruce and Tim—we also call Tim, 'Cubby.'"

I nodded and shook his hand.

"Hey Steeeeve, hey Bruuuuce." He said and nodded his head in return. "Cubbeeee—like baby bear?"

"Yes, exactly—it's a long story." Tim shook his hand.

"My name is Panuk."

"Panuk?" I asked.

"Yeah, Panuk." He then offered a warm and genuine gap-toothed smile. "Fred Panuk Takirak."

"Were you one of the guys who watched over the camp this winter?" Steve put a wad of Copenhagen behind his lip and I noticed Panuk watching intently.

"No, that was Leon. Leon and his brother." He smiled again. "But I would come out and visit sometimes." Another smile. "Bring them food—supplies. Maybe stay awhile."

"Do you live in Kaktovic?" Tim asked.

"Yeah, that's my home. I live with family, but go hunting a lot—I travel, go lot of places."

"Do you fish?" I had been wondering how the fishing was on a remote arctic island near the border of Canada.

"Sometimes, but mostly hunt."

"Want some?" Steve held out the Copenhagen toward Panuk.

"No, I don't do that." Panuk squinted his nose.

"We're almost at the end of our work shift." Steve put the tobacco tin back in his pocket. "You going to be 'round for a while?"

"I'll be here," Panuk said, his grin a punctuation mark after every sentence.

"We'll meet you back here in about . . ." I realized he most likely did not have a wristwatch. "In a little while."

"I'll walk around, then come back." He motioned with his hand toward the end of the gravel reach.

We hurried back to camp for a quick dinner. Tim kept a regimented reading schedule during his free time and remained on the *Oliktok*. Steve and I had moved to a unit on the longshoreman's barge and were in no hurry to get back to our quarters. As we gulped down a couple of sandwiches, our excitement to talk more with Panuk was difficult to hide. Bourke did his best to douse our enthusiasm.

"Be careful," Bourke said. "Those fuckin' 'skimos are always looking for somethin'—trying to get whatever they can. They really trashed the *Lassen*, ya know."

Again, I held back from saying anything and wondered if Bourke spoke from experience or simply bought into erroneous stereotypes.

Discrimination perplexed me. I grew up in a culturally diverse east San Francisco Bay Area neighborhood. A couple of best friends in grammar school were black, neighborhood buddies were Asian, and my girlfriend and some of my closest friends in high school were Portuguese. But during this same time, I often witnessed extreme bigotry and racism; memories of the East Bay riots of the early '70s where friends and their brothers bragged about fighting "those fuckin' niggers," and listening to racial slurs made by some family members, excused years later with comments like, "... it was different back then," or "... you like those people?"

We bolted out of the *Oliktok* and down the icy embankment until our boots touched down on the shore of Barter Island. Across the spit of land, Fred Panuk Takirak awaited our arrival.

"Hey, Steeeve, hey Bruuuce." He waved and walked toward us without reservation.

"Hey, Panuk." Steve nodded his head and smiled. He had a natural tact for putting people at ease, and we could sense Panuk's comfort grow as we barraged him with questions.

From what we understood, Panuk seemed to be more outgoing than most of the others in the village, kind of the character around camp who spent most of his time hunting and hiking the ice fields. An occasional trip to Barrow usually resulted in trouble, and they had arrested Panuk several times. Most of these brushes with the law revolved around hunting without a permit, but other times alcohol or acting out in public came into play. The North Slope Borough Police were his nemesis, and his face frowned whenever he talked about them.

"The Borough Police are no good." Panuk shook his head. "They always make up something to arrest me—can't leave me alone, always make trouble for me."

The Iñupiat lifestyle would never be the same, and a battle for survival had morphed into a struggle for social adaptation. With a share of oil company money came the purchase of new snow-mobiles, bigger guns, and a shifting value system. An avalanche of social changes had dictated much of Panuk's life.

We walked to the old whaling camp, and this time I had my camera. I took several images of the wooden posts, the fleet of AMF tugboats, barges, cranes, and heavy equipment in the background. Surrounded by ever-shifting, ever-changing ice floe, everything was in a state of transformation in the Arctic, even its residents.

We walked around a plank of wood, and Panuk took a stick out of his pocket. About six inches long, with the ends whittled round, and one of them had a sharpened nail sticking out, about an inch and a half long.

"Here's a game." He straddled the plank and tossed the stick in the air. It twirled around several times before falling, then pierced the log with the nail-end. He pulled it out and repeated the action, sometimes bouncing it off the back of his hand in mid-flight or bumping it with his shoulder. Sometimes it stuck into the log, other times it bounced to the side. Panuk's success rate was high in a game of both chance and skill.

"You try." He handed me the stick.

Not nearly as accomplished as Panuk, and we laughed as the stick bounced awkwardly to the side of plank or missed completely. I handed it to Steve and took my camera out of its case.

"Mind if I take some pictures?" I asked.

"It's okay," Panuk said, admiring my camera.

I took photos of Panuk, the whaling camp, and our fleet in the distance. A welcome moment of contentment in sharp contrast to nearly disappearing into a fissure of ice less than twenty-four hours ago. What if I hadn't made it out of the gap between the ice and barge and they found me later—too late. But I had pulled myself out and couldn't help thinking there was a reason. I wasn't a huge believer in divine purpose. I knew if you didn't pay attention around camp it was easy to make a fatal mistake, and your own damn fault. However, I felt as though something was leading me. We may be our own keepers, but a sense of purpose connects us to something larger, something we might not understand.

The one thing I felt most strongly about was that I needed to keep moving, working, and searching.

"You know what this is?" Steve pulled a pipe out of his pocket and showed Panuk.

"Ahhh, kaaq." Panuk grinned. "My friends in Barrow get some for me somtimes."

Yes, the outside world had touched the Iñupiat in all ways. Steve lit the pipe and passed it around, each of us inhaling the NorCal bud, and exhaling into the arctic wind. Maybe it was finally meeting and talking with a native Alaskan, or a feeling of camaraderie and brotherhood between fellow adventurers, or maybe it was merely three stupid twenty-year-olds getting high—whatever the reason, we all stood on common ground as we shared the pipe.

We walked back over to the ship plank and sat down. I held my camera and thought of the photos captured on the roll of film, wondering if they would turn out okay when developed—images of discovery. I would find my direction. But not in one day, one month, or maybe even a year. It continued to arrive in incremental moments.

Two grunt workers from a castaway tugboat and barge company, and an Iñupiat from a centuries-old whaling village, sat on a sea-ridden ship's plank on a thin spit of land jetting out into the Arctic Ocean. All three comfortably buzzed, smiles on their faces, and eyes searching for answers somewhere across a frozen sea.

A SLIPPERY SLOPE

I SIT IN FRONT OF A COMPUTER at my office at least eight hours a day, Monday through Friday. Much of this time is dedicated to designing and maintaining websites. I live in the digital world. But a devout appreciation for the printed word bleeds over to how I read the news.

This morning, like most others, I walk outside my Tahoe home before sunrise (being careful not to stumble across a bear or any other neighborhood wildlife) and retrieve the newspaper from the driveway. The September 28, 2015, issue of the *San Francisco Chronicle* rests alongside a plate of breakfast—two fried eggs atop several leaves of spinach, cream cheese, and an open bagel. The edge of a page is curled against a steaming cup of black coffee. A headline reads, "Shell abandons controversial arctic drilling plan."

Shell's abandonment of oil exploration in arctic waters is big news but not surprising. It's expensive to mine this part of the world for crude, in more ways than one. Shell spent about $7 billion on exploration in Alaskan waters, and it could cost the company an additional $4.1 billion to pull out of the Chukchi Sea, where a recent dry hole was dug. Environmentalists have also posed strong resistance and a growing number of the native population, who once hesitantly approved of oil exploration, is having second thoughts. Negative publicity is stacking up, especially with more headlines focusing on global warming. All of this, combined with the falling price of gasoline (mainly the falling price of oil), has resulted in Shell suspending operations—at least for now. The situation in the world of ice and oil is in constant flux. More headlines are bound to appear within a few months' time.

For environmentalists, there's optimism that this increased pressure on the oil companies will force them to pull out of the northern region entirely, but it's highly doubtful it will truly slow down future exploration. Geologists estimate the Arctic holds a quarter of the world's undiscovered oil and gas. Although native Alaskans have always been leery of big oil, it's brought many benefits to their people. If the cost of gasoline increases, renewed efforts will follow.

Any news about my former home on the North Slope catches my eye, and a few years earlier, I paged through my morning paper and found the headline, "Oil and two ways of life in Alaska: drilling debate divides native villagers." The article focused on Kaktovik, describing the community and its situation as, "a village at the northern edge of the oil-rich coastal plain of the refuge (Arctic National Wildlife Refuge), 280 Iñupiat have been waiting over twenty-five years to find out if they can drill on land they hold inside the refuge." A contrasting viewpoint featured the Gwich'in people. The Gwich'in are a caribou-hunting tribe whose 8,000 members are scattered across fifteen villages in Canada and along ANWR's southern border in Alaska. This group fears the possibility of drilling in the calving grounds of the Porcupine caribou herd, believing it could jeopardize a major food source and destroy their culture.

It was odd to read about Kaktovik, a remote Iñupiat village high above the Arctic Circle. It's a place few people have ever heard about, and where I spent most of the summer of '83. I wondered how Panuk was doing, and how he felt about all the recent attention his home was receiving, or if he even realized what was happening.

I turned on my laptop, brushed the newspaper aside, and poured another cup of coffee. It only took a couple of minutes to find a video about Kaktovik on YouTube, and their position on oil exploration. The community of Kaktovik made the video to counter anti-oil news stories. It features villagers who talk about the positive aspects of development and how oil money has helped their community. Many of the villagers see enormous benefits, including self-sustained electrical power, upgraded housing, education for their children—everything that would help a community continue to evolve and grow. Before the influx of oil money, even adequate sanitation was a challenge as villagers hauled five-gallon "honey buckets" of human waste to dump sites for disposal.

The people of Kaktovik subsist mainly on whaling and hunting caribou. Although the community receives funding through the Alaska Native Claims Settlement Act, the survival of their culture depends on hunting as a way of life. But in a short time, there has been a shift. Many of the villages rely on oil money to further their people and provide needed resources. Even after concerns after the catastrophic gulf oil spill, Inuit leaders in Kaktovik sent a letter to Republican moderates who opposed drilling, pleading that "the survival of our culture depends on nurturing new economic activity."

To further complicate the issue, is the debate over offshore drilling versus drilling on Alaskan lands. The Arctic National Wildlife Refuge comprises 19,286,722 acres in Alaska's North Slope region. It's the largest national wildlife refuge in the country and is totally off-limits to oil drilling. Many Iñupiat believe it would be much safer to drill on land rather than risk a blowout at sea, where the ice could hinder any type of cleanup operation.

An Iñupiat whaling captain was interviewed in one of the news articles I read. The subsistence of his people depends upon Alaskan waters, and there was no question where drilling should occur when asked. He nodded toward the direction of the refuge, where clouds capped the reddening tundra and snow-dusted the mountains of the distant Brooks Range. "Responsible oil development," he said, then cocked his head toward the beach, "versus irresponsible bullshit."

Finishing the last of my breakfast, I think back to how I viewed oil development in Alaska my first few seasons at Prudhoe Bay. It all seemed to make sense. I made good money during a time I was trying my best to find a direction and carve out plans for the future.

I saved a large portion of what I made in Alaska and tucked it safely away in the bank. When I got married and started a family, it paid for the deposit on our first home in Tahoe.

I often wondered if money channeled to the Iñupiat was a positive thing for them or if it would eventually destroy their culture entirely. The world's energy reliance continues to be fueled by oil, and it was probably inevitable the path of exploitation swept the Iñupiat along with it.

I recently visited the Southern Ute tribal offices in Colorado during a conference, and as we toured the four-story building, I noticed a model of a drill rig under a large glass cube in the corner of their reception area. I asked one of the tribal members why it was there. He said it was a model of a drill rig the tribe owned in the Gulf of Mexico. Besides managing oil fields in southern Colorado tribal lands, they had diversified and bought several rigs in the gulf. When I walked out of the office building, I told a tribal friend of mine how I hoped the Southern Ute Indian Tribe wasn't as reliant on oil money in future planning.

She spoke without hesitation. "Yeah, they were questioned a lot about it at first. But listen, people talk bad about where some money comes from—call it 'dirty money.' All money is dirty money. The money the Tribe made from investing in oil production paid for their children's education, provided homes—made a better life for all of them."

I take a sip of coffee and look outside the kitchen window. The first hints of fall are making their presence. Patches of frosted dew cover the lawn, and in a few weeks our aspen trees will begin turning gold. Hopefully, this year will end California's five-year drought, and we'll receive a healthy dose of snow and an accompanying snowpack.

I hear the ignition switch of our heater click to life. The pilot light ignites a wisp of natural gas, and the roar of the unit comes to life. The heater's fan pushes warm air through the maze of ductwork and out of the floor vents, reducing the morning chill from our Sierra home.

KAKTOVIK

SWIRLING CIRCLES DOTTED the sea on both sides of the jetty, a signal of life awakening in the early summer thaw. Arctic char rose along expanding stretches of open water, signaling a change of season. After living the entire winter under a layer of thick ice, the fish broke through the surface to touch open air.

The Blue Goose tossed us around like a carnival ride, but with a lack of seat belts to constrain the constant jerking back and forth. Bourke operated the controls as we made our way toward the airstrip, the tracks of the Air Force vehicle grinding across the long shoal of Barter Island. The plan was for Steve, Tim, and I to get out at Kaktovik, then Bourke would drive to the airport to drop off the two Coast Guard inspectors who were riding with us.

It had been a long couple of days of opening all the barge hatches for the inspectors. With most of the vessels approved to sail, we began buttoning up many of the manholes and getting the decks seaworthy. The big event of the week was gaining hot water on the *Oliktok*. After a week of hard work in frigid weather, a hot shower never felt as good as that one.

It was weird not having Lee around to direct us during the daily grind. He most likely was busy telling a string of stories back at West Dock, managing a crew, and possibly training another greenhorn.

He had been my mentor the first season and taught the new guys most everything they needed to get by. But at Barter Island, we had to manage without him, make our own decisions, and work through the tasks at hand.

Panuk visited us most every day after work. I never understand how he knew the exact time without a watch. The sun circled the sky without rising or setting, voiding any delineation of night and day. Other than a slight shift in its northerly position, it wasn't a tremendous help in accurately determining the time. But shortly after each workday, our Iñupiat friend stood on the shoal of Barter Island waiting.

By catching a ride into town on the Blue Goose, we could visit Panuk at his home and see the village where he lived.

"I'll be back here at eight." Bourke's voice was barely audible over the racket of the Blue Goose's engine and rattling metal shell. "Don't make me wait—I won't have second thoughts of leavin' your asses in Kaktovik."

We climbed out of the back of the vehicle and shut the rear hatch. The engine roared to a higher RPM. Bourke, along with the two Coast Guard inspectors in the Blue Goose, lurched off toward the airstrip. Bourke would spend a few hours at the Barter Island Social Club and enjoy a few cocktails, and we'd have time to meet up with Panuk and check out the village of Kaktovik.

It had rained for almost two days, but sunshine broke through a blanket of overcast sky as we walked through the village. The temperature was still frigid, but each day got warmer in the twenty-four-hour daylight. What was once nothing but frozen earth was evolving into varying degrees of mud and potholes. The streets of Kaktovic served more as pathways or open areas between rows of simple box-shaped houses.

"Man, look at this place," Steve said as we walked down a dirt road through the village. "Why the hell is that here?" He pointed to a bus parked near a longer. With the tires of the vehicle partially deflated, the vehicle hunkered into the village landscape as if it had become a permanent structure.

"Apparently, it's not used very often." Tim walked closer to the bus. "And even if it was in prime running condition, where would one go?"

The building next to the bus was a simple shelter, much like the others, but longer and apparently featured several rooms. A sign above the door read, "Slim's Bunkhouse." Underneath the name of the establishment was the nightly rate: one hundred seventy-five dollars per night.

"I wonder if it has a four-star rating." Tim lit a cigar. He was one of the few crew members who didn't chew tobacco, but preferred a daily after-work cigar.

Panuk told us that less than three hundred people lived in Kaktovik. Originally a traditional fishing village, Kaktovik meant "Seining Place." A seine was a large net used to enclose and catch fish. The villagers' major source of food relied on subsistence fishing, whaling, and hunting. Dall sheep, moose, caribou, and arctic fox hunted in the nearby area contributed to the residents' diet.

"There's Panuk." Tim took the cigar out of his mouth and pointed toward a side road.

Panuk negotiated his way around a couple of mud puddles and made his way to us.

"Hey Bruuuce, Steeeve—Cubeee," he said, followed by his Panuk smile. "My house is this way. Follow me. I show you where I live."

We came to a small yellow house set on the tundra. A deck with railing had a short stairway leading to the front yard. A dysfunctional kitchen stove, apparently carried down to the bottom of the steps, sat without plans to move it much farther.

A wide variety of castaway containers and hunting tools littered the area, strewn around the front yard. Various sized sheets of plywood, five-gallon plastic buckets, a couple of unopened metal cans, and remnants of poly tarps complimented a haphazard menagerie of items. An antenna attached to the side of the house hinted that they might have a television. Next to it, a ladder leaned against the roof—most likely used when adjusting the antennae for better reception or shoveling piling snow during the winter. A couple of snowmobiles and a small sled rested a few steps from the house.

I noticed three polar bear pelts draped over the deck railings.

"Those are some nice hides." I opened my daypack and took out my camera.

Panuk's face reflected approval of my photo taking. We continued to walk around the yard, experiencing a visual assault of items used to survive life in the Arctic. I focused the camera on the bear pelts.

"Polar bear is good meat. The hides we sell for money—or maybe make clothes." He smiled a gap-tooth grin. "Come here—I show you something."

We followed him past a small shed to the side of the house. A rusting snowmobile and motorcycle rested against a square storage tank. Next to it was a blue ten-gallon drum and shipping crates of various sizes. In front of the eclectic collection, a dog rested next to a wooden palette with large slices of whale meat.

"More meat," Panuk said. "We don't get hungry."

"It must be slightly tempting for your dog," Tim commented.

"We keep him tied." A short chain ran from the animal's collar to a log. "He watches—make sure nothing takes the meat."

"No way—what are those?" Steve pointed to three skulls lying on the ground. A thin nylon cord ran through their jaws, connecting them together. Their angular teeth were long and pointed, like crescent moons.

"Polar Bear heads," Panuk said. "The skins out front."

Two of the mouths were open, the other one clenched. They were fairly clean, with only patches of black where tissue once covered the bone. I tried to imagine what the animals looked like when alive, roaming the ice and swimming in arctic waters as hunters, before becoming the hunted. Panuk told us that some bears arrive in mid-July or early August, and remain until the ocean freezes, usually in October. Others wait on nearby barrier islands until the whale harvest, then take the short swim to Barter Island and feed on the remains of bowhead whales harvested by the villagers during the fall hunt.

I walked closer to a smaller skull behind the three large ones. Its fangs, although not as long as the polar bears', appeared much sharper.

"Fox." Panuk pushed at the skull with the toe of his boot.

I turned my attention back to the large skulls. "Those are gnarly teeth—they're huge." I knelt down and took another photo.

"Yeah." Panuk reached down and rubbed a finger over one fang.

"We sell them to someone who make pictures on them."

"Scrimshaw," Tim said.

"Yeah, scrim-shaw." Panuk nodded his head.

I had written a paper about scrimshaw for my art history class final. Scrimshaw originated on Pacific whaling ships in the mid-1700s, where sailors carved fine scrollwork and engravings n bone or ivory. They used the bones and teeth of sperm whales, walrus tusks, and baleen. Baleen is a strong, yet flexible material made of keratin, a protein that is the same material as hair and fingernails. It hangs from the sides of a whale's mouth and filters food from the seawater. It dries to a hard, black material that almost resembles plastic, perfect for scrimshaw.

Crude sailing needles, a ship's constant movement, and the skill of an artist all resulted in drawings of varying levels of detail and quality. Candle black, soot, tobacco juice, or ink were used to highlight the etched lines of the design in bone or ivory. Later on, they also used colored pigment in more elaborate engravings. In the far north, walrus teeth, baleen, and polar bear teeth, all provided a perfect canvas for arctic artisans.

I stood in the center of Panuk's world, visions of crude scrimshaw pictures etched into my brain. Three polar bear skulls, a fox skull, an empty fifty-gallon drum, and a rusting snowmobile surrounded me.

"I like this place—very cool."

"It's my home." The Panuk smile appeared once again. "And next week is Nalukataq."

"Nalloo ka what?" Steve asked.

Panuk repeated the syllables slower. "Nalukataq. When we have blanket toss—you guys wanna come see? Everyone from the village will be there."

"I'd love to make it to the blanket toss." Tim said. "We'll need to see if we can get off work, though."

I continued to shoot photos and ask questions as Panuk described a life of hunting on ice and tundra and the celebration of Nalukataq. I wanted to see the inside of his home, but unless invited, thought it rude to ask.

"Hey guys, we've been here awhile. We better see if Bourke is back in town." Steve pointed over his shoulder with a thumb.

We left Panuk's home and walked back through the village, nodding at some residents along the way. Bourke was waiting for us near Slim's Bunkhouse and we piled back into The Goose. The engine clattered and sputtered as we made our way down the reach toward camp. Every bump and gully tossed us around the compartment like gulls caught in a windstorm.

Along the coast, Arctic char continued to rise along the water surface. After months of living in the frigid depths, they now joined the cycle of life at Barter Island—experiences etched across pieces of white ivory tusks and crescent-shaped polar bear teeth.

UNDER THE ICE

MUCH OF THE CREW got high on a daily basis; it was the only way for some to make it through the season. The soothing effect of THC dulled the sharp edges of tedium, and made the hours easier to digest, the work a little more bearable. The downside was we were around a lot of heavy equipment, and it was a wise decision to keep fully focused when working around forklifts and cranes throughout the day. In addition, The Bear constantly peered down with binoculars from the comm shack, and he had a sense of who was dealing with a full deck, and others who might be a few cards short.

Barter Island was different. It was quieter, and the crew much smaller. Robert Rothman, a Crowley "White Hat," had flown in the day before, so now our total workforce was seven. "White Hat" was a designation for anyone in upper management, since they wore white hardhats. Our duty included getting the camp as organized as possible and preparing it for the long journey back to Prudhoe Bay. Free from the watchful eye of The Bear, I joined Steve in the occasional after-hours pipe-load.

Steve and I walked back to our quarters on *Barge 218* after our camp cook, Casey, had stuffed us with a hearty meal. The generator supplying electricity to the barge had been droning endlessly for the past couple of days, and we had turned on all the heaters in the units to get everything thawed out. Our room had finally gotten to a point where it was warm. We walked inside and took off our work boots.

"What the fuck is that smell?" Steve's nose rose higher, wrinkles forming across his forehead.

A foul odor had consumed the room. It had a putrid smell like rotting fish or something else that had died quite some time ago. We searched the room, looking for the culprit of the foul odor. There was nothing under the bunks or table, and we couldn't see where anything might have spilled or puddled under the chairs.

When we moved into the quarters, I used the locker near the window, and Steve took the one near the door. The middle lockers were never checked and I opened one.

"Ah, shit, here's the culprit. But I don't want to touch the damn thing."

An open Folgers Coffee can had rested in the confines of the locker all winter, the coffee grounds long gone. Inside the can was a worker's urine from the prior season. After an entire winter of refrigeration, the makeshift urinal had now thawed to room temperature when we cranked the heaters to high, releasing the gag-inducing aroma.

"Jesus Christ, someone left their fuckin' piss can in there?" Steve began laughing.

"Holy shit that thing reeks." I pulled my sweatshirt over my nose. "Why the fuck do these assholes use piss cans around here?"

"Because they're too damn lazy to walk to the head when it's freezing outside. The gross bastards would rather piss in a fucking can. Throw it over the side of the barge."

"I'm not touching that damn thing."

"Neither am I."

"All right." I kept my nose tucked under the collar of my sweatshirt. "Get me something to hold it with—I don't even want to touch it."

The past week we had shoveled snow, broken up ice with axes, mucked out a rusted barge, opened and closed every manhole on every barge, fixed a shattered wheelhouse window, and cleaned dead animal bones out of the wheelhouse of the *Lassen*. A lot of shit-jobs had met completion with minimum complaints, but the piss can pushed the limits.

"Here, use this." Steve handed me a plastic bag out of the trash-can, the same one that once held packages of film for my camera. It made for a somewhat adequate glove, and I carefully lifted the can out of the confines of the locker. As I hustled to the doorway, the sweatshirt slid off my face, and I held my breath.

"Open the fucking door," I shouted as Steve laughed. I got to the edge of the barge and hurled the contents overboard, careful not to let the wind blow it back in my face.

"Chuck the can, too," Steve yelled.

As much as I wanted to throw the can as far as I could, an environmentally sensitive conscience forced me to the corner of the catwalk where I put it into the plastic bag. "I'll take it down to the garbage later."

Steve opened the room's one window and left the front door open. He then reached inside his travel bag and pulled out a film container of pot and his pipe.

"This will help douse the smell," he said and smiled. "Let's do a pipe-load or two and go fishing—let this place air out."

"Sounds like a plan—can't we smoke that outside, or wait until we get to the island?"

"Nah—after that experience, I need a bowl right now. And I saw Bourke poking around out there. He acts like he's not watching, but I know he sure as hell checks on us every now and then."

I grabbed fishing gear out of my locker and pulled out a small box that contained an assortment of spinners as Steve packed the pipe and lit it. He took a long drag, then slowly released the smoke into the room, the smell comingling with the residual aroma of year-old piss. He reloaded, then handed me the pipe.

The smoke burnt the back of my throat and expanded in my lungs. I held it as long as I could, fighting the urge to cough. I immediately felt more relaxed, and we took a couple more hits, then put on our boots and gathered the fishing gear. A little higher than

I wanted to be, I thought it best to leave my camera behind on this expedition.

We hopped down the catwalk laughing about the piss can, then made our way to the ice floe connecting the camp to the shore. It had been breaking apart the past couple of days, but was still tightly compacted and solid enough to walk across.

A clear sky and bright sun made everything shimmer across the lagoon, and my dark Vaurnet sunglasses, combined with a healthy buzz, accentuated the glistening terrain. A seagull flew overhead. I felt the edges of my mouth stretch into a wide smile. We continued to laugh about the piss can as we made our way to the island to catch some Arctic char. With worries that clogged my head the week prior temporarily numbed, life was good.

"Let's cross here." Steve stepped down onto the ice.

"Sounds good."

We hopped from one ice patch to another, and it reminded me of jumping across boulders along the rivers in the Sierra Mountains where I used to fish.

We continued our rhythm of ice hopping and were about halfway across the ice field when I lunged for what appeared to be a lumpy patch of ice. In reality, it was nothing more than sea foam and slush ice.

I descended into the frigid arctic waters like a lead weight, my boots filling with water on the way down. The weight of my coveralls clung to my body as if they were a second layer of thick skin. Downward I fell, the sense of sound completely numbed, only my heartbeat audible.

I felt my feet touch the bottom of the bay, and I bounced a few times, like an astronaut taking a lunar walk. Weightlessness, and the acknowledgment that I was experiencing a distinct crossroads in my life, filled my consciousness. Live or die, this was definitely a key event. Full awareness often requires all five senses, and I think sometimes a sixth one slips in on rare occasions. It was impossible to define this feeling, and if I somehow made my way out of the situation, I doubted I would ever experience it again.

The sub-zero water temperature sucked the air out of my lungs.

The contraction felt as though it would not stop until my chest completely flattened.

When a person is first exposed to Arctic water, there's a weird response called "cold shock response." Victims often hyperventilate immediately. For one to three minutes, they breathe fast, deep, and uncontrollable. If you fall underwater, like in my situation, it is easy to swallow water and die.

They never really provided our crew any real hypothermia training. An image of the small ten-page safety booklet flashed through my head. I was told to "read this" and had promptly chucked it to the bottom of my duffle bag. Lee's words of wisdom again reverberated in my head: "Whatever you do, don't fall in the fucking water!"

I could see the bottom side of the compacted layers of ice about ten feet overhead—so close, yet so far. It was necessary to crane my neck as far back as possible to locate the hole I fell through. I obviously had only one shot. There wouldn't be enough time to find another opening. I was out of breath.

Sunlight shined down through the opening like a miner's lamp in a cavernous pit.

I pushed up from the subsurface of the bay. Pulling with my arms and kicking with my boot-covered feet, the buoyancy of the seawater helped lift my body upward. I gained momentum and floated to the opening.

Grabbing onto the edge of the opening, I inched my elbows onto the ice. A hand grabbed onto my arm and pulled me out of the water. I slid onto the surface of the ice. Jumping to my feet and extending my arms, I gasped for air, but my lungs were shut tight like two steel doors. Numbness entered my body.

A look of concern slowly dissolved from Steve's face. "Are you cold?" He smiled.

I finally took a breath—my first in what seemed like an eternity.

"What the fuck do you think?" I then clenched my teeth, trying my best to rid my body of the ache that the coldness had brought upon it.

Steve laughed and patted me on the back. "You okay, man?"

"Yeah—I couldn't breath…"

"I rescued this—it flew off when you went down." Steve held the cap I had been wearing. "You sure as hell got out fast."

"Didn't seem like it."

Once again, my life didn't flash before my eyes. Only a few days earlier, I had found myself trapped between a wall of ice and a two-hundred-foot barge—scared, frantic, but contemplative.

This time was different. Something had changed, although I couldn't quite put my finger on it—a shifting path repositioned, another significant moment. I knew it would take a long time to comprehend why it played out the way it did; years, a lifetime, or maybe I would never completely understand what had changed and why.

I reached for my cap and realized my hand still clenched my fishing pole. The entire way down into the frigid darkness of the bay, and back through the opening in the ice, I had never let go.

THE RISING

AFTER WEEKS OF SOLITUDE, word from the outside world finally arrived at the Barter Island encampment. Bourke had picked up Swan at the airstrip along with a bag of mail and several week-old newspapers. We also learned news of mandatory R&R for the Fourth of July holiday. The Bear annually tried his best to schedule a week off around Independence Day for several reasons: it was about the midpoint of the season for most of the crew; many families got together to celebrate during that time; and AMF wouldn't have to pay triple-time wages for working on a major holiday.

"It makes even more sense this season." Derald poured himself a cup of coffee in the galley of the *Oliktok*. "There's nothing going on at West Dock with everything stuck out here. By the time we return from R&R, maybe the ice'll have cleared out and we can get everything back to Prudhoe—need to be ready for Sealift."

Bourke held the mail sack upside down, and the contents slid across the galley table—several letters, a couple of dog-eared newspapers, and a package wrapped in brown shipping paper, its seams neatly taped. Tim received the most mail, along with the package. His girlfriend wrote to him most every day and it wasn't unusual for a package to arrive like the one on top of the envelopes. He took his time pulling off the tape and shipping paper, a smile on his face as if he somehow felt the fingers that had applied it. After uncovering a box of cigars, he slit the seal with a knife and opened the lid.

"Would anyone like to partake in an evening smoke?"

"Stogies?" Swan said. "I gladly accept the offer."

Steve, Swan, and I each took a cigar out of the box and passed around a lighter. The thick haze and sweet aroma of burning tobacco engulfed the confines of the galley. Derald waved a hand in front of his face then went below deck to grab his fishing gear.

Chris and I had talked on the telephone only once since I arrived at Barter. There was a phone at the airstrip, and I called her a few days earlier when I rode in with Bourke, Steve, and Tim to pick up supplies. Her voice, soft and warm, provided a welcome taste of home as I peered out at the desolate arctic landscape and surrounding bleakness of the island. She said I sounded different, and I told her it must be the connection. But she said it was something about the way I talked. I told her it was most likely a remnant of crude and direct "crew-talk" when working at the camp. It was difficult to turn it on and off. I didn't tell her about falling through the ice or sliding under the bow of the barge.

After re-reading Chris's letter a few more times, I diverted my attention to a newspaper dated June 18th and skimmed across the headlines of world news.

Sally Ride had become the first American woman in space as a crew member of the space shuttle, *Challenger*. That seemed to be the only good news.

Stories of increasing tension around the world smothered most of the stories. Reagan was still on the warpath, favoring a strong-handed approach to winning the cold war. The president proposed to launch a Strategic Defense Initiative (SDI) in March. The ambitious project included the construction of a space-based anti-missile system aptly dubbed "Star Wars." Constructing both space and earth-based battle stations could direct laser beams toward Soviet targets. Theoretically, the system would tilt the arms race back in the favor of the United States, and establish first-strike capabilities against the Russians. U.S. arsenal was also stacking up in Europe.

The Campaign for Nuclear Disarmament had organized marches and rallies because of the deployment of cruise missiles in the United Kingdom. Over 200,000 attended the protests as Margaret Thatcher began her second term as Prime Minister. In the Far East, Iran moved farther into northern Iraq and casualties topped 13,800 within ten days. Iraq was fighting back hard, and in recent years had been the beneficiary of the oil boom that fueled its war machine. The country had amassed over $33 billion in oil money, allowing the government to go on a spending spree of military projects. The Gulf War was on its way to being the 20th century's longest conventional war.

The Doomsday Clock ticked closer to midnight.

There was something different in reading the news within a cramped tugboat galley, a vessel frozen fast in arctic ice. Contemplating the spiraling state of world affairs as I smoked a cigar made me feel like a character from an old Twilight Zone episode. From afar, outside the frenzy of daily routines and bombardment of the news media, the absurdity glared brighter than ever before. I pondered the idea of abstaining from any kind of newsfeed while working the rest of the summer.

"How's Lee doin'?" I asked Swan, trying to dilute the thoughts bouncing in my head.

"Same Lee," Swan snapped. "Tellin' bear stories."

It seemed weird working without Lee and listening to his stories and his view of the world. During long hours of working alongside him, he had a lot to say about world news, most of which I didn't totally agree with—comments grounded in experiences of World War II, Viet Nam, sailing around the world three times as a merchant marine, and years as a hunting guide. His perceived solutions usually required the simple conquering of whatever nemesis reared its head, whether it was a hulking bear or "fuckin' tree hugger." His black and white comments lived in deep, murky waters.

"Let's catch some fish." Derald stood at the entrance of the galley holding a fishing rod.

Steve, Tim, and I grabbed our gear and joined Darrel in exiting the *Oliktok*. We made our way to the island, and a section of open water between the shore and an expanse of ice. It was the same stretch of beach where only a few days earlier we met Panuk, a rifle slung over his shoulder. Taking turns with the firearm, we shot at drifting ice in the distance as Panuk told us stories of hunting, whaling, and fishing for *iqaluk*, commonly known as Arctic char.

Arctic char are a subspecies of salmon, abundant along the Arctic coast. They breed in freshwater lakes and rivers, and wherever possible, migrate to the sea. Char return to their river of origin every year and spend the winter there—they couldn't survive living in saltwater the full year. Similar species of these fish live in other places around the world, including Britain, Scandinavia, and Siberia, and normally ranged in weight from two to five pounds, but larger ones grew as heavy as twenty pounds.

In the calmer stretches we could see the char rising, dimpling the water's surface. Fins occasionally popped out of the water as the fish grouped together. We quietly approached the individual schools and took our place along the shoreline. I cast my line against a light wind, the lure quickly swallowed by a white-capped wave.

I reeled in slowly, the spinner's blade churning through the water, its resistance tugging at the tip of the rod until I felt a hard tug. Pulling back and setting the hook into the fish's mouth, the pole bent sharply toward the water.

"Woo-hoo," I heard Steve yell from farther down the beach. His fishing rod was bent in a "U," and I could tell he also hooked into a char on the first cast.

The fish on my line ran several times, stripping line from my reel as I let it play out. When it had tired, the fish took one last leap before surrendering, and I reeled it into shore. The char flopped against the gravel as I shoved it farther up the shoal away from the water's edge. I reached to the side of my belt and took a Buck Folding Hunter knife from its sheath. Using the backside, I struck the fish three times in the back of the head, and it quivered for a few seconds before finally succumbing.

The side of the fish was bright silver—a female. Males had hooked jaws and were darker. Later in the year, each female char would deposit up to five thousand eggs and would not die after spawning like Pacific salmon. Each female could spawn several times. The cycle of life and death was straightforward and without compromise, dependent on many outside factors.

As I cast my lure back into the sea, I thought of Chris' comment about how I sounded different. Her perceptions had been correct—I had changed. I had flirted with tragedy twice in two days, and I now viewed everything with a fresh set of eyes. From our relationship to world affairs and everything in between, it all felt different. It had changed in a way that might take some time to fully understand, if understanding was at all possible. Like other crewmembers of the same age, I had taken for granted the days ahead. The only major worry had been what direction to take and where our lives would lead us. With a sense of invincibility challenged, reality set in—future possibilities could end as easily as a misstep into frigid arctic waters. Life and death was a connected circle, every second an opportunity.

In less than an hour, all four of us had landed our share of fish on the beach. The char were lined up along the shoreline, lifeless on a bed of stones and pebbles, glittering in the sunlight like silver statuettes. Only moments before, the fish had risen to the ocean's surface in search of food. In a last celebration of tenacity, they fought nobly against the pull of taut lines. Out in the sea, schools of char continued to rise. Life continued, the confluence of destiny effecting each second, minute, hour, and day.

Somewhere overhead, Sally Ride worked aboard the space shuttle as it took another orbit around the earth.

BLANKET TOSS

THE IÑUPIAT VILLAGE of Kaktovik looked about the same as when we visited a week earlier. Dirt roadways, serving as streets, appeared fairly deserted and the town was quiet. Mike and Jeff had flown in a few days earlier and joined Steve, Tim, and I, as we searched for the blanket toss celebration.

"I think we missed it," Steve said.

"Well, it shouldn't take long to check out the entire town." Mike put a wad of tobacco behind his bottom lip.

Panuk had described *Nalukataq*, the blanket toss festival, to us during one of his visits. After a successful spring whale-hunting season, the entire village held a celebration. The event took place in June, scheduled to avoid conflicts between other villages so friends and relatives from all communities could attend. Some of Panuk's family from Barrow would attend Nalukataq at Kaktovik, then he planned to travel to Barrow for their celebration. The actual date also depended on how many whales they caught and the success of the hunting season.

Nalukataq was a celebration of thanksgiving. It was the first of several times during the year when the sharing of whale meat took place. Whaling captains, who always gave large portions of their whales to the community, earn great stature and respect within the village for every whale they catch. The act of sharing is very important in Inuit cultures.

The Nalukataq celebration begins with a prayer, then the raising of the whaling crews' flags. Afterward, the gathering spends a short time enjoying bread, coffee, various goose and caribou soups, and sometimes whale flippers and intestines. Singing and storytelling then take place as the whaling crews share the catch with each family. The first meat distributed is the *quaq* (whale meat frozen raw and cut into cubes), then the *avarraq* (the flukes of the whale cut into thin strips). The last of the meal served is *muktuk* (whale blubber with the skin still on).

As everyone enjoys the feast, the Nalukataq blanket is set up. It's made from either walrus or seal skins sewn together in a circle or square. A rope extends from the edges then pulled tight between four wooden beams using block and tackle. This raises the blanket to waist height, where thirty or more men and women hold the edges. Pulling out on the blanket throws a dancer into the air. The tradition originated from a time when tossing Iñupiat hunters into the air enabled them to see game across the horizon.

The tradition has evolved over the years, and the goal of a dancer is to maintain balance and return to the blanket without falling over. Whaling captains and their wives go first, and the person tossed throws gifts, like candy, into the crowd, and again, the importance of sharing emphasized throughout the celebration. If the dancer loses their balance, they lose their turn. The actual blanket toss lasts several hours and everyone gathers for a traditional dance when it concludes.

"Hey, is that it?" Jeff pointed down a street that led to an open area at the outermost end of the village.

"I think we found it." I swung the daypack off my shoulder, unzipped it, and reached inside for my camera.

We arrived at a circular structure framed with two-by-four and two-by-six boards with Visqueen sheeting stapled to the outside—a layer of plastic skin to block the wind. The residents of Kaktovik sat against the perimeter of the arena, and in the center was a large blanket of caribou hides sewn together. The people of Kaktovik wore festive clothing, including highly decorated mukluks and parkas of seal, caribou, wolverine, wolf, and fox. I knelt and took a photo of a little girl wearing a brightly colored parka with fur trim. Panuk walked out of the crowd with a friend and greeted us. "Hey, Bruuuce, Steeeve—Cubeee." Panuk introduced us to his friend, Leon, and Steve introduced Mike and Jeff. The blanket toss had ended, but the community of Kaktovik was busy dividing the whale meat, visiting with each other, and telling stories of the whaling season. I walked over to the blanket and ran my hand across the hides, the fur smooth but strong.

Panuk walked over to me and held out a piece of paper.

"Hey, Bruuuce—you ask a lot about the way we talk—how to say our words. I wrote some down for you, and will get you more before you leave Barter. Maybe this will help."

"Panuk, this is great. Thanks so much."

I looked at the shortlist of words, many of which I had asked Panuk about during our visits. I always stumbled over the pronunciation of most of the phrases he tried to teach me, and it often led to periods of repetition and laughter. His handwriting was neat and clear, and once again, he was happy to share. The Iñupiat culture depended on the strength of an entire community, and each individual did their best to offer something, whatever and whenever they could. Panuk was no different. In my short time as a neighbor of Kaktovik, I would be forever grateful for the opportunity of getting a glimpse into the life of the Iñupiat.

qaa/nuuq/qik/pin/	How are you
na/quu/ruŋ/ŋal	I am fine
na/nooq/	polar bear
ag/vak	whale
nat/chiq/	seal
eee	yes*
nau/mi	no

* This was said a lot in conversation as an acknowledgement.

sun/na	what
un/na	this one
qu/yaŋ/naaq	thank you
qu/yaŋ/naag/puk	thank you very much
qaau/si/nuk/paun	what time is it
at/chu	I don't know
oolaaq	slang for "horseshit"*
kaaq	marijuana

* Requested by Steve and implemented into our workday jargon.

THE PROPERTIES OF ICE

OUR BOOTS CRUNCHED against the pebbled shoreline as we hiked to the tip of Barter Island. The Fourth of July was only a few days away and Steve, Swan, Tim, and I took one last trek before journeying home. The Brooks Range hovered across a hazy horizon to the south. To the north, an expanse of ice stretched to a faint terminus where it met the sky. I never realized frozen water had a smell, but it does. Carried along on a slight wind, a tinge of salt hit the back of my throat, and the frigid, coppery arctic air filled my lungs.

"I don't see how they'll get the boats through all this ice." I wiped the mist off my camera with the corner of my shirtsleeve.

"It will be quite interesting." The ice field reflected in the round dark lenses of Swan's welding glasses. "There's nothing quite like the reverberation of metal boats and barges slamming against compacted ice. I wonder who will win…"

Swan viewed most everything in formulas and equations. Physics and chemistry defined his world—complexities (and simplicities) demarcated by the components from which comprised. From highly sophisticated classical music to minimalist two-chord punk music; certain rules and laws defined the natural state of things, and rebellion aside, everything had a hierarchical structure, a sense of purpose. Results based upon sets of determining factors depended on observation and calculation and solving the correct equation. There was a reason for everything—or at least, there should be.

Besides other badges of quirkiness, Swan showed up at camp the second season with his wrist wrapped in three layers of electrical tape; a black band of pressure-sensitive insulation. Whenever asked why he maintained this practice through the season, the question received the same curt reply: "I can't tell you."

Swan shared a gamut of musing and insights with whoever wanted to listen. But the ones closer to his heart resided in private property—highly guarded, no trespassing allowed. As many times as I asked him why he wrapped black tape around his wrist, he offered no answer. I sensed it related to something emotionally heavy and personal, a weight only he carried.

"Go out there and I'll take a photo of you." Steve pointed to a pressure ridge of ice about a hundred yards out.

"Sounds good." I handed the camera to him and made my way across the floe, the muted memory of falling through the ice stashed away where it wouldn't hinder my progress. Pushing fears or concerns to a place where they did the least harm was a standard mode of operation while working on the Slope. But like schools of Arctic char that swam just below the sheet of ice I walked upon, such thoughts floated directly below the surface.

Although I had switched my major to Fine Arts in college, science and geology still held my interest, especially when trying to comprehend the surrounding environment. The reason ice floated, and I wasn't at the bottom of the bay a few days earlier, resulted from millions of ice crystals clinging together to form a solid less dense than seawater. This chemical composition, hydrogen bonding, creates ice molecules that exhibit up to sixteen different phases (packing geometries) dependent on temperature and pressure. Crystals can develop from an initial prism into numerous symmetric shapes—hexagonal columns, hexagonal plates, dendritic crystals, and diamond dust were a few types. My artist mind imagined the various patterns forming as the environment changed.

Winds, currents, and temperatures influenced the dynamic nature of the frozen terrain. Ice floating in the sea is "drift ice." "Fast ice" remains fixed to a shoreline, and "anchor ice" attaches itself to the sea bottom. Ice that calves (breaks off) from a shelf or glacier becomes an iceberg. Currents and winds could also force together separate ice floe to form pressure ridges up to forty feet tall. Navigation through this dense floe was only possible through openings called "polynyas" or "leads," and normally required the use of an icebreaker. Taking a fleet of tugboats and barges through long stretches was tricky.

About seven percent of the earth's surface and about twelve percent of the world's oceans are covered by ice. The wind-driven arctic circulation pattern has two primary components. The Beaufort Gyre is a clockwise circulation (looking from above the North Pole) in the Beaufort Sea, where our camp was located. This circulation results from an average high-pressure system that spawns winds over the region. Sea ice that forms or becomes trapped in the Beaufort Gyre could circulate around the Arctic for several years. A second component is the Transpolar Drift Stream, where ice moves from the Siberian coast of Russia across the Arctic basin and exits into the North Atlantic off the east coast of Greenland.

I climbed onto what the Iñupiat called an *agiukpak*—a perpendicular pressure ridge. An agiukpak could often be unstable, and it was not a good idea to spend too much time on top, or near one. For the Iñupiat, the ice is intimate terrain where they live for much of the year. They study and understand every section and ridge as they travel across its surface. The ice serves as a highway and hunting ground for their people, and it represents life itself.

Steve took a photo of me on the pressure ridge, then I carefully worked my way back toward the crew. Swan, Steve, and Tim stood about twenty yards from the shore, all of them looking down at a single spot on the ice.

"What is it?" I walked to the side of Swan to see what they were looking at.

"Eider," Steve said. "It's barely alive."

The eider duck sat placid on the ice, its black and white feathers clean and smooth. It did not evade our presence. Its chest expanded slightly every few seconds, gasping for breaths of air. Steve handed the camera to me. I crouched lower to the ice and viewed the dying bird through my viewfinder. Its bill remained slightly open, and its eyes were miniature ebony marbles.

Flocks of eider ducks had floated in the open water the past few days—several thousand white and black spots sprinkled across a darkened sea. Eiders are sea ducks, a group of diving birds that breed inland but spend the rest of the year in coastal marine waters. The range of their species includes the arctic coastal plain of northern Alaska and Russia. Migrating long distances between their breeding and wintering grounds each year, they fly side by side in long lines, skimming the water.

The eiders travel along coastlines or follow open leads in the ice. Migration northward to the breeding grounds in Alaska begins in late April and they reach their nesting sites in the arctic tundra in late May to early June. Males leave the breeding areas by early July, so I assumed the one on the ice was a male—females remain on breeding grounds until the chicks fledge. When winter approaches, they all travel south to molting areas. The eider that sat in front of us had been free to fly wherever it wanted, but it now took its last breaths.

Swan walked closer to the eider and knelt. He reached slowly toward the bird, then rested his hand on the bird's back. Swan wasn't wearing his leather jacket, black jeans, and a studded belt. A long day of grind work had ended only a few hours earlier, and like the rest of us, he wore dull brown Carhartt coveralls stained with grease and oil spots—a sympathetic figure kneeling over a fading life.

We remained silent for about fifteen minutes. Swan reverently stroked the eider's back as its body heat slowly dissolved into the arctic ice. I imagined the warmth flowing through the molecular structures of ice, intertwining with hydrogen bonds, its energy dissolving back into the water that once gave it life.

Swan's wrist exposed, the black band contrasted against his pale skin. I took one last photo before he stood, and we all walked across the ice and back to the island together without saying a word. I never again asked Swan about the black electrical tape.

We retraced our meandering footsteps along the shore and back to the fleet.

FAMILY DINNER

GOING HOME DURING R&R meant more than a respite from the North Slope. A sense of normalcy gave way to the realization that the short time off afforded only a quick taste of summer and the season only halfway completed. Within a week of arriving in California, I'd repack my bag, then board the plane to fly north for a couple of more months of work. I would need to savor every minute of being home.

Chris and my brother, Don, greeted me at the San Francisco Airport. Hugging them at the gate, I realized how long it had been since I held another person. We spent the first night at my brother's house with his wife, two sons, and daughter. As several bottles of wine emptied, tales of Alaska commingled with stories of the children's summer fun. Chris had been doing excellent as usual in her classes and well on her way to gaining her degree in Education.

The next morning we all piled into Don's van and started off to my parent's home in Calaveras County. The congestion of the San Francisco Bay Area gave way to fields of green and thin earthen rows etched into the landscape like grooves across a vinyl record. After months of seeing nothing but arctic ice and gravel shorelines, it was as if I were seeing the fertile Sacramento valley for the very first time. The van negotiated the winding roads of the Sierra foot-hills, through small rural towns, then dense backwoods choked with pines, cedars, oaks, and manzanita. My parent's house, at the top of a steep knoll, was exactly how I had envisioned it during brief daydreams over three thousand miles away.

When we walked into the house, I took a deep breath and the smell of roast beef blended with the rest of the meal my mother was cooking. During holidays, birthdays, and other special events, my father enjoyed cooking meat on a rotisserie, or what he called, "the spit." My sister, Jo, was in the front room along with her husband and two daughters, and they all laughed at my beard and long hair when I entered.

"Hey, barbers in the Arctic are few and far between—wait until you see me in a few more months."

After greeting everyone, Dad made sure all of us had a drink, whether it was beer, wine, soda, or a glass of water. One of his many quirks was the ability to know everyone's preferred refreshment—that, along with their favorite candy. The candy jar sat on the coffee table in the front room and my father would always ask new guests, "What kind of candy do you like? What do you like to drink?" The next time that person visited my parent's place, their favorite candy would be in the jar and their beverage of choice on ice in a cooler on the back porch.

"I'm glad you're home, even if it's only for a short time." Chris rested her head on my shoulder as we sat in the comfort of my parent's couch watching the news.

"It's good to be home—back to you and the family."

"I wish we had more than a week together."

"I'll be home early this year so we can spend some time on the coast—maybe head down to Monterey."

"Sounds good." She gripped my hand.

Chris was patient, understanding, and supportive, but everyone has a limit. I knew what felt like enduring love could easily fade if taken for granted. She would complete her plans of graduating with a degree in science and education in the spring semester. I still struggled at school, but my focus on fine arts had given me new motivation and passion. If I took a heavy load the next three semesters, I would actually graduate by the winter of '84. The big question: what was an Alaskan laborer going to do with a fine arts degree and a minor in geology and art history? I was accumulating an odd mix of skills and wasn't entirely sure how to leverage all of them together. And once I graduated, I wasn't sure if I'd remain in Colorado, move back to California, consider Alaska, or continue to travel the country and live out of my duffle bag.

I walked into the kitchen where Don and his wife sat on barstools at the counter talking about how hot it had been when we drove through the valley. My mother was preparing green beans next to the stove and had her back to us, steam swirling from a pot of boiling water. She cut the beans into precise lengths and dropped them into the pot. The knife she used was old and the blade thin, its mass shaven down from years of sharpening and cutting. The handle, worn and smooth, had once been held by her mother, and her grandmother. My mom's arthritic fingers were bulbous at the joints, but she could still wield the cutlery as precisely as when she cooked for us as kids.

"Smells great—I can't wait to fuckin' eat." I knew once I let the f-bomb fly, it had been a mistake. Don and his wife were quiet.

My mother turned to face me. "You're not at camp—you're home now. Watch your language." My mother held the knife in front of her, and with the tip bobbing up and down, emphasizing each word.

"Sorry, Mom. It's hard to break old habits." But I knew my vulgar crew-talk wouldn't be an "old habit" for very long. I'd be back at Prudhoe in less than a week. By the time I began speaking like a college student, I'd be stepping off the plane in Deadhorse.

"You know," I said, "you're scary as hell with that knife in your hand."

Don and Jo laughed, and I walked over and hugged my mother.

"Good to have you home," she said and smiled.

Our family laughed a lot when we were together, a gift handed to us by our father. He smiled and laughed more than anyone I have ever known. Sometimes I find myself laughing at inappropriate times, so I often have to maintain some sense of checks and balances. But on the upside, like my father, I also know how to laugh at myself and I believe this to be a valuable asset, especially when questioning one's life path. A little laughter makes uncertainties more bearable.

Dad carved the roast beef, my brother and sister set the table, and Chris helped my mom carry in the food. I walked outside to get another beer. Dad had stocked the cooler with my favorite brew since moving to Colorado—Coors. I popped the can open and took a deep breath of country air. The pungent aroma of incense cedar, black oak, and summer-dried earth brought back memories of other family gatherings at my parent's house in the country. Long shadows formed across a panoramic view of the California foothills. I took another sip of beer, then turned to walk back into the house.

At the porch, I stopped.

Behind the kitchen and dining-room windows, Chris and my family were taking their places at the table. I heard Jo ask, "Where's Bruce?" and Don answered, "Always the last one to the table."

My brother's and sister's children were sitting at the "kid's table," a folding card table my father had taken out of the hall closet. They were goofing around, happy to see their cousins, and acting like the kids they were. My dad checked to make sure everyone was comfortable and had a place at the table. I was sure he would pass around the candy jar after the meal.

Laughter and the sound of shuffling chairs filled the house and floated out the open window.

I heard the words my mother had spoken earlier: "—you're home now."

INTO THE FOG

OUR PLANE SLICED A FOG BANK, and turbulence slammed us against the sides of the cabin. I yanked the end of my seatbelt to make it as tight as possible. We had taken off in the twin turboprop from the ARCO airstrip on our way back to Barter Island. The Trans Alaska Pipeline had been a fading jagged line on the tundra below until we passed over the sea smothered by fog.

Besides the pilot and co-pilot, there was only Squirrelly and me as passengers. The rest of the plane was overloaded with supplies to bring out to the fleet. Squirrelly earned his nickname by being a little high-strung when situations intensified. The more excited he got, the higher pitched his voice became. Sentences often ran together unhindered, and words melded into one other.

As our bodies rocked back and forth in a flying metal tube high through the whiteness, Squirrelly's speech pattern accelerated, and his voice grew a couple of octaves higher as he peered out the side window.

"Fucking-can't-see-shit-out-there."

I sat across the aisle from him, looking out my window. It was a short flight to Barter from Prudhoe Bay, but flying blind made every minute seem like an hour. I had been happy to hear I was returning to the island when I got back from the week of R&R, but now was having second thoughts.

A lot of pilots in Alaska flew an excessive amount of time in order to acquire their commercial licenses. As a passenger, you were never sure how many straight hours or how many days a pilot had racked up—or what kind of experience they might have.

"Look-at-that-shit." Squirrelly nodded his head toward the cockpit.

I noticed the pilot and copilot weren't talking much. They appeared mesmerized by the sheet of white in front of them, along with a navigation system that didn't seem to be a lot of help.

"Look-right-there." Squirrelly pointed with his finger this time.

That's when I saw the copilot's knees shaking.

Squirrelly pulled a folding knife from his pack.

"If-we-go-down-I'm-slitting-my-fucking-throat-before-we hit-the-ground."

The knife clicked open.

"You're going to feel pretty damn foolish if you do that, and then we somehow manage to land safely."

I closed my eyelids and rubbed them, hoping I might reopen them to find myself somewhere else. It didn't work.

"Son-of-a-bitch-whythehelldidwegetinthisfuckingthing!"

I couldn't believe it. I had experienced life-threatening situations twice at Barter (three times a charm?) and now I'm trapped in a twin-engine plane with a near-lunatic and two nervous pilots flying through a dense fog bank high above the Arctic Ocean.

Was this really happening?

I should have attempted to talk Squirrelly down, but I was doing my best to keep my head together. It was every man for himself, and I was clutching tightly to my own emotional lifesaver.

Damn, I should have brought those rosary beads my brother gave me—the ones he brought back from Rome.

After fifteen intense minutes of sitting next to a knife-clutching Squirrelly, we descended to an unseen airfield. I pulled a tin of Skoal from the pocket of my Carhartts and jammed a wad of tobacco behind my lower lip. The last thing I told Chris before I left home was that we'd be together again—soon. She only smiled. Most of me left that day.

Squirrelly wiped the blade of his knife with his denim shirtsleeve. "It's-a-damn-good-thing-we-smoked-that-fatty-before-taking-off."

The pilots craned their necks from side to side, but there was only the flat whiteness surrounding us. I tried to convince myself it's probably best not to look, anyway.

Close your eyes and think of something else... anything else. Maybe you should go to grad school if you graduate. Either that or the Maritime Academy is a possibility...

"HOLYSHIT," Squirrelly shouted.

I opened my eyes to see a crane boom less than fifty feet from the right side of the plane. The engines screamed as the pilot throttled up and we arced to the left. Air whistled through the crane's stanchions as we skimmed past. The copilot lost most of the pigmentation in his face.

Drifts of sand and ice sped underneath us until a faint light appeared, a beacon signaling the end of a runway. The pilot took a deep breath and zeroed in.

The plane skipped twice on the gravel before settling down. As we bounced across the washboard surface, I noticed the whale jawbone just past the Quonset huts and radar tracking screens. Past that, the village of Kaktovik came into view.

The plane rolled to a stop in front of the doorway to the Barter Island Social Club.

Squirrelly closed the knife and stuck it back in its sheath, saying the flight was a piece of cake and he's had worse trips. "No big deal."

Across the runway was the road that led to the Arctic Marine Freighters camp—a fleet of tugboats and barges trapped in arctic ice over one hundred miles from where they normally docked—and my home away from home.

RIDING WITH THE WIND

"OKAY, LET'S TRY IT on for size."

Casey turned the storage bag upside down and shook it. An orange neoprene bundle flopped onto the deck and a sheet of paper floated to his feet. "Instructions." He kicked them to the corner of the galley, then unfolded the cold water immersion suit.

I picked up the paper and scanned the numbered illustrations. "Someone's opinion on how it should be done—this'll only slow you down."

I imagined a tugboat on the high seas, its engine room on fire, the stern sinking deeper into the abyss, seawater pouring through the hatchways, and some sorry-ass crewman reading the instructions on how to put on his survival suit. Robert Rothman had gathered some crewmembers into the *Point Oliktok* for cold water safety instruction. The survival suit was the last thing you wanted to have to put on—a thin shell of synthetic rubber between one's body and the life-sucking frigidity of arctic waters.

Steve, Tim, Dave, Mike, Jeff, and I stood around as Casey put his foot into the suit. Swaying back and forth, he forced the other foot in. He bent over, grasped at the neoprene, and yanked it up over his knees. Pushing his arms into the sleeves and struggling to stuff his body into the suit made him appear as though he was wrestling against it rather than attempting to wear it. He grabbed onto the large metal zipper and jerked it inch by inch until it finally reached the bottom of his neck. His arms arced outward from the sides, the bulk of the suit pushing them away from his body. We stood in a circle around what looked like a large, puffy, bearded lobster-like creature.

"Jesus, the boat would have been at the bottom of the ocean by the time you got that damn thing on," Steve said.

"How the hell do you swim in it?" Dave asked.

"You don't." Rothman stood from the galley table. "You float on your back on the surface of the water and wait for someone to come along and fish you out."

"Rettig could have used that a couple of weeks ago," Steve said, and everyone laughed.

"We're going to be sailing through a lot of ice." Rothman halted our laughter. "We'll be out there for a couple of days, maybe longer. You guys need to learn how to put these things on—quickly."

The frigid arctic environment had bitten me twice: once between the bow of a barge and solid ice, and a second time in the water itself. Floating calmly and waiting for help in a turbulent ocean sounded like the rational thing to do in order to survive a catastrophic situation. In reality, it would be a living nightmare as heat slowly dissipated from one's body.

Hypothermia is not a fun way to die.

When exposed to prolonged cold, a person's internal mechanisms struggle to replenish lost heat and the body's core temperature eventually drops. The temperature range required for normal metabolism and body functions is 97.7–99.5 °F. If it gets below that range, the situation steadily spirals downward. The body sends blood to protect vital organs, depleting the brain. Sluggish thinking and amnesia follow shivering and mental confusion, accompanied by a difficulty to speak. In severe hypothermia, there may be paradoxical undressing, where a person removes their clothing—if they can still move. Soon, the inability to use one's hands and legs occur. Cellular metabolic processes then shut down.

Below 86 °F, exposed skin becomes blue and puffy, muscle co-ordination is very poor, and the person exhibits incoherent and irrational behavior—they may even fall into a deep stupor, feeling warm and euphoric. As body temperature continues to decrease, further physiological systems falter. Pulse rate, respiratory rate, and blood pressure all decrease, but an accelerated heart rate can periodically kick in (a racing heart.) Finally, major organs, including the heart, fail, and clinical death occurs. Basically, a person fades into the cold.

I had only been in the water for a short time when I fell through the ice, and the arctic waters had only robbed me of my breath, a few degrees of body temperature, and a minute piece of dignity. For most of the crew, it was only another story to laugh about. Rothman was upper management, and a voice of reason. When he heard I had fallen in the water, he was the only one who showed genuine concern and it had worried me. An accident-prone worker was a liability, and I tried my best to keep a low profile and do my job as safely as possible.

"I'm piloting the *Oliktok* back to Prudhoe," Rothman said, "and you, Tim Payne, and Casey will be on board. You ever sail as a deckhand?"

"No, I haven't. I got my Z-Card at the Coast Guard station when I went back home last summer."

"I'll tell you what to do—just pay attention. It'll be slow-going through the ice."

Other crew members had flown to Barter Island and joined us in the effort to get the fleet ready for the hundred-mile trek, and our ice-breaker barge, *The Arctic Endeavor*, had sailed from Prudhoe Bay to assist in the journey. The ice had pulled away from the barges and most of them were now afloat. Engineers scurried from vessel to vessel, preparing for departure the following day.

"Panuk's on deck." Steve peered out a porthole.

"He can come inside." Robert turned and walked toward the stairs that led to the wheelhouse. "Make sure all you guys practice putting on a survival suit."

Steve leaned out of the hatchway and signaled Panuk to come

aboard. Our Iñupiat friend entered the galley carrying a large, curved object. It was almost four feet long, about one-quarter of an inch thick, and shaped like the tip of a crescent moon, but ebony black. "Hey, Steeeve, Bruuuce, Cubeee—Casey." He nodded at the rest of the crew gathered in the galley. "I brought you guys some baleen—whale tongue."

Panuk handed small pieces of cut baleen to all of us, the same material as the longer complete piece he held in his other hand. It felt like hard plastic, and I had seen scrimshaw etched into similar slices at a gift shop in Anchorage. I imagined how flexible it had been when it hung alongside a whale's mouth, filtering microscopic plankton that nourished the giant marine mammal.

"You can keep those," he said. "Steve, you have this." Panuk handed Steve a polar bear tooth.

"Thanks man, this is cool." Steve held the tooth in his open palm so we could all see it.

"Hey, do you have any more polar bear teeth?" Casey squirmed out of the flotation suit and it flopped onto the deck like a shed layer of skin. "I'll buy one from you."

"No, only one," Panuk said.

"How about that baleen?" Casey walked closer, eying the pristine piece. "I'll give you fifty bucks."

"No, Casey—it not for sale."

"One hundred." Casey looked Panuk in the eye. "Okay, I'll give you two hundred dollars—deal?"

"No, I don't think so." Panuk smiled.

"I give it to Bruce." Panuk handed it to me.

I held the section of baleen, admiring the smooth texture that narrowed to filamentous edges. "Are you sure?" I asked.

"Yes. You keep it."

Casey stormed out of the galley. We walked out on deck and talked with Panuk for a while longer, but the camp differed from our prior visits with him. The quiet comfort of freedom afforded by spending long days on a remote island had vanished. Diesel engines rattled to life and the clatter of tools and shouting voices bounced across the decks of boats and barges. A thick smell of diesel hung in the air, flecks of carbon fluttering out of exhaust stacks and ascending into the arctic sky.

"I have your address. I'll write to you." I shook Panuk's hand.

"Sounds good—happy travels." He grinned the Panuk smile.

We all said goodbye to Panuk for the last time, then walked to our quarters to get some sleep before the journey ahead. The sound of the fleet coming to life drifted through a partially open porthole as I lie in my rack. I put on the Sony Walkman headphones and Jimi Hendrix sang "Little Wing," muffling the sound of machinery.

Well, she's walking through the clouds

The next day we would leave the island, and I might never see it or the village of Kaktovik again. I'd serve as a deckhand for the first time as we sailed through a sea of ice, a fleet of tugboats and barges searching for whatever open water we could find.

With a circus mind
That's running wild

I ran through a mental checklist of my duties on deck. I had worked aboard boats and barges for the first season, and Lee had taught me a lot. This time it would only be Steve and I. Rothman would tell us what we needed to do—was he good at directing, or would he yell and scream orders like many other captains had last summer? He seemed level-headed and showed a concern for safety. I had heard that once the boats set sail, some captains experienced distinct personality changes—a Jekyll and Hyde syndrome. It was probably bullshit crew-talk but I could see how it might happen. Would we sleep on board, or be on the clock the entire time? What if I made a mistake on deck? No telling what the upcoming days presented.

I took a deep breath and quieted my thoughts. Jimi's voice drifted along as my racing mind eventually faded into semi-lucid sleep and a montage of dreams.

Riding with the wind...

I stepped into the college photography lab back in Colorado. An image slowly appeared on a sheet of photo paper floating in a tub of developer. Stars sprinkled across an ebony sky; in two years of working in the Arctic, I had never seen an Alaskan night. Another image faded to life: Van Gogh's "Starry Night" swirling across a projector screen as my professor droned on about the artist, and his passion for textural color. Pairs of eider ducks flew by my side. I turned to watch the flock as the sky lightened. High above, a current of wind held me aloft. I turned and peered down through a hole in the clouds. More stars—orange, not white—wedged between jagged channels of indigo against ivory. A group of mariners looked up at me with eyes composed of small spheres of ice. They floated on their backs in orange survival suits, arms and legs outstretched—a thin layer of neoprene between flesh and frozen sea.

DEADLINES

NEWS ON THE RADIO about an oil spill in Prudhoe Bay drifts out of the Jeep's open window as I'm filling it with gas at the local Chevron station. I think the report said the spill covered several acres, but it's difficult to hear over the sound of weekend traffic. Skiers and snowboarders pack Lake Tahoe in April as they squeeze a few last days into another short winter. It took several minutes of waiting in line to get to a pump—I should have known better than to drive into town on the weekend. There are several tight work deadlines coming up, however, requiring extra hours to meet them.

As the dollars, cents, and gallons blink across the screen, I realize how much I now dislike fueling up. I began pumping gas when I was fifteen years old, working at my brother's service station in the San Francisco Bay Area. My first paycheck was from Shell Oil Company. The money earned while working at the station went toward the purchase of my first car, a 1967 Chevelle SS 396. Working at the Shell station was a great opportunity to learn about auto repair and maintenance, and I often helped many of my friends work on their cars. There were a lot of good times back then, and I cherish those memories. Unfortunately, other events now also pierce my thoughts whenever I see an ARCO, Exxon, BP, or Shell logo.

In 2002, a San Francisco Superior Court jury found three companies responsible for poisoning South Lake Tahoe's drinking water supply with a possible carcinogen found in gasoline. They determined two of the firms knew the chemical's dangers for years but failed to warn water officials. Pollution by Shell Oil, Lyondell Chemical Company, and Tosco Corporation resulted in the shutting down of over one-third of South Lake Tahoe's thirty-four drinking wells. The jury also concluded that Shell and Lyondell withheld information about the dangers of MTBE (methyl tertiary butyl ether) and that the gasoline additive is a defective product. Shell pulled out of South Lake Tahoe for several years after the ruling, and only recently returned to the area.

As much as I decry purchasing gas and ride my bike to work as much as possible during the summers, relying on this commodity is still mandatory. Until electric cars become more affordable, alternatives remain limited. Like every other consumer waiting in line at the Chevron station, I justify my gasoline usage and top off my tank.

After a moment of cussing, I'm able to wedge my way into the snaking line of traffic and drive the rest of the way to my office. Working on weekends is never enjoyable by any means, but it's a good time to get caught up. The phone remains silent; the building is quiet, and the only sound is the buzz from one of the fluorescent lights above my desk. I turn on the computer and browse the Internet for news about the oil spill.

Apparently, the pipeline rupture in Prudhoe Bay first hit the newswires on Tuesday, and I had heard the follow-up story on the radio. A leak occurred in a six-inch-diameter pipe exiting a wellhead in a section of pipe referred to as a "flow line" or "well line." It connects to a manifold that channels fluid to a transit line and then on to a processing facility. An unknown amount of crude oil, natural gas, and water sprayed across twenty-seven acres of snow-covered tundra. The release of oily mist occurred at a well operated by BP Operation Alaska, and they contained it in two hours after isolating the line and depressurizing it. The mixture covered such an extensive area because the leak occurred at the top of the pipe, and pressurized gas forced it into a thirty-mile-per-hour wind.

This latest blowout was a little more than a mile from a 2006 leak in a transit line that ultimately became the largest recorded spill on the North Slope. The 2006 accident lasted five days and discharged over 267,000 gallons spread over two acres. BP ultimately pled guilty to negligent discharge after failing to address corrosion issues in the system. It also reached settlements on four other spills: a discharge on October 15, 2007, when about 1,932 gallons of oil mixture spread over nearly an acre of tundra wetlands; a discharge on November 29, 2009, when about 13,482 gallons of oil mixture covered 8,400 square feet of tundra wetlands; a discharge on December 21, 2009, when about 504 gallons of oil mixture spread across tundra wetlands; and a discharge on July 18, 2011, when about 1,764 gallons of oil mixture covered approximately 2,040 square feet of tundra and 4,960 square feet of a man-made gravel pad.

I was unaware of any major spills during the years I worked at the end of West Dock in Prudhoe Bay. To my twenty-year-old eyes, it appeared the oil companies did everything they could to reduce their impact on the environment. At the same time, I often wondered how the increase in oil field expansion would impact such a fragile area. One catastrophic event would cause irreparable damage.

The Prudhoe Bay field, along with twenty-six other oil-producing areas, sprawls across one thousand square miles of Alaska's North Slope. There are now over 4,800 exploratory and production wells, 2,223 drill pads, over five hundred miles of roads, 1,800 miles of trunk and feeder pipes in over six hundred miles of pipeline corridors, two refineries, twenty airports, 107 gravel pads for living quarters, and other support facilities, five docks and gravel causeways, thirty-six gravel mines, and twenty-eight production plants, gas processing facilities, seawater treatment plants, and power plants. In short, the vast complexity of this sprawling infrastructure is staggering.

The Prudhoe Bay oil field and Trans-Alaska Pipeline have caused an average of over five hundred spills annually on the North Slope since 1996, according to the Alaska Department of Environmental Conservation (ADEC). Forty different toxic substances, from acid to waste oil, have spilled during routine operations. There were

4,532 spills between 1996 and 2004, totaling over 1.9 million gallons of toxic substances. These were most commonly diesel, crude oil, and hydraulic oil.

I was living in Sacramento, California, when the Exxon Valdez ran aground on March 24th, 1989, less than four years after my last day of employment at the slope. It's estimated that between eleven to thirty-eight million gallons of crude oil dumped into the Pacific Ocean, transported south from Prudhoe Bay via the pipeline.

Considered as one of the most devastating human-caused environmental disasters in history, The Valdez accident resulted in a slick covering 1,300 miles of coastline and 11,000 square miles of ocean. I watched the news on television, footage taken by helicopters high overhead as Crowley tugboats and emergency response equipment worked to contain the spill. I recognized many of the boats and felt a sharp pain in the pit of my stomach. The personal connection forever changed how I viewed oil development in Alaska or anywhere else in the world. The words "Drill, baby, drill" scorch my soul.

I often wonder how routinely they upgrade the oil infrastructure and the percentage of company profits reinvested back into the system? In many of the past oil spill settlement cases against BP, the court concluded, "BP had been aware of corrosive conditions for over a decade, and yet chose not to address them." I fear that the companies who oversee the Prudhoe Bay oil field and the Trans Alaska Pipeline have already failed to create and manage a crucial maintenance schedule necessary to keep the system safe and up to par. Their record is not very strong as the pipeline continues to age. It's only a matter of time before the next spill happens, and hopefully it will not be a catastrophic event. And of course, there's always the random act of idiocy to factor in, like in 2001 when a drunken hunter shot at the main pipeline and the resulting hole led to 285,000 gallons of crude oil flowing into the Alaskan forest.

I turn my attention to the stack of papers on my desk. It'll take a few hours to complete the work. After it's done, I'll turn off the computer and light, lock the office door, get back into the Jeep, merge into the bumper-to-bumper traffic, then pass the Chevron station and the long line of cars waiting to fill their vehicles with gasoline. I'll drive to my mountain home along an asphalt-covered road, the surface a product of petroleum, and tires made from a mixture including oil. I'll park in the garage and walk into a warm house heated by natural gas.

Once again, the work completed, and deadlines met.

BREAKING ICE

THE WIRE'S WEIGHT pulled me closer to the edge of the barge before I regained my footing and yanked the cable eye onto the deck. Tim was at the bow of the *Oliktok* and had thrown the lead line up to me, then fed the wire hand over hand. I grabbed the open eye and walked it to the stern's port side and dropped it over the corner bit. One down.

Another lead line was thrown up, and I pulled it and the wire to the starboard side and dropped the eye over the other corner bit. With both wires in place, Rothman operated the winches from the wheelhouse. The whine and clatter of machinery filled the air as the tug pulled tight to the stern of the barge. It was time to depart Barter Island and transport the fleet back to Prudhoe Bay. I worked deckhand aboard the *Point Oliktok*.

The *Oliktok* was a pusher boat, as compared to a towboat. Used for pushing barges or floats, these vessels feature a square or rounded bow and "push knees," large plates mounted to the bow for pushing barges of various heights. These boats usually operate on rivers and inland waterways. Because of their low draft, they are perfect for sailing the shallow waters of the Beaufort Sea and maneuvering close to the shoreline.

We had spent most of the morning throwing lines and pulling the fleet out of the lagoon and into deeper water. As I worked the decks along with the other hands, I continued to hear Lee's voice and things he taught me the prior season. "You have to watch your ass around this shit. You've heard the expression 'the bite of the line?' Well, it really will fuckin' bite if you're not payin' attention— these lines'll cut you in half faster than you can realize what the hell happened."

The door to the wheelhouse of the *Oliktok* was open and we could hear chatter from all the other captains as they communicated directions to each other. One by one, each boat and barge made its way around the tip of Barter Island, their headings set northwest to deeper water and the long expanse of ice. As we rounded a thin jetty, I noticed two Iñupiat on three-wheelers on the shore of the island, and a third one standing next to them. It was the last time I would see Panuk and the Kaktovik villagers.

The *Arctic Endeavor* took the lead as we sailed into the pack ice, pushed forward by the *Point Barrow* with Jeff and Steve working as a deckhand. The *Endeavor*, built in 1982, sailed to Prudhoe the same year. Designed specifically for ice management, it had a pointed bow and a strengthened hull. The success of this barge relied on a pusher boat driving the vessel up onto the ice, and the sheer weight of the *Endeavor* would fracture the frozen surface. With the ice spread apart, it created a navigable channel. It was a simple concept, but the procedure did not always yield a consistent result.

Arco, Exxon, and Sohio closely monitored the progress of the fleet. A cameraman rode aboard the *Endeavor*, hired by the oil companies to film our progress as we struggled to break our way through. Overhead, a helicopter periodically circled over the fleet each day. It was important for the oil companies to record how, and if, we could sail the frozen waters—for two reasons. One, if we could navigate efficiently, it would increase the amount of work we could get completed during a season; and two, it would help their efforts in convincing interested parties we could perform successfully in an emergency, like an oil spill.

Effectively navigating arctic waters has long held the interest of the oil companies, and many much longer voyages are legendary. In 1969, Humble Oil commissioned the ice-breaking oil tanker ss *Manhattan* to conquer the Northwest Passage. The Northwest Passage is a sea route connecting the northern Atlantic and Pacific Oceans through the Arctic Ocean, along the northern coast of North America via waterways through the Canadian Arctic Archipelago. The goal of the *Manhattan* endeavor was to establish viable transportation of Alaskan crude from Prudhoe Bay to the east coast of the United States. Shipping oil by tanker is the most cost-effective form of transportation. The ss *Manhattan* completed the journey twice from the east coast to Prudhoe Bay and back again, the first commercial ship to navigate the Northwest Passage. The effort, however, also demonstrated how arduous it was to transport crude oil using an icebreaking tanker. Once again, the ice had won.

We set out slow the first couple of days, and the pace would only continue to bog down. Our fleet snaked its way through the ice, a meandering line of tugboats and barges following whatever open water the *Endeavor* could clear for us. I wondered if there was anything more unpredictable than sailing through a stretch like the one in front of us, but it was my first duty as a deckhand, so I really had nothing for comparison. Ice pounded the hull of the *Oliktok*, jolting everything inside the vessel back and forth with each impact, relegating sleep to brief catnaps.

I made my way to the bow of the barge to relieve Tim, who was on ice watch.

"There really isn't much to tell Rothman, other than there's nothing but ice as far as you can see." He handed me the radio transceiver and binoculars. "Some larger chunks drift in back of the *Endeavor*, and get pushed along in its wheel-wash, then hit our bow—let him know when they're going hit. I'm getting a few minutes of rest."

I had already spent several days standing at the bow, watching brash ice slam against the steel hull, then slide along the length of the barge. In the distance, the occasional phenomena called "water sky" appeared—dark streaks stretching along the undersides of low clouds, indicating water beneath them. It seemed we were at a dead stop much of the time, and I wondered how long it would take for us to return to Prudhoe, or if it was even possible. Maybe we'd sail aimlessly in pack ice until the end of summer, and it would again freeze solid. Several times, we unhooked from the barge to assist other vessels in the fleet. I had come aboard the *Endeavor* during one of these assists and talked with Dave who had also boarded the icebreaker barge.

"How's life on the *Oliktok*?" Dave asked.

"Doin' all right— Rothman's a good captain." I took the camera out of my pack. "Not much sleep, but I'm heavily amped on tugboat coffee."

"Yeah, each day blends into the next—we're not making fast headway, by any means."

I walked across the deck and took some photos of the cameraman who focused on the *Endeavor's* bow creeping up and over a large sheet of ice. A helicopter flew overhead, shadowing our slow but methodical progress. The *Oliktok* was alongside the *Point Barrow* at the stern of the *Endeavor*, the whine of diesel engines echoing across the deck. I climbed down one of the *Oliktok's* push knees and back onto its deck. Rothman was in the wheelhouse, the radio blaring as I brought him a cup of coffee. I could hear The Bear, who was piloting the *Point Thompson*, talking to another captain. There had been a fire in the engine room of one boat, and they had put it out.

Hour by hour, we pushed our way through, smashing through whatever pack ice blocked our way. I had spent forty-one days aboard the *Oliktok* including my time at Barter Island. We had sailed approximately one hundred miles along the northern coast, and finally, a structure appeared on the horizon. I lifted the binoculars and peered across the expanse. The AMF comm shack with all the antennae atop its roof, came into view; we were less than a day's journey from West Dock.

It had been my first duty aboard a marine vessel, serving as deckhand. We had navigated through what I thought of as an impassible stretch of ice, and the fleet had returned to Prudhoe Bay.

LEARNING CURVE
ON THE SAG RIVER

JONESY SCREAMED directions from the wheelhouse, his voice crackling through the loudspeakers—"... starboard—starboard side—make it fast!"

I ran across the deck, pulled the line through the H-bitt, and made three quick figure eights. The high-pitched whine of the diesel's blower pierced my ears, and the deck rumbled underneath my work boots. The line stretched from tugboat to barge, its diameter narrowing as it pulled tighter. Increased tension compressed the wraps around the bit—strands of nylon squeaking across steel. My breath puffed into a fading mist toward the wheelhouse.

We'd been back at West Dock for only six days when I had been told I'd be serving as a deckhand aboard the *Sag River*. The tugboat's name originated from the Sagavanirktok River, a stream that originates on the north slope of the Brooks Range and flows into the Beaufort Sea near Prudhoe Bay. Colberg Incorporated of Stockton, California, built the boat in 1975 for Crowley Maritime. She had a square bow, flat hull, and designed to run in three and a half feet of water. Known as a "triple screw," she had three propellers powered by three individual diesel engines combining for 1,095 horsepower. The Arctic Marine Freighters' fleet included four triple screw boats, all referred to as "river boats." The *Sag River* was sister boat to the *Colville River*, the *Toolik River*, and the *Kuparuk River*.

Two captains had flown up from Seattle the past week: Rich Jones, who piloted the *Sag River*, and Hank Tucker, pilot of the *Toolik River*. I knew both from my first season, and was well aware that they were shouters, and relished the opportunity to yell orders down to deck crews and barge workers. Loudhailers, mounted on the wheelhouses, allowed the captains' boisterous voices to echo against nearby vessels or bounce across the bay, fading into a salty hinterland where all captains' seemingly relentless rantings finally die.

I spoke with a couple of crewmembers who had sailed with both captains and learned it best not to screw with either of them—do your job and keep a low profile. Rich Jones, referred to as "Jonesy," was a large man with a full black beard, and often ended his sentences with the phrase, "Don'tcha know?" Hank Tucker had earned the colorful moniker "Captain Fuck," because of seemingly endless sordid tales of sexual exploits with whatever women he preyed upon, along whatever Alaskan waterway or bar he pillaged. I felt very fortunate in not having to sail on the *Toolik* and wished the best for Mike (or rather pitied my friend) who worked her decks.

I had plenty to learn aboard the *Sag*, and Jonesy's method of teaching anchored in telling greenhorns, in no uncertain terms, exactly how little they knew. Then it was up to them to figure out the rest. He was inherently a decent person—loyal to his wife, whom he often mentioned, and a fan of sea story books. It was a tough love kind of situation, and as much as I had secured my footing around camp, I needed to become mentally stronger when living on a thirty-foot tugboat piloted by a hard-nosed captain.

"You need to stand up to Jonesy," Jim, the cook, said to me one morning in the galley.

"What do you mean?" I was doing a decent job and enjoyed working on the *Sag*. Jim and I had become good friends in the short time we had sailed together, and he told me things straight up, no B.S. Ben, the engineer, was a good guy and took time to show me around the engine room and helped me on deck when needed. I thought I had no problems with any of the crew, including Jonesy.

"You're too polite—always letting him go first when he's in the galley, or making way for him when he's walking around on deck. It bugs the shit out of him."

"He's the boss. I thought he was old school—a Captain Bligh type."

"Yeah, but you need to understand he's used to lifers—guys who've been around boats before they could even walk. In his eyes, you're just a college kid from Colorado."

I sat down at the table and took off my cap. My upbringing in a German-Irish Catholic family, and my father's experience as a Navy man, had guided me with teachings of respect for both superiors and elders. Jonesy was both. I pondered the idea of how to act and work in a way that wouldn't annoy him—if that was even possible.

"You're trying too hard." Jim poured me a cup of coffee. "Just slow down, go with the flow, and you'll learn along the way."

Lee had taught me a lot, and I had never known such a seasoned worker than he. I thought about what Jim had said and the way I acted around Jonesy as compared to Lee. I was more relaxed, more myself, when I was on one of Lee's crews. I had plenty of respect for Lee, but it was like working with him, not for him—and he took time to teach me. I always thought the primary goal was to work hard and get the job done, nothing more. Now it appeared as though it was also about something more.

Over the next couple of days of working the decks of the *Sag*, I felt a growing resentment toward Jonesy. All I wanted to do was complete my duties in the best way possible, learn the ropes, and not have to worry about how I was merely a "college kid" and not a company guy. I stood at the bow of the *Sag* as we approached a barge and pushed the thoughts out of my head. We were several miles out from camp, sailing north into the Beaufort Sea, about to assist a barge loaded with drill rig equipment. I pulled the shortwave radio out of my pocket and switched to the same band as Jonesy as he finished up a conversation with another captain.

"... yeah, we'll hook up on the stern and take it the rest of the way. Over." Jonesy said.

"Roger that. Over."

"Send your deckhand out to help—mine doesn't know shit. Over."

I don't remember running across the deck, only a short time when my feet touched every other step on the stairway leading up to the wheelhouse.

"What the fuck was that?" I said as Jonesy sat down in the captain's chair.

"What?" He turned to me.

"I heard what you said to that other captain—that I don't know shit."

"You don't."

"Hey, I'm breakin' my ass out there, trying to do the best I can. I'm part of your crew—you should be stickin' up for me, not talking shit to other captains. I'm trying to learn this stuff as fast as I can."

"You're green—still have a helluva long way to go and have to earn it, don'tcha know?"

With my ego and pride obliterated, I returned to the deck and Ben and I threw lines up to the deckhand on top of the barge. I knew the crewman from the other boat. We had worked on pump crew together the prior year. He was about my age, a company man, lived in Seattle, and worked in the harbor all year. He climbed down onto the deck of the *Sag* and walked over to me.

"How's it goin'?"

"Not bad."

"How ya like workin' with Jonesy?"

"It's okay—except when he's talking bullshit about me on the radio."

"Huh?"

"Yeah, he told your captain over the shortwave that I didn't know shit."

"You don't."

The deckhand laughed, opened up a can of tobacco, and handed it to me.

A myriad of responses clogged my head: *What the hell is there to know… how hard is it to pull lines across a deck… I sailed on the Point Oliktok, bashing our way through a sea of ice—I know what I'm doing… do you want to settle this here and now?!*

Instead, I took a deep breath, sucked up the arctic air, and grabbed a wad of tobacco from the tin. Standing at the bow of the *Sag River* with the other deckhand, I surrendered to the fact—at least for the time being—that I didn't know shit.

LAST DAYS OF '83

MINUTES, HOURS, AND days crawled along at an agonizingly la-borious pace to the constant drone of the camp generator. Addi-tional crews, who were full-time company workers, had flown up from Seattle to sail on the tugboats. Most all the grunts like myself found themselves transferred back to laborer and dockhand duties. Swan was the only camp worker still on a boat and held onto his position as captain of the tug, *Prudhoe Bay*, to prepare it for the upcoming Sealift.

The "Prudhoe Stare" was already appearing on many of the worker's faces—the time of the season when one's mind drifted to somewhere far from the Arctic, a mythical place that numbed the fact that many long working days were still ahead.

We stood on the causeway, about to organize pallets and Pee Vees into stacks—the same ones we moved off the barges the day before. I was back on Lee's crew, which was an upside, and helped prevent a downward spiral into a quagmire of eternal doldrums. It was the calm before the storm, the dog days of preparation before the frenzy of another Sealift and the accompanying weeks of non-stop overtime.

"I'm tired of driving that fuckin' forklift." Lee reached into his coveralls. We winced as he took out his pocket watch. "Someone else needs to bring it over here."

"I'll get it," Mike said.

"Take your time. We need to milk this job."

Mike turned toward the direction of the forklift, then hesitated. "Hey Lee, since we have some time to kill, why don't you tell us one of your industrial accident stories?"

We all laughed. Lee's accident stories were the most colorful and graphic of his tales, and always involved a tragic miscalculation or gross human error. When long workdays reached their most tedious tenure, and the crew's morale took a nosedive, a couple of these yarns put grins on our faces. Lee turned to face us and we huddled around him in anticipation of hearing one of his many experiences with death.

"Yeah, tell us about one of the grossest things you've seen." Jeff wedged a wad of chewing tobacco behind his lip.

"Did I ever tell you guys about when I used to work as a logger?"

"In Washington?" Jeff shoved the tin of tobacco back in his coveralls.

"It was after I got out of the service—I worked this loggin' camp a couple a years. Well, there was this one time when we was workin' a ridge up in the northern Cascades. Beautiful country, but steep as all get out. It was tough as hell hikin' those damn mountains."

Thoughts ran through my mind of a young Lee, a chainsaw or ax slung over his shoulder. I wondered what he was like back then. He certainly wouldn't have had the large cache of stories as he did later in life. I wondered if strong storytellers were born with a gift for reciting colorful narratives, or if they honed this skill over the years—memories stacked on top of each other like worn crates filled with ship line, waiting to be opened. I imagined it was probably a little of both.

"Anyways, we were fallin' some big trees along this sidehill—big-ass lumbering rigs all around us." Lee's eyes gleamed as he continued the story. "A guy knew that when a tree was felled, you'd run parallel with the ridge, out of the way of where the log was gonna roll. They roll downhill—every dumbass knows that. Gravity *always* wins. Well, one day one of the guys wasn't payin' attention, or must have had something on his mind besides the work at hand. I can't even remember what the hell his name was, it's been so damn long ago." We all leaned in closer, smiling.

"Right above us, up near the very top of the ridge, a huge fuckin' tree was felled—shook the shit out of the ridge when it hit the ground. Well, I don't know what that poor son of a bitch was thinking—or not thinking—but he ran *down* the mountain as that tree came rolling toward him. He didn't run *across* the ridge-like he was supposed to—like we'd been doing all week long. It was like he lost his mind and tried to outrun the fuckin' thing."

"What the heck?" Mike said. "He must have panicked."

"Yeah, I don't know what the hell was rattlin' around inside his head." Lee rubbed spittle from the corner of his lip with the back of his hand. "Of course the tree rolled faster than the guy could run—there's some things you just can't outrun. Sure enough, it went right over the top of him."

"Did it kill him, Lee?" Jeff asked, egging Lee on.

"Oh hell yeah," Lee said indignantly. "He was deader than a turd."

Jeff laughed and a piece of tobacco flew out of his mouth.

"So Lee, did you see him—what did he look like?" Mike asked, prying for more details.

"He was smashed flatter than a pancake—his eyes were all popped out, brains pushed out of his ears. Shit, he was a fuckin' mess."

We all smiled. Our amusement certainly wasn't at the cost of the poor worker's ill fortune and untimely death. We were all working in a dangerous environment and knew serious injury or death was only one poor decision away, and we didn't need to jinx our luck. The allure was in the way Lee told a story—a simple and non-eloquent recounting of an event, even one with such an ill-fated ending. His recitations evoked a sense of wonder, as if he re-lived the events during each retelling. An encyclopedia of industrial accidents, Lee remembered most every detail of the incidents, and always marveled at how a split second of poor decision-making resulted in such tragedy. I wondered how many of these gruesome deaths he had seen in his lifetime.

My professors at college often told of their experiences, memories from years of passionate work in whatever their field of expertise; intricately woven tales, recounted with rich, precise language, carried along by the unique voice of the teller. Lee's stories stood as ragged testaments of a life spent as a dockworker, deckhand in two wars, lumberjack, bear guide, and merchant seaman. They were as straightforward and colorful as the storyteller himself, their edges roughened by a lifetime of hard labor.

Once Sealift arrived, the days sped by as I once again worked on a pump crew and racked up as many overtime hours as possible. It wasn't long before it was time to head back to school. With my duffle bag stuffed tight, a daypack slung over my shoulder filled with a couple of books, cassettes, and Walkman, I carried the long strip of baleen Panuk had given to me and walked down the gangplank onto the shoreline. After taking one last look at the camp, I loaded everything into a company Suburban and we made our way to the Deadhorse airstrip.

When we transferred planes in Anchorage, the flight attendant asked me if I would like a drink. I ordered a double scotch and water.

"That probably won't fit in the overhead, so you can keep it next to you," the flight attendant said and nodded toward the piece of baleen. "What is it?"

"Baleen."

She had a puzzled look on her face.

"From a whale," I explained, the answer met by another perplexed look. "Whale tongue—hangs down from the sides of their mouth."

"Eww." The flight attendant took a couple of steps back, then reached into her cart and grabbed a miniature bottle of Cutty Sark. She set a plastic cup filled with ice and the bottle of Cutty onto my tray, keeping an eye on the baleen as if it might somehow still be a living organism.

"So, where'd ya find that thing?"

I smiled then took a sip of the scotch. The plane was only half full and I was sitting in the very last row. Apparently, the flight attendant wasn't in a great hurry, so I told her a story of flying out to a place named Barter Island, traveling along the shore in a vehicle called the Blue Goose, and onto our stranded fleet of boats and barges at the end of a gravel reach. I related the experience of living near an Iñupiat village, and of a friend I had made—days of fishing, shooting a rifle across a frozen sea, and the time we attended a blanket toss celebration. The colorful stories flowed easily, but it seemed impossible to convey the long work hours, monotony, and isolation our crew had encountered; experiences abbreviated to a few sentences. The fading remnants of the Prudhoe Stare, and the dark circles underneath my eyes, told those stories better than any words.

When the flight attendant returned to her station, I reclined into the softness of the airplane seat—the scotch had adequately warmed and relaxed my body. I reached into my daypack and felt the pocket watch I had bought back in Seattle at the beginning of summer. It was the same kind Lee carried throughout the work season. The drone of *Barge 213's* generator continued in the back of my mind as I wound the timepiece and watched the minute hand spin along its endless path.

DRY CAMP

I LEARNED THE ROPES my first two seasons at Arctic Marine Freighters, both work-wise, and how to relax during the short periods of being off the clock. AMF, like all the other camps on the slope, was a dry camp; no alcohol or controlled substances allowed. Like most other challenges in the Arctic, if there's a will, there's a way.

In my third year, I considered the camp expediter as one of the most important people to know—they held the key to providing provisions that took the edge off a relentless work schedule. An expediter's job was to ensure efficient movement of goods or supplies in and out of camp. He or she drove to Deadhorse every morning and afternoon, picked up any new arrivals at the airstrip, collected the mail, and swung by the Prudhoe Bay General Store. If you needed camera film, another roll of chewing tobacco, or wanted the latest edition of your favorite magazine, the expediter could pick it up it for you if it was available at the store—and occasionally could also obtain a case of beer.

"Man, it'd be great to have a cold beer right now," I had mentioned to my roommate, Ken. I was lying in my rack, daydreaming of sitting on the porch at my parents' house on a hot summer day, having a cold Coors with my dad.

"Sometimes the expediter can get beer." Ken lit a cigarette.

"Beer?" I sat up, squinting at the harsh light reflecting off the ice outside our window. It seemed like everyone had weed stashed somewhere in their quarters and many rooms I visited reeked of reefer, but I hadn't seen any beer.

"Some of the truck drivers carry it up on the Haul Road."

The Dalton Highway, referred to as the Haul Road by slopers, was the only road leading to Prudhoe Bay. The so-called "highway," constructed in 1974, served as a supply road to support the Trans-Alaska Pipeline System. It's named after James Dalton, a lifelong Alaskan and an engineer who helped supervise construction of the DEW Line. Dalton was an expert in arctic engineering and worked as a consultant in early oil exploration in northern Alaska.

The Haul Road directly parallels the pipeline and is one of the most isolated roads in the United States. It's over four hundred miles long, begins at the Elliott Highway, north of Fairbanks, and ends at Deadhorse and the Prudhoe Bay oil fields. There are only three towns along the route: Coldfoot has a population of approximately ten, Wiseman hovering around twenty-two, and Deadhorse with twenty-five permanent residents (3,500–5,000 or more seasonal workers depending on oil production). Two other settlements, Prospect Creek and Galbraith Lake, are uninhabited except for seasonal residents. The road is primitive in places, and the nearest medical facilities are in Fairbanks and Deadhorse.

"That's a long way for a beer run," I said. "I thought there wasn't supposed to be any alcohol, nothing at all even at the Prudhoe Bay store—and AMF is a dry camp."

"The entire slope is dry—designated as no alcohol, and no controlled substances." Ken flicked ashes into a coffee cup. "Even though weed is everywhere, it's still a big deal if you get caught with it. In the oil field camps, they bring dogs through to sniff out any pot. I've never seen them do it out here, but every year they talk about it—probably to keep it under control, or at least behind closed doors."

"Who's 'they?'"

"Upper management," Ken said and took a drag off his cigarette.

"A scotch and water sounds good," I said, not so much as a desire to get drunk. It was more of a need to relax after the long workdays, and ease the numbness in my carpel-syndromed hands.

"A scotch drinker, huh?" Ken said. "I can bring you some when I get back from R&R."

"Really—you can do that?"

"Yeah, I'm a Black Velvet drinker myself, and figured I'd bring some reserves to camp. I can probably fit some scotch for you in my sea bag."

"Man, that'd be great."

"What's your flavor?"

"Huh?"

"What kind do you drink?"

"Oh—Dewar's."

True to his word, Ken came back from R&R with a supply of alcohol to get us through the season, or a few weeks, anyway. He opened his sea bag upon returning and pulled out two large plastic water bags, the kind you take camping and hang from a tree; one filled with Dewar's, and the other with Black Velvet, the tops carefully wrapped in duct tape to avoid a blowout of alcohol on the airplane. We ripped the duct tape free, and I went down to the galley and grabbed two cups of ice, then ran back to our room.

"You can hang it in your locker," Ken said and showed me how the bags hung perfectly on a coat hook inside the locker (coat hooks were a valuable commodity at AMF). "Kind of keep it hidden behind some shit in case anyone comes snoopin' around. All you have to do is open the spout, and fill 'er up."

We poured a couple of drinks and sat at the table, looking out the window at the sea of ice. I rubbed my wrists—a sensation of thousands of crawling ants spread across my hands. Ken noticed me holding my wrist as he lit a cigarette, then opened the window a couple of inches.

"I'm working on the winch on the 213. It got fried last year after Sealift when everything blew over to Barter. I'll tell Bourke I could use some help. It'd get you away from grinding boat hulls for a while. Maybe ask Homan, too—you get along with him?"

"Yeah, Kevin's cool. Sounds great."

"It'll make the day a little less monotonous." Ken kicked off his boots. "The parts finally came in."

The 213's towing winch was on the aft deck, a black piece of machinery with a huge metal spool where steel wire, as thick as two to three inches, wound around it up to eight or nine layers deep. The machinery and supporting steelwork for the spool were even larger. Standing almost as tall as most crewmembers, it covered about fifteen square feet of space. It weighed somewhere around 50,000 pounds—the wire alone weighing between eight to ten tons.

Just aft of the spool was a level-winding device, a couple of vertical posts that moved back and forth with the wire between the posts, much like the guide on the level wind fishing reel I had back home. Behind the posts was a set of H-bitts, welded to the deck of the 213. The bitts served as the wire guides.

After working on the winch each day, Ken and I returned to our quarters, poured a cocktail or two, and discussed the completed work. It was a welcome addition to my daily routine of book-reading, or watching an old western or war film in the movie room. We kept our after-hour ritual to ourselves, except for the occasional invited guest—Kevin was a coworker on the project, and Swan was partial to scotch. The tingling in my hands faded as the days went by.

Working on the winch with Ken opened doors to more jobs with engineers, welders, and other skilled workers. In my third season, I became a reliable assistant, and although I hadn't completely escaped all the mandatory grunt work, at least I found some welcome respite. Some of the workdays concluded with a styrofoam cup filled to the brim with scotch and water, or an occasional beer that had traveled the long journey down the Haul Road.

SOLSTICE

FOR THE FIRST TIME since I had worked at Arctic Marine Freighters, a crewmember walked up the stairway to the comm shack each morning who wasn't a male worker. A young woman, about the same age as the other college-attending seasonal laborers, had traveled north to work at AMF as an expediter for the summer. Her name was Ann Johansen—affectionately and respectfully referred to as Annie, or "Tugboat Annie." She was cute, smart, hardworking, and knew how to handle herself in a camp full of men. She also was the daughter of the vice president of operations at Crowley Maritime and had attended high school with Mike.

The crew was protective of Annie, even though we knew she had no problem taking care of herself. We didn't want to put her in the same situation as the past expediters, so it was a little tougher to ask her to pick up beer in town; negotiating with the truckers didn't seem like a good idea—again, most likely too protective on our part.

"Annie's cool," Mike said as we cleaned up after work. "I see her around campus, back at State."

"Whenever you have a woman aboard a boat, or in a camp, it

only causes fuckin' problems." Bourke took a long drag from his cigarette, then blew a puff of smoke out the door of the tool van. His stance was consistent with many of the old-timers.

"Man camps" were the norm in Prudhoe Bay. There wasn't a lot of diversity either—a few black, Hispanic, and Iñupiat workers, but the northern population was predominantly white male. Having Annie as a co-worker wasn't an issue for younger members of our crew, and it was refreshing to see someone without a scraggly beard and a wad of tobacco in their lip.

With ice-breakup at least a month away, shore duty and the monotony of work prematurely wore down the crew. Summer solstice signaled the longest day of the year, and even though daylight remained continuous throughout the work season, that fact did not hinder a solstice party at the ARCO camp.

"Annie said she could drop us off at the ARCO camp when she goes to Deadhorse for supplies—The Bear OK'd it," Mike said to me. "Wanna go?"

"Yeah, when?"

"Now—meet us at the 'burb.'"

After running up to my quarters and making a quick change of clothes, I walked down the gangplank of the 213 where Mike, Jeff, Steve, and Annie waited by the company Suburban. Ronnie and Big G drove to the Exxon camp about every other night to play basketball. The oil company camps made AMF look like a shantytown. Many of them featured basketball courts and workout rooms and better facilities overall.

When we arrived at the ARCO camp and walked through the entrance, I noticed a chart hanging in the hallway. A graph listed temperatures throughout the previous year, the lowest point dipping to -54°F. A mark directly below, listed the same temperature plus windchill factor at -90°F.

Promptly handed cans of beer by ARCO workers, we wound our way throughout the camp, drinking and celebrating. In one room, I picked up a commemorative t-shirt from a stack of boxes. Sprawling letters surrounded a woodcut graphic of a smiling sun: *Solstice Party, South Lake Inn, Prudhoe Bay, 1984*. There was no place named

"South Lake Inn" that I knew of, so I assumed it was an inside joke by the ARCO crew.

Summer solstice occurs when the tilt of the earth's semi-axis is most inclined toward the sun, the word "Solstice, derived from the Latin words sol (sun) and sistere (to stand still). Midsummer was also a crucial time of year for Nordic seafarers, who met to discuss legal matters and resolve disputes. They visited wells or bodies of water thought to have healing powers, then built huge bonfires. In Prudhoe Bay, this same time of year apparently ignited a reason to party.

As much as it felt great to be out of the AMF camp for a night, inevitably, the season of '84, with a larger than normal Sealift on its way, would be a long one. The comfortable numbness afforded by a night off and a cold beer quickly dissipated over the following workdays. Word came down from The Bear that most of the crew would work through the Fourth of July holiday—Annie, and only a few other workers, planned on heading home for a week. There was a possibility of an optional R&R a few weeks later, depending on the progress of the Sealift fleet rounding Point Barrow. I had called Chris and told her I would most likely not take R&R if offered, and I still questioned that decision—especially after hearing the disappointment in her voice.

To keep morale from sinking into a deeper arctic chasm, the Fourth of July holiday would be celebrated at the end of West Dock, AMF-style.

"What's this?" I watched Tim as he attached a sheet of paper to the door of the head with a couple of pieces of masking tape. Written in blue felt-tip pen:

Arctic Marine Freighters 1st Annual Softball Invitational
Will's Wimps (elderly gang) vs Bruce's Bruisers (the boys)
Umpire: The Bear
* *Watch Lee tell a hunting story and pitch at the same time!*
* *Are the Buff Brothers as explosive on the field as they*
are in the bilges?
July 4th, Dock 3 Field, 7:00 pm.

I laughed after reading the line about the Buff Brothers. These two workers had spent an inordinate amount of time the past few weeks, as we all did, mucking out the bilges of all the boats. This grimy job involved days in the belly of a tugboat pumping out a mixture of diesel fuel, oil, water, and anti-freeze into fifty-gallon drums located topside. Once completed, we used 3M synthetic sorbent pads to wipe the hull clean. Often referred to as diapers, the 3M pads gave way to the name "Diaper Dan," another one of our fellow workers who spent a lot of time in the bilges. A chemical called Westlode, a powerful petroleum-based solvent emulsion was then used to complete the cleaning process.

"Softball game, huh?" I said to Tim.

"And bonfire," he replied, a cigar wedged in the corner of his mouth.

Swan strutted to the entrance of the head, turned, and read the flyer. "They only used your name because 'Bruce' and 'Bruisers' go quite nicely together." He then stomped his way through the doorway.

The following week, the crew stacked scrap wood and any other burnable items of no use in the middle of West Dock. Each day the pile grew higher, a haphazard heap comprising both oil-soaked and sun-bleached timbers.

Any kind of baseball gear was well over three hundred miles away, so the crew got innovative. Lance, who managed and ordered all the equipment for camp, fabricated a ball from a variety of materials found in the tool van, including a large, rusted steel nut, about three inches wide, wrapped with layers of duct and electrical tape until its denseness felt as close to that of a softball as possible. Everyone kept an eye out for anything that might serve as a bat, including shovel handles and boards from shipping pallets. Work gloves became mitts.

Over thirty AMF workers walked onto the gravel surface of West Dock on the Fourth of July and took their positions—old-timers up first. A square board, hastily spray-painted white, served as home plate. The Bear stood behind it.

"Plaaaay ball!" he growled.

The jeers began. "Hey, batter, batter... old farts can't hit... swing for the fence—or the end of the dock... this guy's got one foot in the grave, another on a banana peel..."

Getting a hit required not only a perfect swing but also a tremendous stroke of luck that might enable the duct-taped ball to hit a rock and ricochet in the opposite direction of a charging fielder. To say the game was exciting would be a stretch, but it was definitely interesting, with both sides sharing a lot of laughs as the game plodded onward. Lee did a good job at pitching but struck or grounded out each time at the plate. Ronnie's athleticism helped the old-timers get some runs, and some others showed grit, but the younger guys had more enthusiasm and more than an ample amount of cockiness.

I'm not sure if anyone kept score, and if they did, I don't remember which team came out on top. For all intents and purposes, I like to believe it was both.

At the end of the game, there was plenty of diesel fuel to douse the pile of splintered deck planks, broken pallets, smashed crates, and other scrap wood that had grown to over twenty-feet high the past week. The welding crew lit the pile with propane torches, and a wave of heat blasted our faces. The fire burned hot and fast, the crew slowly trickling back into camp until it was only The Bear, Tim, and I watching the glowing embers. I read in a book later that Ancient Nordic seafarers came together to meet around the summer solstice to resolve disputes. They built huge bonfires and bonded in a seasonal ritual that spanned generations.

"Get a shovel and cover it up when it's done." The Bear turned and made his way back to the 213.

Tim and I stood in silence, each of us in our own thoughts, watching the last of the flames slowly die out. I pondered the delicate balance of keeping a crew's morale high, maintaining their focus, and attempting to limit conflicts or resentments. It takes wisdom to look into the flames in order to see the light.

Bourke said women had no place in camp—that they only caused problems. All I had for reference was Tugboat Annie. I saw how most all the other workers welcomed her, how she more than pulled her own weight, and how quickly she became an integral part of the crew. Her father let her work at the camp, surely a difficult decision—the letting go, and trust in the belief that everything would be okay for her. When, or if, I ever had a daughter or daughters, I realized the same decision most likely awaited.

REFLECTIONS

MY DAUGHTER FOCUSES her camera on a weathered television antenna atop a seaside trailer. Click—another image captured. The welcoming aroma of the sea fills our lungs as we walk through the trailer camp. We continue our early morning photoshoot, searching for subjects of interest.

"These are going to make some cool black and whites." She scans a group of trailers lined up like giant snails, their shells all the same grayish hue, void of color. "Perfect."

Our family makes a trek to a northern California beach at least once a year. My wife, Robbin, and I spent our honeymoon near Mendocino, and like migratory fowl, we journey back to the coast each year. It's about a six-hour drive to Mendocino from our home in South Lake Tahoe, or a four-hour trip to Bodega Bay. These are two of our most visited coastal retreats. We rented a house in Dillon Beach this time, a mile and a half stretch of sandy coastline and dunes near the mouth of Tamales Bay, south of Bodega Bay, looking out at the Pacific Ocean. The Northern California coast is a place where memories float as thick as early morning fog. The allure of the ocean, and the many reminiscences and thoughts of the future that ebb and flow within its tides, remain a soul-cleansing experience with each visit.

We had set our alarm clock to awaken us around daybreak, before the sun crept over the rolling hills to the east. A couple of deer perked their heads toward us as we drove down the curvy road from our rental and made our way past the Dillon General Store and out to Lawson's Landing.

Each trailer along the landing reflects the personality of its owner. Homemade wind chimes shaped as plastic pelicans, starfish, and seashells dangle from day-glo mobiles in front of a twenty-foot Airstream, clanking their flat notes. Taped to the front window hangs a line-drawing of John Lennon with the word "Imagine" underneath. Two slips down is an Overland, painted olive drab with khaki trim. A POW/MIA flag flies out front. On its window is a bumper sticker with rifle crosshairs and the words "This is *my* peace sign." Fishers, beach bums, and a couple of seasonal surfers are residents of the other trailers, sixty-three in all. It's a perfect location for early morning photography.

My daughter is using a film camera, the one my father gave to me at Christmas many years ago when I left for college. It's an old Canon AE-1, the same one I took to Prudhoe Bay when I worked up in Alaska. It's also been to Europe to capture iconic images in Austria, Switzerland, Italy, the Netherlands, and Germany, including the Berlin Wall when it was still standing. Packed carefully within my duffle bag, it made a later trip to Nigeria's Ivory Coast, along with all the other gear stowed aboard a one hundred and twenty-five foot seagoing tugboat.

Now, my daughter was creating her own images and memories with the camera.

Leaving her digital Nikon at home, she decided to shoot film instead. She took a photography class the previous summer to learn how to develop film, retouch, and create enlargements. She also understood how traditional photographic techniques are still a viable medium and has maintained its stature as an art form. Film interprets subtleties, tones, and the transference of light, differently from digital. It has a unique warmth and feeling. Most importantly, it forces a person to look more carefully through their viewfinder.

Knowing that there are a limited number of shots on one roll of film makes a photographer examine their subject with a more critical and observant eye.

We wander through the narrow, meandering roads between the trailers. It's an eclectic mix of dwellings huddled against the Dillon Beach dunes. The sky lightens, the mist is less dense.

"Let's walk to the store—I need another cup of java." I swing the camera strap over my shoulder.

"Sounds good."

A neon sign flickers "OPEN" at Lawson's Landing Store & Tackle. The left side of the building is a marine repair shop—the right side, a general store that sells fishing gear. I pour a cup of coffee, walk to the counter, and hand the clerk a couple of bills. She hands me change—the cost is cheap, the taste bitter and strong.

We walk out of the store and head to a long pier that stretches into the bay. It's the same place we went crab fishing the day before with her sister. Wooden planks squeak against the rusty nails that hold them in place as we make our way to the end.

"We'll have to come back at low tide with the nets," my daughter says.

"Yeah—it's going to be a nice day." I squint my eyes at the glare reflecting off the water surface in kaleidoscope patterns. The smell of the ocean and sound of squawking gulls provide an early morning comfort, a familiar feeling filled with memories.

My father often took us to the beach when my family lived in the San Francisco Bay Area. Martin's Beach, south of the city and about twenty miles down the coast, was one of our favorite destinations. It was what one visualizes when thinking of a stereotypical California Beach, with both its idyllic natural features and idiosyncrasies. Martin's was a family beach, and since we mostly visited it on the weekends, this particular beach scene included crowds of people, screaming children, and the smell of overcooked hotdogs drifting from a nearby food stand. Our skin, heavily marinated in suntan lotion, collected sand like a magnet, legs encrusted like the Shake 'N Bake chicken drumsticks my mother made for Saturday night dinners.

On one of these visits to the beach, late in the day, my father took me by the hand and we walked along the surf to wash off all the sand stuck to my body after a day of making sand castles. The sun sank low in the sky, a golden sunset about to take center stage. Then I felt something brush against my leg.

"Uh, Dad," I pointed to the side of my thigh which had turned midnight black.

"What the heck?" My father lifted me out of the water. "Son of a gun."

"What's the matter?" my mother asked when my father set me on the beach and grabbed a towel.

"Damn oil."

"Is it from the spill down south?" my mother asked.

"I doubt if it could travel this far. Probably from a boat or maybe a tanker."

I was ten years old when I heard the news at school about the oil spill near Santa Barbara. A friend told me oil was nothing more than dead animals buried deep inside the earth. All of our cars were burning dead stuff. Now it was spilling into the sea, he said, killing everything it touched.

"Is there more out there?" I asked.

"Maybe." My father did his best to wipe off the sludge with a beach towel, but the tar-like coating only smeared deeper into the pores of my skin.

The horizon turned burnt orange as seagulls swept across glittering waves, red diamonds reflecting across the ocean's surface.

"What about fish and birds—what happens if they get in the oil? Will they die? Wouldn't they drink it, or get covered and not be able to move?"

"I doubt they'd drink it," my father said. "We'll have to clean you off better when we get home—probably take some turpentine to get it off. You, and the fish, will be fine."

My father did his best to assure me that everything was all right. That was his job.

Fifteen years later, he hugged me, said goodbye, and I boarded a plane at San Francisco International Airport. With the film camera he gave me at Christmas packed safely in my duffle bag, the same bag he used when he sailed aboard an aircraft carrier in World War II, I traveled over 3,400 miles to the North Slope of Alaska. Once again, like many times before, he would trust that it would be okay.

One day, while working on a tugboat tied alongside a towering oil rig in the Arctic Ocean, I would think back to the time at the beach when I was ten years old, my father trying his best to rub remnants of an oil spill from the side of my leg.

"Ready to go, Dad?" My daughter's deep brown eyes looked up at me.

In a few years, she'll be traveling to college. I'll watch her go, the film camera tucked away in her luggage. And after her, my younger daughter will be heading out. They'll be all right—they'll be safe navigating the waters on their own.

"Yeah, sorry—my mind kind of drifted a bit."

The sea signals to us as it has many others, like the buoy a half-mile out from shore, dancing in the glittering sunlit swells of Bodega Bay.

DOG DAYS

"HERE'S THAT BOOK I was telling you guys about." Lee tossed a bound document the thickness of a small-town phone book onto the table. Titled *Veterans and Radiation*, it had a Veteran's of Foreign Affairs logo on the cover.

I picked up the publication and leafed through its pages, stopping at a section named *Mortality of Veteran Participants in the* CROSSROADS *Nuclear Test*. I skimmed the first page, then read a paragraph near the bottom: "Among Navy personnel, the primary analysis group for the study, participants at the CROSSROADS nuclear test experienced higher mortality than a comparable group of nonparticipating military controls. The increase in all-cause mortality was 4.6 percent and was statistically significant."

"You ever have a doctor check you out?" I turned the page.

"I take a yearly, as required, so I can work up here—just like everyone else. I hate those fuckin' things. I feel fine." Lee puffed out his chest. "Hard work makes you strong—live a hell of a lot longer than a guy sittin' behind a desk all day."

There was a lot to be said for a job requiring hard labor. Lee was right; I had never been stronger, and aside from the carpel tunnel syndrome and constant tiredness, I felt better than I ever had.

At the same time, I wondered how many chemicals and toxins, and at what concentrations, a body could tolerate and filter from its system. Exposure to diesel fumes most every day, along with Westlode, a powerful petroleum- based solvent emulsion used to clean boat bilges and machinery, couldn't have been healthy for the crew. A month of sanding hulls, then breathing in the toxic fumes of epoxy paint and experiencing the resulting dizziness, most likely wasn't the safest work conditions either.

Hull paint, or "bottom paint," is enhanced protection that improves a ship's performance and durability. The chief ingredient is Tributyltin (TBT). TBT is used as a biocide in antifouling paint that's applied to the hulls of ocean-going vessels. It reduces the rate of biofouling, which is the growth of organisms on a ship's hull.

The effects of anti-fouling paint go beyond the organisms that it's intended to kill. By poisoning barnacles, algae, and other organisms at the bottom of the food chain, TBT is biomagnified up the marine predators' food web. It can harm many layers of the ecosystem, including invertebrates, vertebrates, and humans. A couple of weeks prior, we also had to muck-out the inside of a barge that had hauled diesel fuel. By the end of the day, my skin radiated a reddish hue, a result of breathing in the diesel fumes for too many hours. These were all minute exposures to toxicity, paling in comparison to radioactive particles floating into one's lungs.

I read further into the document Lee had handed me and waded through statistics of increased cancer, leukemia, and mortality among CROSSROADS sailors. At the bottom of the section was the conclusion. "These findings do not support a hypothesis that exposure to ionizing radiation was the cause of increased mortality among CROSSROADS participants. Had radiation been a significant contributor to increased risk of mortality, then significantly increased mortality due to malignancies (particularly leukemia) should have been seen in participants thought to have received higher radiation doses relative to participants with lower doses and to unexposed controls. No such effects were observed. This study, however, was neither intended nor designed to be an investigation of low-level radiation effects, per se, and should not be interpreted as such."

"Does any of this stuff worry you, Lee?" I asked.

"It's just a bunch of bullshit—gives some paper-pusher something to do. We were ten miles from the blast at the Atoll and didn't spend more than a couple a days cleanin' up the boats afterward."

I imagined it was better not to think too much about past exposures to whatever toxicity one receives. There was no taking it back, and didn't matter in the here and now. With the cards dealt, it was only a matter of time to see how it played out. We were living in the present; each day bled into another for the crew, and thinking too far into the future only drove you crazy. The most important goal was maintaining one's sanity and clinging onto anything that helped navigate the unrelenting tedium.

When we found out that Steve's birthday was only a few days away, we planned a party. Although alcohol and drugs drifted into the AMF camp, gatherings with more than a few crewmembers were rare. Various workers socialized in smaller groups, but like the softball game, this would be one of the few times when the entire camp took part in one celebration. The Bear and upper management surely heard about the plans, but at that stage of the season, and in order to help maintain morale, they looked the other way.

Like all the other living quarters on *Barge 213*, Steve's was a small room filled with two bunk beds, a table, and a couple of chairs. Workers moved in and out of the confined space and meandered into other rooms as the celebration grew.

"Grab a brewski," Mike said when I walked through the doorway. Tugboat Annie had aptly negotiated the beer-buying waters in Deadhorse and procured alcohol for the special event. Several cases of Old Milwaukee and Olympia were piled on one of the beds. "Oly" was my father's favorite, and I thought of him working around the house back home, a beer constantly within arm's reach. I smiled and popped open a can, holding onto the memory as long as I could before it faded into the revelry of the party.

"Special delivery." Big G entered the room. "One for us all." The tall Croation opened a box of cigars and passed it around. Several of us already had our lower lips packed with chewing tobacco, but everyone grabbed a cigar to celebrate.

Tugboat Annie followed G through the doorway carrying a

large chocolate cake with Happy Birthday, Steve, sprawled across the top of it. "A birthday has to have a cake," she said and put it on the table along with a stack of plates and napkins.

"C'mon Annie, try a chew." Mike held out a tin of Copenhagen.

"I guess I at least need to try it once," she said and smiled.

Digging her fingers into the tobacco, Annie took a small pinch and put it into her mouth. Her squinted face caused everyone to laugh, and it wasn't long before she spit the tobacco into an empty cup.

"It really burns."

"You get used to it," Mike said. He had a lot of experience with the effects of chewing tobacco. At the end of the prior season, he had taken a trip to the doctor for a skin graft in order to repair the inside of his lower lip.

"Have cigar." G held the box to Annie.

"Okay, that might be more my speed," Annie said as Mike lit it for her.

I took photos as crewmembers continued to circulate through the room, congratulating Steve on his birthday, and enjoying a beer, a slice of cake, and a cigar. The ice would break in a few weeks, and everyone would scatter into different work crews or assigned to boats. The days would finally speed up as Sealift approached, and a departure date for home would appear on the horizon.

It was good to see Lee with a beer in his hand—the first time I had seen him with one in nearly three summers of working on his crew. It had been a long season and there were still many days ahead of us. He looked happy and not as tired as previous days, when I noticed he had slowed down a bit, his face a little more drawn.

I thought back to the book titled, *Veteran's and Radiation*. The document had arrived in Lee's mailbox, tucked within the rest of his mail. No one reached out to the vets that I knew of, or explained what all the numbers and graphs listed on the pages actually meant. Lee said he didn't care to know. But if it truly didn't concern him, why did he keep the book—was it merely another item to help him launch into one of his many stories, or was it something deeper, something that pervaded his soul like the bombardment of radiation so many years before?

Lee, like every past crewmember he worked with, every animal he hunted, and every sexual partner in his many colorful encounters, seemed to fade into one of his own stories. I pondered how many more seasons he would travel to the Arctic to work at AMF, and I pushed the question out of my mind as if it were a harbinger of bad luck to follow. For the time being, the crew was all together, making the best of a long season. We drank, smoked, chewed tobacco, talked, and most importantly, we laughed.

AN ISLAND IS BORN

"TIME TO GET UP—we're headin' out." Jim, the cook, turned and walked out of the sleeping quarters after giving me a wake-up call, although I had already opened my eyes and assessed my situation. Yes, I was still aboard a tugboat in the Arctic.

The roar of gravel cascading onto a barge deck had lulled me to sleep during my six-hour break. When the sound stopped, so had the brief slumber. The muffled roar of triple Caterpillar diesel engines; gnashing metal of a conveyor belt; gravel crashing against a metal deck—these all constituted the right conditions for a deep sleep aboard the *Sag River*. Any change in the constant drone was my alarm clock, causing me to open my eyes and look out of the porthole next to my rack, wondering why the noise had stopped and what duties the next shift presented. I surrendered to the fact that I had become a part of the same machinery that dictated my rest cycle—another gear within the larger scheme.

A few weeks prior to my assignment as deckhand aboard the *Sag*, Lee had sat down in the galley during our lunch break and grinned. "Looks like we have a side-job this year."

"Yeah, what's up?" I asked, before taking another bite of my grilled cheese sandwich.

"AMF landed a contract to build an island."

I did not know how, or why, such an endeavor was to take place, but like most everything at Arctic Marine Freighters, it was another learn-by-doing-or-watching experience. I learned that offshore drilling in the Arctic required islands to serve as drill rig platforms to fight off the forces of ice and turbulent seas. If a natural island wasn't available, the obvious solution for the oil companies was to build one.

After a two-hour rest, I was back to performing duties as deckhand. Ben, the engineer, stood at the bow. Our boat was soon to depart Thetis Island and push a three-hundred-foot barge with several hill-sized stacks of gravel atop her deck.

"What's up?" I rubbed the sleep from my eyes.

"Stand by to stand by." Ben lit a cigarette.

Several vessels in our fleet would work the "gravel haul" and the building of Mukluk Island. The island, planned for construction during the winter of '82 and summer of '83, was a project of Standard Oil of Ohio (Sohio.) The site was in the most remote, exposed, and deepest water of any island built in the Alaskan Beaufort Sea. Sohio had one year to plan, design, and complete the man-made island, including obtaining the thirty-three necessary permits from various regulatory authorities. The estimated cost of $100 million made it the most expensive offshore exploratory drilling project at the time.

The basic design concept for an artificial offshore gravel island is simple. The goal is to use materials with enough height and bulk to protect the island against ice and water damage over the life of a drilling project. For winter island-building, ice roads are built and maintained over a frozen sea. Large water tankers spray water on the roads to increase thickness and durability. These surfaces provide a flat driving route void of obstacles for the vehicles, and occasional stress cracks repaired with large steel plates. Upon arriving at their destination, the trucks deposit gravel through a hole cut into the ice and it sinks to the seabed. It eventually piles high enough to break the water surface; an island is born.

The Mukluk Island project combined both winter and summer transportation techniques. During the winter, they had trucked gravel over an ice road from the mainland and stockpiled it at Thetis Island. Our job during the summer work season was to haul the gravel from Thetis by barge about twenty-two miles out into the Beaufort Sea.

"How many of these runs will we have to make?" I asked Ben as we pulled away from Thetis, diesel engines screaming from the engine room.

"Who knows—it all depends on the ice floe, and it seems to have a mind of its own. There's a Canadian icebreaker out there helping manage it—and the *Challenger* is also pushing things around. They have to get 'er done before winter sets in. I heard one of the crane operators say it'll take somewhere over 800,000 cubic yards of gravel to build this thing—way over a million tons."

"Sounds like we'll be out here for a few weeks." I grabbed a tin of tobacco out of the top pocket of my coveralls.

"After this run, we'll head back to camp to fuel up—I'll show you some things around the engine room." Ben, much like Ken Townshend, instructed me on some basic marine engineering. My father and brother had taught me how to work on cars since I was old enough to crawl under one, so I had some basic mechanical skills. Many members of my family had spent their share of time in airplane hangars, shipyards, and automobile repair shops. My uncle had learned engineering during World War II while serving aboard several Navy vessels, then became an engineer for Crowley Maritime, and eventually worked his way up the ladder to become vice president of the company.

"Cool—anything you can show me would be great," I said.

After three hours of dodging ice, a crane boom appeared on the horizon, and the slow birth of an island came into view. The *Arctic Challenger*, Crowley's ice-breaking barge, floated in the distance, its crow's nest perpendicular to the surrounded ice. Another barge floated in the expansive ice floe, along with the Canadian icebreaker—a vessel at least ten times as large as the *Sag*. Painted bright orange and dark blue, its massive bow towered over the ice. Near the barge, a black ring protruded from the ocean's surface, a gravel-bag armor system that would serve as the island's slope protection. We would dump gravel from our barge into this encirclement.

The drill site was far from supply sources, service depots, and work camps. Access by vehicles to the site was only available during the winter months, and intermittent due to changing ice conditions. Because of this remoteness and isolation, the island needed to be large enough for self-contained operations to minimize the risk of shutdowns due to resupply needs, weather, or other problems. The island surface would have space for a drilling pad, drill equipment, a towering drill rig, storage area to stockpile pipe, drilling mud, cements, lubricants, and other supplies. It also needed to support a power plant, shop facilities, water and fuel storage, onsite utilities, communications, crew quarters, helipad, barge ramp or dock, and everything else required for uninterrupted drilling into the earth's surface.

The construction of Mukluk Island was impressive, and I felt a sense of pride in being involved in its construction. I contemplated whether it was the idea of completing a massive project that made me feel that way, or some god-like power rush of conquering the forces of nature (at least temporarily). Were such endeavors overextending our reach into somewhere we shouldn't be? Minute sea life crawled along the ocean floor, and fish, seals, and sea lions swam the frigid waters. They were as hearty as everything else that lived in extreme arctic conditions and adapted to most all changes in landforms and adversities. I imagined that these same species teetered on the edge of survival.

"Stay alert," Jonesy shouted from the wheelhouse.

"No shit," I said under my breath.

The whine of the diesel slowed as we approached the construction area and drifted nearer the other barge. The bitter-sweet smell of diesel exhaust filled my lungs as it swirled across the deck. Once Jonesy maneuvered the *Sag* and barge into position, the crane boom lowered slightly, and the process of moving gravel began. The scraper dangled from a main cable, rigged with an inhaul and backhaul cable. A pulley pulled the scraper back and forth as the gravel cascaded into the bay, falling between our vessel and the crane barge.

"Not much for us to do—we don't need to tie off," Ben said. "Just be alert in case we're needed. Round trip, it should be about a nine-hour gig."

I thought of the gravel descending through the water and what it must have looked like from the ocean floor. With each load of gravel, layer by layer, the manmade island would extend toward the surface of the sea until it finally reached daylight. Lifted onto the island, dozers and front-end loaders would move and flatten the surface when the gravel was high enough. In a few weeks, workers could walk across the pad and construct a drill rig to explore what lie several thousand feet below. As a former geology student, diagrams of the completed island and multiple layers of earth filled my head. No one knew how much oil was down there. I assumed it must have been a significant amount if Sohio spent that amount of time, money, and effort to build an entire island. They referred to it as an "exploratory well," which meant it might not be producing oil for several years. The fact of the matter was that Mukluk Island construction costs would eventually exceed one billion dollars, and the project gain notoriety as the most expensive dry hole in oil industry history.

In geologic time, small natural islands such as the ones in the Arctic remain in constant flux. The sea and ice, relentless forces powered by winds and winter storms, carve new shorelines and shape the contours of the land. In the case of a man-made island, the gravel-bag armor system eventually breaks apart. After years of harsh weather, when the drill rigs and support equipment are long gone, the sea will reclaim control over another small land mass. Everything is in a fluid state of transformation. Nothing is permanent.

Another six-hour shift ended when we sailed from Mukluk Island. The *Sag River* pushed an empty barge through a jagged channel in the ice floe, maneuvering through the jigsaw-puzzled terrain. I grabbed a book from my duffle bag, *The Discoverers* by Daniel J. Boorstin, and sat in the galley reading. I yawned as the hum of the engines droned on, ice banging against the side of the hull.

DECISIONS UNDER FIRE AND A GLIMPSE INTO THE ABYSS

THE METAL STAIRS CLANGED and rattled with each step I took up the catwalk to the Arctic Marine Freighters' Com-shack, the resonance dampening into the arctic air. The AMF communications shack served as a ship's crow's nest for the camp. As the tallest point, it housed the camp's radio equipment and served as a place of observation and communication. But like a ship's wheelhouse, it also functioned as the nerve center—a place where The Bear made final decisions.

I opened the door and The Bear was talking with a Crowley White Hat who managed many of the company's operations. Joel Burckhalter sat in front of a couple of shortwave radios. They were in the middle of a conversation and although they acknowledged my entry, they continued as if I wasn't there.

"No one knew what the best option was—which direction might be the correct one," The Bear said in his gravelly voice. "But I made a decision."

"That's the most important thing," the company White Hat said.

"I don't know if it was right or wrong. Hell, it could have been debated for weeks. And it could easily have turned out bad." The Bear grinned. "Very bad. But the main thing, is that I made a decision."

I later learned that The Bear's decision pertained to taking on a side-job that put some boats and equipment at risk. It had been a gamble since the ice floe in the proposed project was so unpredictable. I had made my way to the com-shack to tell them I wanted to work through R&R this year. My decisions paled compared to the ones The Bear had to make each season.

After making Joel aware of my intentions, I descended back down the stairway to the warm-up shack. The next step was to call my folks and Chris and let them know I'd get home later than first planned. With several of the crew waiting their turn to use the one phone in camp, I contemplated the conversation I had overheard in the com-shack.

I had always been under the premise that making a correct decision was a primary goal. I thought of friends back home and people I had worked with in other jobs. They were always happy when they made what they perceived as the "right choice." People are proud of themselves when they think they've made a correct assessment and judgement, and the importance of being right provides a sense of assurance.

For The Bear, it wasn't so much about making a right or wrong decision, but more about choosing a direction and going with it— decisions under fire, void of the luxury of time to contemplate and weigh the pros and cons. They relied on gut instincts. I could hear the confidence in the resolution, not so much in The Bear's words, as I did in the tone of his voice. Possibly perceived as a "fly by the seat of your pants" or a caviler assessment under pressure, I'm willing to bet that in most cases, first intuition is usually the best.

I often got bogged down by indecision and tended to over-analyze every likely outcome of very minute choices. Over analyzing slows down the process of whatever venture, whether it's a choice about taking time off work, or making a major decision involving an entire work camp and millions of dollars of heavy equipment and an entire flotilla of tugboats and barges.

"I'm thinking of skipping R&R this year—working as long as possible until school begins." As my words floated across the thousands of miles to both my parents and Chris, I was already questioning my option to remain in camp without a break. I had made plenty of wrong choices in the past, and I was trying to swing the tally to a more favorable record.

"Can't you get back to Boulder a week or two earlier…" Chris asked. I could hear in her voice that she held back much of what she wanted to say.

"If I get back too late for registration, I can take some night classes again, like I did last year."

"Do you really think that's a good idea? You can do what you want of course, but consider the options. I thought you wanted to graduate this year, and you can do it if you sign up for a full class schedule. And it'd be nice to have a few weeks together before classes begin."

I knew she was right. It would take me a semester to graduate if I carried a full load, and I could be out by the end of the year. I promised her I would be back before the semester began, and I'd do my best to not cut it too tight.

I hung up the telephone and walked out to the end of West Dock to take some photos of the camp. It was quiet, and most everyone was in their quarters, finishing up dinner, or in the movie room. Although AMF was smaller and not nearly as accommodating as the oil field camps, there was something about working for Arctic Marine Freighters that bore a sense of pride and attitude. Maybe because many of us were sailors, compared to oil workers working in the oil fields. The oil companies continued to mine the vast reserves of the North Slope and rake in record-setting profits, but AMF was one of the few that could get into their pockets. It was as if we were pirates, pilfering some of the richest bounties in the world.

Although AMF was relatively small, the parent company, Crowley Maritime, had grown substantially since its founding in 1862. That was the year Thomas Crowley purchased an 18-foot Whitehall rowboat in order to provide transportation of personnel and supplies to ships anchored in the San Francisco Bay. Within a few years, services quickly broadened. In addition to acquiring larger vessels, the company expanded in the 1920s into Los Angeles

Harbor and Puget Sound, with tugboats for ship assists and barge transportation. Bulk petroleum transportation joined the list of services in 1939.

In 1958, Crowley moved into arctic transportation with an agreement to resupply the U.S. government's Distant Early Warning Line on the Alaska coastline. It was the first private company with commercial tug and barge services in the Arctic. Crowley's Alaska common carrier services provided containerized and bulk petroleum cargoes to over 130 villages, many of which lacked docking facilities.

Beginning in 1968, Crowley began summer sealifts of equipment, supplies, buildings, and production modules to Prudhoe Bay. Since that time, 334 barges had carried nearly 1.3 million tons of cargo to the North Slope, including modules the size of ten-story buildings and weighing nearly 6,000 tons. The company had several subsidiaries, including ocean liner cargo services and trucking lines. Crowley also provided specialized marine transportation services, including petroleum product transportation and sales, tanker escorts, contract barge transportation and ocean towing, logistics and support services, marine salvage and emergency response services, spill-response services on the West Coast of the United States, and all-terrain transportation services. A company that began as a one-person operation with an 18-foot rowboat had grown to become the largest company in the maritime industry.

I made my way back to *Barge 213* and our living quarters. I stopped and leaned against the railing, gazing toward the sea. The receding ice continued to morph over the past few weeks. It clogged Prudhoe Bay solid one day—on the next, it might drift out to sea and reveal indigo blue waters, nearly black, with white caps dancing across the surface. I was off the boats for the season and would soon be back on pump crew. How the heck had I worked in this bizarre world for a third year, or the very first year? Of course, I had weighed the options and sacrifices of being away from home, my girlfriend, family, and friends. Instead of summers spent at beaches and lakes, I spent my days on the frigid steel decks of tugboats and barges surrounded by arctic ice. How had that decision made any sense? Ah, yes—money. Amazing how it almost always comes to that.

We were most likely the quirkiest group in Prudhoe Bay; a ragtag camp located over three miles off the mainland on a gravel causeway stretching due north toward the north pole. Our logo was a polar bear with the Crowley "C" encompassing it, and three of the world's largest oil companies contracted with us.

I thought of how The Bear made decisions and the pirate mentality of the camp. Leaders with renegade attitudes make bold and brave decisions and aren't afraid of making mistakes. They see opportunities everywhere, striving for excellence and consistency, not perfection. Taking action and setting sail, they navigate toward their dreams, capable of dealing with wind and tide, adjusting their course as needed. They have all the skills to repair anything on a ship, and the fortitude to find out how to make seemingly impossible ventures somehow possible. But sailing without fear into the unknown can reveal things that are deeper and darker than imagined. My mind drifted to a story Lee had told us only a few days prior.

". . . it was the time we were sailing the Indian Ocean. I was on a merchant ship. We entered the Bengal Sea right after the Bhola cyclone had hit. The swells finally died down to where we weren't getting thrown around like a fuckin'cork in a bathtub. I'd been on ships that sailed into some god-awful shit, but I'd ever seen anything quite like what I saw that morning I walked onto 'er deck."

I watched Lee tell many stories, and the expressions across his face and the glint in his eyes were always an important aspect of the storytelling. But in this recounting, there appeared to be something different, something deeper—a face void of expression, eyes as dark as the iceless bay.

"The Ganges Delta, south of Dhaka, had been hit the worst. Estimates put the dead at over a half million—the deadliest cyclone in history." Lee squinted his eyes and looked toward the sea. "The Hindus burn their dead—cremate them on a pyre of wood. With the amount of bodies piled up everywhere, there wasn't time for a full ritual, so a burning coal was stuck in each of the mouths of the corpses and they were set to sea. When I woke up and looked out over the bow, the water was covered with dead bodies. I had never seen such a thing—thank god, most likely never will. As they drifted by, some of their mouths had been scorched into round holes. Bloated bodies and animal carcasses drifted across the surface as far as you could see—the stench of death stronger than anything I'd ever come across."

The images of Lee's story haunted me. Whenever I walked on deck, I was thankful for seeing nothing but a wide-open sea, or an expanse of ice that appeared to cover the entire world.

Lee was a simple guy, a hardworking sailor and laborer who took things as they came. His interpretations of events he experienced and decisions made were treasure chests of colorful narrations. The story of the Bengal Sea, however, and what he had witnessed in the Gangas Delta was different. He had sailed into the unknown only to be met by a sea of death. It might have forever changed him in a way that he had never fully comprehended.

Experiences shape and mold lives into ways that are difficult to describe. The acceptance and acknowledgment of these experiences, and the questions they present, compels us to keep searching, to keep looking beyond the horizon in search of seemingly unobtainable answers. The quest challenges my vision like a long expanse of ice, its image refracted over the horizon, seemingly afloat in the sky high above the surface of the ocean.

Decisions, choices, and divergent paths; we all choose what seas to sail and how to navigate them. Inevitable squalls present challenges in our thoughts and interpretations. How we meet and negotiate them is often more important than the events themselves.

TUNDRA

I NAIVELY ASSUMED during my first season at Prudhoe Bay that everything would be the same when I returned home as if frozen in a place void of time and space. Even though it often felt like time stood still in Prudhoe Bay, I quickly learned the world had moved on. Parents grew older, friends began careers, and Chris and I drifted further apart with each spring I journeyed north. Time and distance eventually cause relationships to fade like shadows entering an unlit room.

Changes at camp from season to season were also inevitable, normally discerned the first few weeks in camp. After then, the monotony and tedium of long workdays consumed chunks of time until sealift. My first assessment of the '85 season included a head-check of who had returned for another year and who had not. Jack Bourke stood at the doorway of the tool shack, a cigarette in his mouth, hands in the pockets of his worn coveralls.

"Decided to come back for 'nother round, eh?" The cigarette bobbed in his mouth, ashes floating through the air like tiny insects.

"Yeah—couldn't stay away."

"Thought you might be smarter than that." He smiled. "Oh well—every day's a holiday, every meal's a banquet."

"You're bunking with Cubby and Johansen," Bourke finally said, then flicked the cigarette butt across the deck where it landed in a spray of sparks, then tumbled over the side of the barge.

"Sounds good," I said, but concerns over rooming with Erik Johansen swirled inside my head. Johansen was a large, loud, and boisterous Norwegian engineer with a perpetual grimace. I never worked with him, but could not avoid his colorful presence in the galley during meals. His heavy Scandinavian accent, jet-black hair, and chiseled face made for an imposing figure. Several of his co-workers frequently referred to him as, "that fucking squarehead."

One redeeming factor to my living quarters situation was that Tim Payne, or Cubby, would be my other roommate. Tim and I worked together the previous season at Barter Island, and I enjoyed our conversations. The Bear often communicated with a simple glance or glare, but his son, Tim, enjoyed entering any lengthy conversation relating to national and international topics, had a habit of reading the Wall Street Journal each morning as he ate a bowl of prunes, and routinely smoked a cigar after work. My season of '85 began with the "Squarehead" and "Cubby Bear" as my roommates.

"Hey boy," Johansen said to Tim. "I need the bottom bunk— my feet hang over the fucking edge as it is—I don't wanna have to climb to the top rack every goddamn night, too."

"No problem," Tim said. "I like to read late at night. Let me know if the light keeps you awake."

"Okay—you take the other bottom bunk, so his light doesn't bother you." Johansen pointed at me with his huge finger.

"Fine with me." I wondered what it was like to sleep only a few feet away from the high-strung Norwegian. What if he snored as loud as he spoke—how do I deal with that? I hoped my Walkman might drown it out. I enjoyed falling to sleep to the sound of classical music. Vivaldi's *Four Seasons* brought back memories of better times with a photo of Chris, who also enjoyed classical music. My mind wandered to when, or if, I would see her again.

Tim took out a photo of his girlfriend and taped it to the inside of his locker door. I did the same with Chris, even though our relationship was on unstable ground. We continued to unpack our gear and stow it into the lockers. I brought my running shoes and planned on taking some runs after work whenever the twelve-hour workdays didn't wear me down. With the length of the causeway about two-and-a-half miles long, to the mainland and back would total five miles, about the same distance I ran in Boulder three times a week—a healthy workout to keep my head clear.

Johansen jammed a large radio/tape player next to a camera bag on the top shelf of his locker.

"Nice boom box," I said. "What kind of music do you listen to?"

"Oh man, I fuckin' love crazy-ass guitar playing with the shit amplified out of it," Johansen said, excited to talk about music. "Dick Dale is the guitar king."

"Dick Dale—he does the beach and surfing music?"

"Yeah, c'mon, you're from California—you musta grown up on him," Johansen said. "He's one of the fastest guitarists, ever. Listen to this shit." Johansen popped a cassette into the boom box and turned up the volume. The sharp licks of Dick Dale filled the compact living quarters, a guitar medley spanning a repertoire of the guitar master's greatest hits. Tim smiled and bobbed his head to the beat of the music.

Johansen leaned back and shouted, "Goddamn boy, this shit is fuckin' great!"

From then on, our 5:00 am ritual began with Dick Dale's Misirlou as we all rolled out of our racks. "Time to wake up boys," Johansen would yell after we opened our eyes and realized we were still in Prudhoe Bay. "Treat yourself to the best music in the world—it'll be in your head all goddamn day!"

It did stick in our heads, and that was a good thing. Anything softening the toll of long working hours was more than welcomed. The repeating guitar licks spiraling inside my head numbed ricocheting thoughts about what could be happening back home. It became apparent that Johansen's crazy temperament was the very thing that kept him mentally focused in the twisted reality of Prudhoe Bay. Physically, he wasn't huge, but he had a body of steel and a blast furnace filled with flaming determination.

"That fuckin' squarehead," one of the other engineers recited at breakfast one morning, "we were trying to figure out how to move a generator so we could work on the damn thing. We unbolted it and was talkin' about riggin' it up with a come-along winch—to get it to a place where we could work on it. Johansen got a crazy-ass look in his eyes, then lifted up the frickin' thing all by himself, and carried it about ten feet from where it had been bolted to the deck, then set it down."

A couple of weeks after that incident, Johansen burst into our living quarters more excited than usual. "Hey boy, I'm goin' out on the tundra tonight—wanna come?" He reached into his locker and grabbed his camera. "The Bear's lettin' me use one a the trucks."

"What's out on the tundra?" Tim asked.

"I saw a bunch of eider duck when we were driving into camp the first week. You have a good camera, huh?" Johansen asked me.

"Yeah—it'd be great to get some shots out there."

I took advantage of getting out of camp whenever the opportunity arose. We packed up our gear and headed toward the mainland. From a distance, the flat gray tabletop of stark landscape appeared incapable of maintaining any life. Less than a quarter-mile after the causeway ended, and the land began, Johansen pulled into a small turnout.

"This is where I saw them." He pointed to the barren sheet of land and we piled out of the truck. "Be careful when you walk on the tundra—watch where you step. Don't screw anything up."

We followed Johansen across the tundra, carefully stepping over any flora or other vegetation. It surprised me how carefully and delicately the amplified-guitar-loving Norwegian made his way across the fragile surface. Frozen for much of the year, the partially thawed Arctic tundra landscape revealed intricate moss, lichens, and a variety of plant life. Yellow and purple flowers dotted the scenery in front of us.

"Look at these wildflowers." Johansen's permanent grimace faded, replaced by a look of awe and appreciation. "Man, they look fragile, but these guys are tough—somehow survive under the ice for almost eight months a year and look at them now—beautiful."

During the winter, temperatures along the tundra drop to -40°F, sometimes lower, and one-hundred-mile-per-hour winds blow large snowdrifts across the rock-hard surface. In the spring, the permafrost thaws only enough for plants to grow and reproduce on the top surface—the ground below the topsoil remains frozen, and water cannot sink any lower. As a result, lakes, marshes, bogs and streams form across the flat terrain.

I attached a macro lens to my camera and focused on the colorful flowers. The soft petals contrasted against thawing rock and pebbles, bright yellow against dull gray. We made our way across the tundra, taking photos but saying little to each other. I felt the comfort of surrounding life, a rhythm free of droning generators, and boats and barges made of steel. I marveled at the vegetation's power to survive as long as it did in the harshest of environments. In a few months, they would vanish into the Arctic winter.

"There's one," Johansen whispered and raised his hand to halt our progress as we approached a long stretch of gravel. "Quiet—don't get too close."

There was a round indent in the gravel, surrounded by small twigs and sticks. Inside the ring, a black and white eider duck hunkered in the comfort of its shelter. Greenish-gray eggs protruded from underneath her. Undisturbed by one of the largest oil fields in the world only a few miles away, the eider kept her eggs warm and protected. I squatted down and zoomed my lens at several more nests clustered across the tundra.

Johansen crawled to one nest on his stomach, careful to keep his distance. He slowly lifted his camera and took several shots. Then he set the camera down and continued to watch the nest. The large Norwegian was the quietest I had ever seen him. He was no longer the boisterous tugboat and barge engineer with the loudest voice in camp. He was just a man, lying on a thin stretch of gravel in the middle of the Arctic, marveling at an eider duck keeping her eggs warm.

THE BIG THAW

I'M STANDING ON A KNOLL next to my father's faded brown '72 Chevrolet short-bed pickup. I'm with my parents. A dirt road snakes up the incline. An expanse of wooded rolling hills surrounds us. A sharp crack, like a shot from a .22 rifle, draws our attention to a spot on a ridge. A massive black oak leans to its side. Like a giant domino, it crashes to the ground.

"That's weird." I point to the tree. It lies on its side, a fallen soldier.

"It's not right." My mother's worried voice drifts softly.

"Trees fall over—happens all the time," I assure her.

"But honey, that oak tree has been there forever."

"Nothing's forever. Maybe it was its time to go."

A sound similar to a crackle of lightning resonates across a thin valley.

Another falling tree. This one, a towering ponderosa pine.

One after another, surrounding trees lean over and crash to the earth. The concern on my mother and father's face weighs as heavy as the fallen timber. We turn to the truck to get away from what is happening around us.

I awake.

I'm in bed at home in Tahoe.

My father passed away over twenty-five years ago, and my mother over fifteen years. When they were alive, we spent afternoons exploring dirt roads around their home in the foothills of the Sierra Nevada mountain range. Dreams often pull me back to those times, lending both comfort and melancholy. But this is different. This feels like a premonition or warning. I remain in bed, piecing the scene together, trying to digest the images before they fade like drifting dust from the fallen trees. From the sound of the fractured timber, I'm certain they were sick due to lack of water. Their roots or trunks severely weakened, they finally surrendered to gravity and toppled over.

I had read a magazine article the night before about a southern section of our country with an opposite problem—too much water. The story, titled "The Drowning," appeared in the *Smithsonian Magazine*. An aerial photo on the first page depicted an expanse of flooded land, and the caption underneath stated, "The U.S. Geological Survey has reported that Louisiana is losing a football field's worth of land every hour." I re-read the statement to confirm the words, "every hour." There's a temptation to turn the page, to move on to the next article and relieve myself of yet another dire depiction of global warming. But the article tugs at me, and a feeling of obligation and concern forces me to continue on. They calculated the total yearly loss of land in this one state alone at seventy-five square kilometers.

The high-pitched sound of coyotes yapping drifts through a tinder-dry forest and enters our room. I get out of bed and look out the window. California is in another drought and the dry seasons get longer each year.

How did we get here?

When working near the Prudhoe Bay oil fields of Alaska in the '80s, concern for the environment often entered my thoughts. The major risks focused on oil spills and over-development of natural habitat. Scientists had introduced theories about the "greenhouse effect" since the late 1800s, but no one really considered it a major concern. It wasn't until the mid-'70s when the term "global warming" surfaced. Even then, it was only a side note in a few newspaper stories. At the first United Nations Environmental Conference in

1972, the topics included chemical pollution, atomic bomb testing, and whaling. It wasn't until the '90's when global warming became regarded as a serious topic and caught the attention of the public eye.

I stare at the ceiling and contemplate a conversation with a fellow writer, and a member of the bi-weekly writing workshop I attend. Tracy Valier is a geologist who spent over fifty years studying the geologic history of Hell's Canyon, Oregon. He was one of the first of a small group of geologists who researched, then accepted, global plate tectonics—the movement of the earth's landmasses. Prior to one of our workshops, I asked him how others in his field viewed the concept of global warming.

"At first, some of the science community were reluctant to accept it," Tracy replied. "There were a couple of reasons for that."

"Politics?"

"That was the main one." He grinned. "It took the same path as when theories of global plate tectonics were first introduced—almost an identical process. It takes a while for data to be confirmed and accepted. Today, the entire science community understands and acknowledges the seriousness of global warming. Now everyone is on board, and they all agree that man is a key factor in climate change—and the trend is accelerating. It's going faster than we first realized. And not enough is being done to correct the cause of it."

"Do you think we can slow it down?"

"Maybe. Right now, however, we're being really stupid."

I feel as though the toughest things are sometimes the most fragile. The arctic environment, a place I once called home, survives some of the harshest weather on the planet. Much of the life there is in a constant fight to survive. My head fills with images I photographed on the tundra—the soft petals of purple and yellow wildflowers, and satiny surfaces of greenish-gray eider duck eggshells. Once thought very rare, tundra wildfires are now a problem in some lower latitudes. It leaves me with an empty feeling as I think of all the other life in the far north.

Maybe more than anywhere else in the world, a wide range of Arctic wildlife is struggling to adapt, including caribou, Arctic fox, and a tremendous variety of waterfowl. This environmental shift affects whale migrations, walrus and seal populations, and other cycles of sea life. One of the largest mammals on earth, the polar bear, is especially at risk.

An adult male polar bear weighs around seven hundred to fifteen hundred pounds. The polar bear, its body built for cold temperatures, is classified as a vulnerable species, with eight of its nineteen subpopulations in decline. Polar bears travel across long distances of snow, ice, and open water, searching for their prey. The loss of sea ice due to global warming looms as the chief threat. Although most of them are born on land, polar bears spend most of their time at sea and feed upon seals living near the edge of arctic ice. When no sea ice is present, polar bears must live off their fat reserves. The reduction in ice platforms limits productive areas for the fish that the seals eat, affecting the seal's nutritional status and reproduction rates. As seal populations decline, so will the polar bears. Everything is connected in a delicate web of life.

The dramatic decrease of ice has implications beyond the obvious habitat loss. The remaining ice is farther from shore, making it less accessible. The larger gap of open water between the ice and land creates rougher wave conditions, forcing bears to swim from shore to sea ice in more hazardous conditions. In 2004, biologists discovered four drowned polar bears in the Beaufort Sea where I once sailed. The total number of drowned bears that year may have been considerably greater. Biologists attributed the deaths to a combination of retreating ice and rougher seas.

As climate change continues to melt more sea ice, the U.S. Geological Survey projects that two-thirds of polar bears will disappear by 2050. This dramatic decline is occurring in our lifetime—only a fraction of the total time these mammals have roamed arctic seas. The species is in crisis and is a clear foreshadowing of more global changes to follow.

I push the thoughts out of my head, get out of bed, and walk downstairs to put on a pot of coffee. It's the weekend, and I always take a Saturday and Sunday walk with my wife, Robbin. It's a time when we can reflect on events of the prior week, and it provides a chance to reconnect and talk without the outside chatter of day-to-day tasks. We grab a couple cups of freshly brewed coffee and make our way down the trail, our yellow lab, Annie, following along.

"The forest is really dry, but at least it looks better since they cleared it." Robbin throws a ball for our dog and it bounces along the trail near a pile of tree limbs and angular stumps.

"Yeah, it'll take a couple of winters—all that slash will decompose. A lot of the underbrush is already growing back."

Much of South Lake Tahoe's forest was clearcut about a hundred years before we moved into our home, the timber used in the silver mines of Virginia City, Nevada. A large section of original growth remains buried underneath the earth, forever shadowed from sunlight. Only a few old-growth trees can still be seen. Due to an aggressive fire suppression program, the new forest with smaller trees grew too dense and became a major fire danger. It soon became apparent to foresters that much of the timber needed to be cut and the forest thinned out.

As we walk along our recently cleared forest, I think about all the heavy equipment that spewed exhaust into the air as the lumber company felled, bucked, loaded, then hauled away the timber in semi-trailer trucks. In order to correct our past mistakes, are we only chasing our own tails? I ponder the idea that maybe we're doomed to rely on fossil fuels for as long as they last, and the earth's environment will continue to warm to disastrous levels as long as we do so.

We stop at a bank overlooking the Truckee River. The water level is much lower than it should be at this time of year, but the early morning sun still glitters across its reduced surface, and trout dimple the pool below us. The cool morning air will soon surrender to afternoon heat, and the land becomes drier each day as summer progresses. I pray for an early and heavy winter.

In a meadow on the other side of the river, coyotes hunt for mice, pouncing between large clumps of grass. In the distance, the sound of summer traffic increases as another Tahoe weekend begins. From the lake, the roar of a powerboat engine drifts across the meadow.

"The sounds of summer." I take another gulp of coffee, the java now cool and bitter.

I try my best to let the river wash away my thoughts, the earlier feeling of emptiness replaced by a sense of resignation. If we can't change our present direction, maybe it's too late to turn back. Maybe it's our time to go.

FLOATING ISLAND

"FIFTEEN FOR TWO, fifteen for four, and a run of four are eight."
Dazzlin' D. finished counting the cards fanned out across the galley table.

Cribbage—the official game of tugboaters. Any free time involved a round or two accompanied by large quantities of coffee.
"Dazzlin' D" served as cook on the tugboat *Lassen* and she referred
to the crew as the "*Lassen* Family." Like Tugboat Annie, Dazzlin' was
one of the few female workers at Arctic Marine Freighters. Most
all the full-time seamen knew her, as she served on Crowley boats
in both Seattle and Alaskan waters.

"I might visit some friends in California after the first of the
year," Dazzlin' said.

"Really? Cool. Maybe we can meet up if you're out my way.
No telling where I'll be—if I have a place, you're welcome to crash
there for as long you want."

"Thanks, I might take you up on the offer. You're not going back
to Colorado?"

"Maybe for a short time—just to visit."

My future felt as jumbled and uncertain as ever. My relationship
with Chris remained on shaky ground, and I desperately yearned for

a clear career direction. Nothing felt concrete. Working at Prudhoe each summer provided an excellent source of income, although I felt as though I was biding my time. I knew if I let the years slip by, I could be the next old-timer like Lee. A career as a merchant marine was a solid possibility, and engineering definitely piqued my interest. But all the years I spent studying art fueled an ingrained passion. The creative process was like an addiction. Although I wasn't completely confident in my skills as an artist, I felt there must be something I could be competent at doing with my mind, as compared to developing carpel tunnel-syndromed hands.

The *Lassen* plowed its way toward its destination: a newly designed drill rig deep in the Arctic Ocean. To further reduce construction costs, Exxon had developed a reusable structure named "CIDS." CIDS is the acronym for "Concrete Island Drilling Structure," a mobile platform specially designed for arctic offshore drilling. Instead of building a gravel island for drill rig construction, this concrete floating island contained its own rig and could be transported across the high seas and re-used wherever needed.

The *Lassen's* mission was to bring a barge of supplies out to the CIDS. Our icebreaking barge, the *Arctic Endeavor,* was also anchored out there. We sailed on a section of ocean socked—in with ice floe. Our progress, slow and arduous, allowed ample time for several binges of crib.

"I was up in the wheelhouse and they were talking to the dispatcher on the CIDS." Dazzlin' shuffled the cards. "He said they chased off a polar bear near the rig a couple of days ago. They had to call in a helicopter to swoop down and scare it off."

An Arctic grizzly had roamed the tundra the prior season near West Dock, and I remembered the polar bear skulls at Panuk's house in Kaktovic. For thousands of years, these mammals have been a key figure in the material, spiritual, and cultural life of arctic indigenous peoples. They symbolize the Iñupiat's link with both the natural and spiritual world. Their significance stems from the belief that the universe is inhabited by both human beings, and spirits known as 'tuurngait.' Each human being has a spiritual essence, 'tarniq' and a breath of life, 'arnirniq', which are passed on to new human or animal bodies when a person dies. In past times, shamans served as intermediaries between the human and spirit world. The shamans received power and strength from tuurngaits, and these spirits often took the form of polar bears.

The *Lassen's* engines decelerated; the whine of the turbochargers slowing to a thin whistle.

"Sounds like we're getting close." Dazzlin' stood. "We'll have to finish up later."

I pulled on my coveralls and headgear, and we both stepped through the galley hatch and onto the frozen steel deck of the *Lassen*. Rosie, another crew member and engineer, stood near the handrail. A puff of breath faded past the hoodie covering her head.

"Pretty awesome," Rosie said as we drifted nearer to the rig.

The CIDS unit towered above the ice floe less than a quarter-mile from our vessel. A field of jagged ice stood between us and the drill rig and a dense layer of fog blended into a sky darkened by cloud cover. I realized it was the darkest day I had experienced since working in the Arctic. Lights from the rig penetrated the haze, and the structure appeared like a spaceship floating in a hazy, faded-white universe.

Dazzlin' climbed up to the wheelhouse. Rosie and I stood on deck as we approached the rig. Willy, the captain of the *Lassen*, navigated through the last stretch of ice to the drill platform, and they tossed lines down to us and we tied them fast. I entered the warmth of the galley to get a cup of coffee as the rest of the crew prepared to board the CIDS.

"We're going topside onto the rig," Willy said to me. "You okay to stay in the wheelhouse—keep an eye on things while we're up there?"

"Sure, no problem." Although I wanted to check out the rig, the thought of being alone in a quiet wheelhouse reading a book sounded like a great idea. I relished the opportunity to have some time to myself.

"Good. We'll only be a few hours—I'll leave the radio on."

I hunkered into the comfort of the wheelhouse and it wasn't long before I became immersed in *The Crying of Lot 49*, by Thomas

Pynchon—the latest book Swan passed on to me as a mandatory read. There was nothing like a satirical, postmodern, conspiracy laden adventure story to pass away the hours in a frozen Arctic Sea. My eyelids soon became heavy, and I decided it might be a good idea to head below for another cup of coffee. That's when I looked out the wheelhouse window and noticed how much the ice floe had moved the *Lassen* backward, along the side of the CIDS unit.

"Crap," I whispered into the emptiness.

The wind had picked up, and wisps of fog swirled snake-like around the CIDS unit. Normally it was difficult to see the movement of the floe, but the jagged house-sized chunks of ice now bunched up against the *Lassen's* bow like a stack of cards. Several pieces slowly angled upward in a machine-like motion. The *Lassen* slipped farther alongside the rig, the lines tightening under increasing stress. If they broke free, the ice would drag the boat deep into the floe.

"Hey, Willy?" I said into the handheld. "Over?"

Silence.

I depressed the audio button again.

"Willy? Do you read?"

I concluded it might be near impossible for the signal to penetrate the thick metal or concrete walls of the CIDS unit.

I was on my own.

As the lines continued to tighten, I fired up the starboard engine. I pondered the notion that this might *not* have been the best decision. Maybe holding tight until the captain came aboard was the most sensible protocol. An unwritten rule on the boats was that you never got behind the wheel without the captain's permission—the wheelhouse was their domain, and you did nothing unless asked. And starting the engines as deckhand alone on the boat breached a major tugboat rule.

But if the lines break free, and the vessel heads out into the ice floe— what the hell will I do then?

"Fuck—if it *can*, it *will*." I heard myself mutter the line I had heard all too frequently by Lee when a situation went awry.

I depressed the start button to the port engine, and it roared to life. I had never piloted the *Lassen*, and could count my experience behind the wheel of a tugboat in hours, not days or years. Having spent only a short amount of time piloting the *Point Oliktok* when we sailed to Prudhoe Bay from Barter Island, and Swan tentatively letting me pilot the *Prudhoe Bay* a few times, docking or tightly maneuvering a boat of any size remained out of my realm of experience. I prepared for a quick on-the-spot training session and kept my eye on the tightening lines. My hands shook, then grasped the wheel of the *Lassen*.

Relief entered the wheelhouse when I noticed our crew making their way down the ladder of the drill rig. They carefully made their way over a patch of ice and across the barge and onto the deck of the *Lassen*.

The captain immediately climbed the stairs to the wheelhouse.

"You started the engines?" Willy asked when he entered.

"I wasn't sure what to do," I said hesitantly. "The ice was pulling the boat down the side of the rig, and the lines were stretching thin."

"You should have radioed us."

"I tried—a couple of times but couldn't get through."

Willy, an experienced captain, looked about the wheelhouse and rubbed his chin.

"Guess I'd do the same if I was in your boots." He took his place behind the wheel. "Go down on deck and help work the lines. I'll get us over to the leeward side of the rig—away from the drifting ice."

Taking my place on deck next to Rosie, I wondered if I had made the right decision in preparing for the worst-case scenario. The last thing I wanted to do was to piss off Willy. I surrendered to the fact that it was better to make a decision that could anger or perplex someone, as compared to doing nothing at all.

We remained alongside the CIDS for a few more days before casting off and making our way back through the maze of ice. I sat in the galley waiting to begin another game of crib, and thought back to when I decided to fire up the engines when the ice floe attempted to rip the *Lassen* free of the CIDS. I wondered about breaking points in larger extreme situations—the time of final decisions. The normal course of action is to remain cool, but also to look ahead and weigh all consequences. There was most likely a thin line between a sensible solution and total denial or ignorance until a situation becomes unsolvable.

The pattered rhythm of Dazzlin's footsteps down the wheelhouse ladder pulled me out of my thoughts.

"Hey, check it out." She grabbed her parka off the coat rack. "The polar bear came back. They just radioed us from the CIDS and said it was about a hundred yards to the north of the rig."

We climbed out of the side hatch and onto the deck. Leaning against the bullrail, we gazed out across the ice floe.

"I think that's it." Dazzlin' pointed.

I peered through the mist and barely made out the tiny dot on the ice near the CIDS. The shape of the mammal, dwarfed by the silhouette of the drill rig, exuded a somber tone that hung in the frigid northern air. The leviathan concrete and steel structure loomed over a species that had survived in the harshest of environments for thousands of years. I felt a sense of foreboding as we sailed away as if something more immense lurked somewhere deep within the arctic fog.

SAILING WITH SWAN
(FREE RADICALS)

"HEY BRUUUUCE…" Swan shouted down from the wheelhouse of the *Mop King* in his best impression of Panuk, our Iñupiat friend from Barter Island a few seasons prior. "We need more beans—immediately, if not sooner."

After working as deckhand aboard the tugboats *Lassen* and *Kern* for more than a month and a half, they had transferred me back to camp. Days of mind-numbing grind-work took their toll. When they assigned me to the *Mop King* with Swan, I halfway knew what to expect the first day I walked on deck and up into the wheelhouse.

"So, The Bear mentioned you're going to be my new deckhand, aye?"

"Yeah, he said I could give you some help for a while." I noticed my reflection in the round dark lenses of Swan's glasses.

"Well, I only have one rule. And it's of utmost importance."

Prolonged silence prompted me to respond.

"And it is…?"

"Always keep the captain—and that would be *me*—adequately hydrated with coffee."

"Sounds easy enough."

"Follow me to the galley. I'll show you all the necessary equipment and materials."

We climbed the stairway down the side of the wheelhouse and into the galley.

"Hah! *See*—that can *never* happen," Swan yelled and pointed at an empty coffee pot. "Your first duty is to brew some beans. The blacker, the better. There's no way you can make it too strong—ever!"

The *Mop King* was a day boat, which meant she spent most of her time stationed near camp performing duties within the bay—a harbor tug. Her sister ship was the *Prudhoe Bay*. Both were smaller boats with long open decks featuring a crane boom. At their bows, a loading ramp swung open for easy offloading of equipment and supplies. Overall, the boats were fairly ugly—exactly what Swan found attractive about them.

"The *Prudhoe*'s the star of the fleet and the *Mop King* is a close second." Swan continued to show me around the galley and engine room. "I'm the only one who goes into the engine room. *You*, never go down there unless I ask you to." He peered over the rims of his welder's glasses. "And that would be today—after a cup o' Joe. We need to muck out the bilges. I'll get some empty drums on deck."

It only took a short time before I became accustomed to the punk-induced metallic reverberations of Swan's music collection. With speakers blaring songs from bands like Dead Kennedys and The Lewd, we spent days preparing the boat for the season ahead, along with performing some smaller jobs around camp—moving barrels or shuttling equipment from barge to barge.

As in previous years, the crew searched for ways to fight the doldrums brought on by the seemingly endless hours of mundane tasks. Ongoing discussions and debates regarding reading, writing, and music kept our minds maintained, and I enjoyed Swan's curt and angry diatribes regarding whatever topic served as a target. As a former chemistry major at the University of Washington, his knowledge of the subject vastly overshadowed my "D+" in General Chemistry at the University of Colorado. His mind worked in creative equations, and several times he spoke in terms of "free radicals," an atom, or group of atoms, that are very unstable and highly reactive. Swan, therefore, referred to anything out of the ordinary or outside of the norm as a free radical.

"Hey Bruuuuce, good news," he said one morning as I walked onto the deck of the *Mop King*. He was hand-rolling a cigarette, and from the look of his oil-smeared coveralls, had been working in the engine room the entire night. "We've been given a task requiring us to depart Prudhoe Bay—they've provided us the opportunity to leave this godforsaken place."

"Finally. Where're we headed?"

"Oliktok Point. It's a little place just west of here—somewhere on the DEW Line. We'll spend today getting the *Mop King* ship-shape, then load the cargo—survey equipment, don't ya know. Pack your bags after work and don't bring a lot. It's only a three or four-day journey—or so they say. We'll head out in the morning. Few opportunities for sleep. Lots of overtime." Swan grinned.

We used the *Mop King's* crane to load survey equipment for a crew scheduled to fly out and meet us at Oliktok Point. The cargo included a couple of large crates and a red three-wheeler. Swan held the keys to the vehicle. "We might need to take this beauty for a little test ride when we arrive."

So we were now sailing out of Prudhoe Bay and heading west along the coast, the flat-bottom tug bouncing over waves with Swan shouting, "More beans!" I went to the galley to get a fresh pot of coffee brewing, maintaining my balance on the undulating deck of the *Mop King*. It appeared as though Swan had lived on the boat the past month, shunning the option to sleep in camp. A stack of dirty dishes in the washbasin clattered back and forth as we negotiated a series of swells. Dark gray blankets, rolled into a large ball, rested on the corner of the rack inside the cramped sleeping quarters. I took a few minutes to clean things up as the coffee brewed, and I actually found myself whistling—a first in all my years of working at Arctic Marine Freighters.

The sound of punk music filled the wheelhouse when I entered with two cups of coffee. I noticed an eclectic collection of books on a shelf. Most of the tugboats featured dog-eared copies of Louis L'Amour and Zane Grey. The *Prudhoe,* however, housed such authors as Thomas Pynchon, James Joyce, and Dostoyevsky. Swan noticed me flip through a few pages of *Finnegans Wake.*

"You can borrow any of my books you wish," he snapped. "When you have completed any one of them, bring it back promptly of course. *And*... I have the third book of the trilogy you've been reading." He held a copy of *Leviathan,* the final book of the *Illuminatus! Trilogy.*

I had already read *The Eye in the Pyramid* and *The Golden Apple,* written by Robert Shea and Robert Anton Wilson. The stories cover topics including counterculture, numerology, and Discordianism, a religion and philosophy based on the veneration or worship of Eris, a.k.a. Discordia, the Goddess of chaos (or as Swan would note, a "free radical"). Chaos—the perfect topic for living and working at Arctic Marine Freighters.

The sea came to a peaceful calm once we sailed farther into the Beaufort Sea and away from Prudhoe Bay. Swan kept an eye on the radar as West Dock dipped under the horizon, and we sailed into wide-open sea and an occasional stretch of drifting ice. With no other vessels in sight, we journeyed alone in the arctic currents.

"I cleaned up the galley."

"No need to. Thanks anyway."

The hand-rolled cigarette hung from Swan's mouth like a flailing appendage. Standing at the wheel, he reached for the throttle and slowly pulled back and squinted his eyes.

"It's time to *do things.*"

"And what needs to be done?"

"Get down to the bow and keep a lookout. I see swirls on the water surface. And the depth finder is erratic—fucking piece of shit. I can't tell how deep we are. There could be some shoals I'm not aware of. It's imperative we avoid running aground, ya know."

"I'm headed down." I set my coffee on the map table and exited the warmth of the wheelhouse and made my way onto the main deck. I craned my neck around the loading ramp and saw what Swan had noticed from the wheelhouse. He often proclaimed himself as "blind as a fucking bat," so either he had better eyesight than he let on, or keener senses compensated for the deficiency of one.

From the depths, small swirls rose like tiny tornadoes toward the surface. Peering into the sea, I could see five to ten feet deep before it became too dark and brackish, blocking my vision. The circular rings continued to rise upward as I strained my eyes to see deeper into the darkness. The swirls formed somewhere hidden from sight and ascended upward like a series of smoke rings. I struggled to figure out where and why they were forming. The depth of the water-limited my vision, and there was no way I could tell where they began as they reached the surface.

I held up my fist and Swan pulled farther back on the throttle, then hit the kill switch. The idling diesels came to a stop. He then turned around and slapped the radio off, extinguishing the raucous music.

"What do you see?" he shouted from the foredeck.

"I wish I knew," I muttered.

"What?"

I turned my head. "It might be getting shallow. It's kind of hard to tell what's goin' on..."

"Hmmph." Swan flicked ashes from his cigarette, then marched back into the wheelhouse. I noticed the greenish glow of the depth finder reflecting in his glasses, then disappearing as he looked toward the bow. He looked back and forth several more times before stepping out on the foredeck again.

"Hey, Bruuuuce. It's a *thermocline*."

"A what?"

"A thermocline. We have plenty of depth—over thirty feet, according to this crappy-ass depth finder. I'm coming down."

I continued to watch the swirls get larger, and fade in frequency as we floated in silence. Small chunks of ice drifted around the *Prudhoe* in an irregular patchwork.

"What the hell's a thermocline?" I asked Swan as he joined me on the bow.

"It's a thin layer in the water where the deeper temperature changes more rapidly than the layers above, thus creating the resulting swirls. The depth and thickness of a thermocline is affected by many things—weather variations, latitude, environment, tides, and currents—all kinds of shit comes into play. Looks like the swirls are abating."

I shifted my gaze from the depths and into the varying shades of blue surrounding us. Lacking any distinct delineation or horizon line, the sky and water melded together as one. Slabs of ice floated in the stillness as if suspended in midair or weightless in deep space—untethered to any worldly body. I thought of grabbing my camera, then reconsidered, fearing an attempt to capture the experience would break the spell. It felt wiser to allow the memory to become etched into my mind where it would always reside, pure and unspoiled.

We stood at the bow in silence. I'm not sure how long we remained without saying a word to each other. Time did not factor into the equation. Both of us stood on the steel deck of an obscure tugboat in the middle of the Arctic, drifting in a calm sea of ice. Deep within our individual thoughts and fragmented imaginations, we respected the moment. I clung to a new sense of clarity—a feeling of being alone, yet totally at peace in the enveloping unpredictability and solitude.

WHALING CAMP

PILOTING THE *MOP KING* required strong faith in the bare-bones navigation equipment on board. Without land in site, and lacking a SatNav system, my eyes remained focused on the gyrocompass if it might spin out of control at any moment. Swan supplied brief instructions before going on break: "Your coffee was inadequate—I'm headed below to get a couple of winks. Keep her headed precisely in the direction I charted—the throttle remains as is—don't fuck up."

When I heard him ascend the stairway to the wheelhouse less than an hour later, I hoped I hadn't navigated us too far off course.

"I kept her as straight as possible."

"Indubitably." Swan walked over to the chart table and rested his thumb on the outline of an island. "Presumably, there is—or *was*—a whaling camp here." I stepped aside and he took over the wheel. He grinned and said, "What do ya say we have a little look-see?"

About a half-hour later, a long gravelly sound resonated from the *Prudhoe's* hull as we slid onto the beach. Swan gunned the engine to push the boat tighter into the shore.

"There's no place to tie 'er off," I shouted from the deck.

"It's not going anywhere," Swan shouted back.

A thick blanket of gray now covered the crystal clear blue sky and wisps of fog rolled off the water, fading across the island's low profile. Diesel exhaust swirled out of the *Mop King*'s stacks, commingling with the mist. Although I knew we certainly weren't the first to visit the island, it felt like few had walked on its ground for quite some time.

The past few days, we had fallen into the comfort zone of the rolling sea and the rattling reverberation of twin diesels. It felt odd to be back on land with gravel crunching under our footsteps, then onto the sponge-like texture of the tundra. We made our way to a cluster of structures, appearing to have been uninhabited for a very long time. Several wooden boats rested atop the tundra, all of them about the same distance from shore. Constructed of heavy timbers, years of harsh arctic weather had sucked any hint of color from their fiber, leaving them bleached in shades of gray. As we walked among the weathered remnants of the encampment, Swan reached down and picked up a wide rack of caribou antlers.

"We should put those on the wheelhouse of the *Mop King*," I said. "They'd look cool—The Bear would love it."

"Na. They belong here." He carried the antlers over to one of the shelters and gently rested them against an outside wall.

The larger of the structures appeared to be built of three separately constructed cabins, all connected. Two of the areas inside looked like sleeping quarters, while the other most likely served as a place where they cut and butchered whale meat. The room contained several small tables, chopping blocks, and a saw, all appearing as if it had been many years since used.

Next to the larger building were several smaller and older cabins. Walls constructed of thick timber supported roofs made of tundra resting upon crossbeams. Blocks of cut tundra also formed stout foundations for the more primitive dwellings. It was almost as though the shelters were living extensions of the island itself, or that the land was taking them back into its own. Within the walls, humans once lived, worked, laughed, and cried.

Once again, our chatter remained sparse as we surveyed the structures that once kept whalers sheltered from the elements and provided outposts as they harvested huge mammalia from the sea.

The whalers struggled to survive in the harshest of environments, cutting and packing their kill, then preparing for the long trip home to their families. The things they carried with them—whale meat, oil, baleen, experiences, and stories of the hunt—would sustain them.

After departing the whaling camp, it only took a day to arrive at Oliktok Point, and the nearby DEW Line station. The *Mop King* once again rested upon a shoreline. Swan walked down to the main deck and took his position behind the crane and ramp controls. Pushing against one of the worn, black levers, the ramp slowly tilted down until resting on the beach.

"Time to take a ride." Swan hopped on the three-wheeler and turned the key. The engine fired to life. He slowly maneuvered the vehicle down the ramp of the *Mop King* and onto the beach. He gunned the engine and sped down the coastline. I walked along the beach and watched him disappear into the mist—a vanishing speck in the harsh landscape.

I turned to the *Mop King* as she sat idling against the shore. The air was dead calm, and I heard the three-wheeler returning, the engine droning louder. Swan pulled up and got off the three-wheeler, letting the engine idle. The smell of the 4-stroke engine lingered in the air, the two cylinders pumping away.

"Take 'er for a ride," Swan said.

"Hell yeah."

"There's another whaling boat off the point."

I hopped on the ATV, put it in gear and took off.

First gear, then second, third, and onto fourth.

As I sped along the coastline, the wind whipped around my sunglasses. Water streamed from my eyes, across the sides of my face, and swept into the arctic air. I realized something had changed inside me the past week. I couldn't quite put my finger on it. It was a definite, however subtle shift in the way I felt—a slight positive repositioning in my psyche. It could simply have been a sense of freedom resulting from being away from camp, however, it felt like something much more.

A final shift to fifth gear.

I turned to take a quick look over my shoulder. The *Mop King* remained resting on the shore far behind. The expanse of shoreline in front of me extended to the horizon. Residual thoughts of thermoclines, whaling encampments, and free radicals filled my head.

SWAN AND I SAT at the DEW Line bar drinking scotch and waters. The outpost was like the one we visited at Barter Island. Musty country music droned from a cheap radio behind the bar. The twanging guitar and sappy lyrics obviously angered Swan. The only country musician he could tolerate was Johnny Cash, and mostly because the singer had experienced more than his share of strife, and was also referred to as the "man in black."

We had met the survey crew the day before, although all the hours blended together in the twenty-four-hour daylight and it became challenging to remember exactly how long it had been since we left West Dock. First, we unloaded all the survey equipment, then assisted the crew as they took measurements.

Wooden markers crisscrossed the tundra as wildlife continued to hunt and roam the area, occasionally staring at us as their home became tattooed with designations that would eventually aid oil exploration. I watched an Arctic fox peer up at us, remaining hunkered along one of the survey lines between two markers. In the afternoon, a herd of over fifty caribou galloped by us as the surveyors worked, adjusting equipment to assure accurate measurements.

"Good trip," Swan said, as we clinked our glasses together in a toast. Swan rarely drank alcohol while in Prudhoe, and on the rare occasion he did, scotch and water was the preferred formula. We walked out of the DEW Line bar and into a thick layer of fog. After a bit of wandering to find the shoreline, we boarded the *Mop King*.

Swan and I worked a few more weeks together aboard the *Mop King* and had one more job assisting the surveyors. I would have liked to have sailed with Swan throughout Sealift and for the rest of the season. As was so often the case, however, management shifted me from job to job, denying the comfort of keeping a steady position on any project. Constant change was the common thread for all laborers at AMF and we had little or no control over most situations. I had come to terms with the reality of this quagmire—and the fact that increased frustration over constant change, or fear of the unknown, most often resulted in unnecessary angst.

Several weeks after my discharge from the *Mop King*, I found myself back at camp with the pump crew. The Sealift fleet had arrived at Prudhoe Bay and they transferred Swan to another boat, the *Agloo*, and Dave served as deckhand. One morning as I helped load pump equipment onto a small barge, an Able Bodied Seaman whose boat had docked at camp to refuel and resupply, walked up to me. He reached out with an envelope in his hand.

"I ran into Swan—he said to give this to you. 'Immediately, if not sooner.'"

"Thanks." I walked to the edge of the barge, sat down on a cleat, and looked at the envelope.

The return address said: *Tyrone Tautemer, 70:24.00 N, 148:31.63 W*. Judging from his longitude and latitude reading, he wasn't far from West Dock. I had no idea, however, who Tyrone Tautemer might possibly be, and imagined that was most likely the idea behind the name. Where a stamp would be affixed, was a drawing of a bugle with five letters underneath—*W.A.S.T.E.*, harkening to Pynchon's *The Crying of Lot 49*, required reading material by Swan. It was addressed to *Rettig, B. 218, ho ho*. Ironically, I actually *was* at the moment, sitting on *Barge 218*. The letter began in true Swan fashion:

Rettig—

The weather sucks, you're glad you're not here... they're rationing sleep... I'm supposed to be on pump crew, but I've been running the Agloo... poorly... alone... it ain't easy ya know. Masiel sends his love (alternate spelling acceptable)... here are your O.T. sheets. If they don't approve all the time we'll beat 'em over the kidneys w/a big stick 'til they straighten out... make the fuckers piss blood for a month...

The letter continued with, *I had a bad dream...* Swan's bad dreams were much more complex and cinematic than most. This one was no different. A full page of writing vividly depicted scenes including white rats, whores in alleys, Nazi Germany, his ex-girl-friend (who he referred to as "The Redhead"), towering skyscrapers, a dark river, and a suicide attempt.

The account concluded with him awakening to the sound of the boat's radio: *Agloo, this is Barge 213... Agloo do you read?...*

The letter ended with a single line:

peals of mirthless laughter in the boisterous company of solitude...

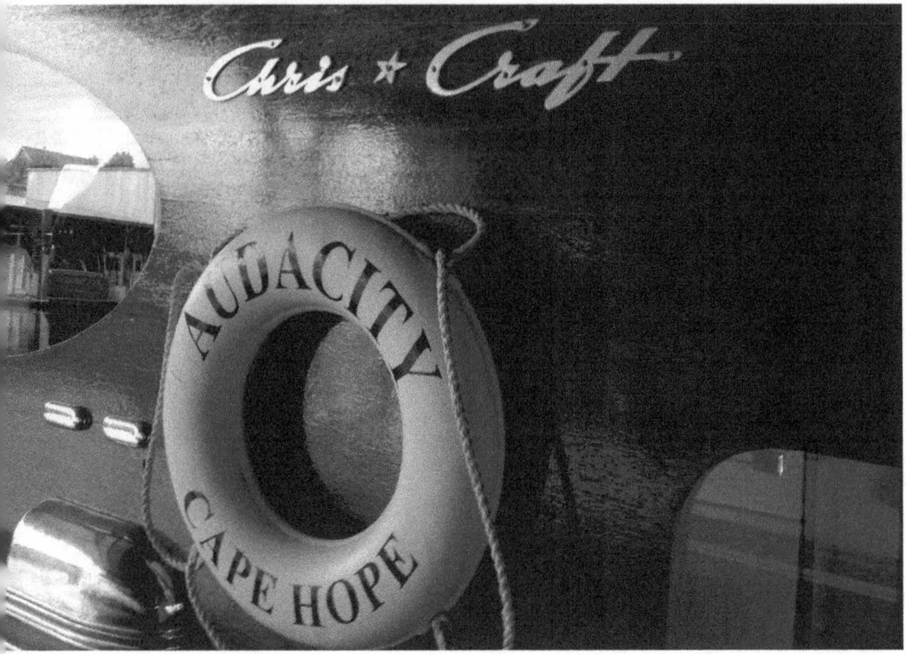
Chris ★ Craft
AUDACITY
CAPE HOPE

AUDACITY

THE SEAGULL HOVERS in the air for a few seconds, then sweeps across the tops of sailboat masts that reach into the sunrise. Instead of a morning walk in Tahoe with views of treetops, a forest of mastheads stretches before me. A hot shower at the Alameda Yacht Club facility slightly cleared my head. I rarely drink more than a glass or two of wine anymore. After one-too-many beers, a late night of swapping sea stories, and catching up with old Alaska crewmates, I feel like the main character from "Lost Weekend."

Once or twice a year, I get together with Dave and Jim, fellow laborers from my days in Prudhoe Bay. In the past, we've taken turns meeting at each of our homes, but Jim's is our recent place of preference. He lives aboard a boat he's refurbishing—a thirty-eight-foot Chris-Craft aptly named *Audacity*. Jim, once considered the most unlikely to go near a boat again after working at Arctic Marine Freighters, is perfectly at home living on the water. As a professional woodworker, he's a perfectionist, and *Audacity* continues to be transformed into a floating work of art.

In the quiet marina, it's difficult to determine which boats are live-aboard and those merely docked there, awaiting their next journey. One small sailboat sports a San Francisco Giants banner. I walk past a powerboat and a woman says hello, a chicken at her feet. Each boat shares the ebb and flow of the tides, despite their varying size, design, age, or individual history.

The day before, we took the ferry across the bay to visit the San Francisco Maritime National Historic Park, at the Hyde Street Pier. On the way out of the Alameda estuary, we sailed past shipyards and tugboats and talked about the fleet up in Alaska. A few years back, Dave had returned to Prudhoe Bay to gather research for an article he was writing for *Outside* magazine. During his trip, he flew to Barter Island and visited our old Iñupiat friend; Panuk still lives in Kaktovik, and his brother held the position as mayor of the village. Dave said Panuk remembers well the year the Arctic Marine Freighters fleet drifted to Barter Island during an early winter storm, and the crew that worked there during the summer of '83.

"He remembers you," Dave said. "He asked, 'How's Bruuuce…'"

The area near Kaktovik has continued to draw attention from the oil companies over the years. Shell stunned federal regulators by snatching up leases in the Beaufort Sea, then bidding $2.1 billion to secure acreage in the Chukchi Sea, part of a record-high $2.6-billion federal offshore lease. In 2015, President Obama signed conditional approval of drilling by Shell. After an exploratory well in 2016 came up dry, and the price of oil decreased in the market, the company backed off on exploration in Alaska. Depending on the political climate and the price of oil, renewed efforts are most likely to take place in the future. As long as the world remains dependent on fossil fuels, the thirst for oil continues.

In reflecting on my time in Prudhoe, I usually tell of the experiences, the people, and the land. How I perceive the lessons learned has slowly shifted over the years, like the many drifting sand bars and gravel islands I once called home. Nailing down my feelings, then and now, remains ever-evolving—I often struggle to interpret them in a deeper context. The journey never ends.

Thirty years ago, we were in our early twenties and none of us knew where we were going, or the direction of our lives—a period filled with an overwhelming avalanche of question marks. I made both good and bad decisions and surrendered to the fact that any hurdles were all a part of the experience.

After my last season, I learned Lee had passed away only a few months after returning home. He was diagnosed with cancer and it spread quickly throughout his body. I often wondered what it felt like to get hit in the chest by the crane's headache ball, and imagined it felt much the same as when I heard the news about Lee. I search for solace in the many stories he told, and how he told them.

I never returned to Colorado. Chris and I had already drifted too far apart to save our relationship. I found work at an advertising agency as a graphic artist and met a beautiful television producer whom I married, and three children came into our lives.

Dave, Jim, and I, of course, moved on after Arctic Marine Freighters. We raised families, established careers, and continued to learn along the way. Although the common thread connecting us is the shared arctic experience, a larger percentage of our conversations focus on life in general—the same waterways everyone navigates. We've all had our struggles and life challenges, but we laugh and smile about it—like when we worked "up in Prudhoe."

Someone once told me dreams are merely random fragments of our imagination, nonsensical thoughts meaning absolutely nothing. They said it's a frivolous endeavor to put any value in their worth, or attempt to decipher what they might mean. They represent nothing more than quirky images leftover from various thoughts bouncing around in our heads. I'm not exactly sure how our dreams develop, but I don't dismiss them as meaningless. Maybe it's because so many seem to evolve out of metaphor, and some are easier to understand than others.

A reoccurring dream of mine remains wedged between images born in deep sleep and those of distant memories. Sometimes it's difficult to comprehend it as a product of my imagination, or a distortion of the past. I find myself on the island with Swan—the one where the old whaling camp resided. We're making our way back to the boat, but it's the *Prudhoe*, not the *Mop King*. The fog is dense and all I can see is a shadow figure of Swan in the mist. Occasionally I see his face, and the mist coating his round wire-framed eyeglasses. I can tell by his expression that he's perplexed and struggling to see through the mist—the same as I. We're walking in the same direction. We pass abandoned whaling boats, and in the distance, they take the shape of beached whales. Visibility becomes even more limited and dwindles down to less than five to ten feet in all directions. We keep traveling over the tundra's irregular terrain, sometimes stumbling, and often cursing. I realize we've recently left the DEW Line bar after drinking a few scotch and waters. In the distance, the *Prudhoe* awaits. We can't see it, yet we know it's there. We'll board her, fire up the engines, turn on the running lights, and sail out to sea.

THE PARTY'S OVER

WITH THE '85 SEALIFT more than halfway completed and most of the pump crew duties dwindling down, some workers came back to camp to help offload barges on West Dock. Laborers could log as many hours as they wanted, enabling them to rack up paycheck-ballooning overtime.

"I haven't slept for three days." Steve leaned against the idling forklift.

Lulls came in erratic streams during the offloading process, and if you worked a forklift, you could get out of the cold. Three of our larger articulating machines featured enclosed driving areas. The diesel engines ran continuously, and the heaters kept the confined compartments comfortably warm.

"Take a catnap in the forklift—turn on the heater," I said.

"Good idea."

"I'm taking a break—and making a phone call. Let me know if anything comes up."

Chris and I hadn't maintained a consistent call schedule like the first years I had worked up north, so it didn't surprise me that there was no answer after I dialed her number. The next man in line shuffled in when I walked out of the warm-up shack. I stomped up the stairs of the catwalk to the movie room. When I opened the door, light streamed into the room and I quickly closed it. A couple of longshoremen I didn't recognize stared at the screen, along with Erik Johansen. Yul Brynner, in a black cowboy hat, filled the frame, and the theme of *The Magnificent Seven* drifted in. The men began humming the song as the other characters came into view. Above the chorus, a loud Scandinavian voice proclaimed Charles Bronson as a badass motherfucker, the comment followed by a round of laughter. I walked over to the popcorn machine at the back of the room, put a couple shovelfuls of kernels into a bag, and left. My mind was numb, not sure if I truly missed being back home, or was only acting the part.

My mind kept drifting to how Lee looked at the end of the season. Everyone noticed something wasn't right with him. The man's life included exposure to large doses of oil and chemical fumes, nuclear radiation, and more than his fair share of rough and tumble days as a sailor and laborer. But the latter appeared to have made him almost invincible. Even at his age, he had been one of the strongest men in camp and appeared to be in excellent shape, until this last season. I reached into my coveralls and clutched my pocket watch, the same kind as Lee's. I felt the faint tick of the minute hand within its thin metal shell.

"What's up?" Jim asked me as I met him on the catwalk.

"Not much."

"You okay?"

"Just a little burnt."

"You need an attitude adjustment." Jim waved his hand and turned. "Follow me."

In a quarter unit upstairs, a door remained almost always locked. Jim rapped his knuckles in a distinct pattern against it. After a brief shuffling sound, it opened a couple of inches and a bloodshot eye peered through the crack.

"C'mon in," Ron said. The blast of pot smoke hit us like an incoming gale, and the door quickly shut behind us. Ron grabbed the bag of popcorn from me and smiled.

"Hey man, how's it going?" Martin, an assistant welder, said, then reached under the table and set a bong on top. "Never can be too careful." He reached over and turned up the volume of the boom-box next to him, and the room filled with Greg Allman's voice crooning, "Midnight Rider."

Martin was another one of the crew that once refused to wear a hardhat. "Listen," he often bragged earlier in the season, "if a piece of iron hit me in the head, that plastic isn't going to slow it down. It's just a fucking bother—more dangerous wearing the damn thing." Shortly after making that statement, Martin was working at the bottom of a barge on a welding job. Near a manhole directly above him, a haphazardly stacked pile of tie-downs sat precariously on a pallet (tie-downs are steel eyelets welded onto the deck as needed, in order to secure cargo). No one knew for sure what really happened, and several rumors drifted around camp. One theory anchored in the idea that someone—tired of hearing Martin boast about working without a hardhat—had kicked one of the tie-downs into the hole in order to scare him. Unfortunately, its trajectory ended directly on top of Martin's head. When they discovered what had happened, a couple of workers scrambled down the ladder to help him. The Bear, leaning over from the top deck and looking down into the manhole, shouted, "Well . . . is he dead?" One worker replied Martin was still breathing, and after a trip to an oil company infirmary, he came back to work the next day. We all noticed something different about him after that incident, though, and how he seemed more disconnected than usual. His frequent gaze into the nothingness had changed from the usual "Prudhoe Stare."

"This guy needs to catch up." Jim pointed at me with an angled thumb.

"Let him fire that puppy up," Ron said to Martin, whose eyes appeared as glossy black marbles.

"Casey's at bat," Martin said after loading and holding the bong toward me.

"Maybe it'll help get my head together." I sighed.

"It'll do something to your head," Ron said and grinned.

I took a deep drag off the pipe and felt the smoke expand in my lungs as my eyes watered—blurry images of my coworkers smiling in front of me. Don't cough. I then found myself holding a plastic cup filled with Jack Daniels. I took a deep chug; the alcohol stinging my freshly singed throat tissue.

"Smooth, huh?" Ron said.

A knock on the door caused Ron to re-enact the same greeting as before. This time Dave walked in.

"How's it going?" he said, then looked at me and laughed. "I thought you were going clean this season—running, keeping in shape."

I could only shrug my shoulders in reply. With a thick wad of chewing tobacco in my mouth and a whiskey in front of me, I accepted a refilled bong from Martin. I had worked over thirty hours straight with no substantial sleep, and my head swirled in a semi-lucid tailspin.

Ron broke into song: "Ain't no sunshine when she's gone, it's not warm when she's away... ain't no sunshine when she's gone, and she's always gone too long, anytime she goes away..."

I made my way back to my quarters after spending the better part of an hour at the party room. Reclining back into the plastic chair, I peered out my window at the ocean and Sealift fleet. No longer a scene of varying shades of gray, the arctic seascape appeared brighter, and glittered in an enhanced definition, drawing me into its seemingly unworldly vastness.

THE DECISION TO REMAIN at the AMF camp to the end of the '84 season was one I made early on, but staying late into the '85 season resulted from a lack of concrete plans. Since graduating, I no longer needed to return to school or get back on a particular date. Besides, I didn't know what to do once I arrived back home, wherever that might be. After the Sealift fleet had departed for their journey south to their home ports, The Bear assigned me as expeditor, shuttling co-workers to the airport as the camp quickly diminished in size. Most of the crew had already left. Only a few remained waiting for the AMF fleet to freeze in; The Bear didn't want to take any chances of having the boats and barges rip free again, like the year they drifted to Barter Island.

"I've been trying a different tactic to get through the season this year," I said to three surveyors I had picked up at Deadhorse Airport. "I try to run on the causeway a couple of days a week. It's about three miles long, so to the mainland and back is over six miles. I started out running every day, but I've kind of tailed off lately."

The truth of the matter belied the fact that I had not run in quite a while. I began a faithful routine the first month of the season, and had sworn off alcohol, tobacco, and turned down any offers to get high. The daily work schedule finally wore me down. The last couple of weeks before everyone left camp, all three of my old vices had reared up once again.

"Want to take a slight detour and see the Kuparuk Oil Field?" I asked the guys.

One surveyor looked at his coworkers in the back seat. They neither nodded approval nor disapproval—only shrugged.

"Sure," the surveyor said. "Why not?"

I made a right turn down one of the major arteries of the oilfield and gunned the truck up to sixty-five miles per hour.

"Have to keep an eye out," I said. "I got a ticket for going over seventy last week. Can't believe I got a ticket up here—over two-hundred miles north of the Arctic Circle."

"They have police in Prudhoe?"

"It was an ARCO oil field security guy."

I pulled to the side of the road and stopped in front of a sign that read, "Kuparuk Oil Field." We stepped out of the vehicle and walked over to read a tailored-down history of the oilfields etched into the sign's surface. I had read about the development of the oil fields in several books, and knew the full extent of the endeavor. They estimated the Kuparuk Oil Field had a recoverable reserve base of over two billion barrels, making it the second-largest field in the United States. The Kuparuk River and Milne Point fields were the only other developments online, despite the size of the Point Thomson and Fort Mcintyre reserves. Other nearby potential oil-bearing areas included the Colville delta to the west, and the Canning River (Point Thomson) to the east.

"Our fleet has four tugboats designed specifically for work up here," I said. "They're shallow draft boats that draw less than two feet of water and named after nearby land points—the *Point Thomson, Point Milne, Point Oliktok,* and the *Point Barrow.* I've sailed on all of them."

We stood and looked at the map on the sign. Sections of pipeline stretched across the Prudhoe Bay oil fields like tentacles, a webwork of oil-sucking conduits that led to the main pipeline heading south. *Those pipes don't bother the caribou at all,* I could hear Lee's voice saying. *All those bleeding-heart environmentalists don't know what the hell they're talkin' about when they say it'll disrupt the herd migration. Shit, all they have to do is come up here and take a look.*

In my first season, I convinced myself that Lee's statement was correct. Technology had made it possible for a major oilfield like Prudhoe Bay to avert diverse effects to both the wildlife and the environment. We were simply using the earth's resources in the most responsible way possible. In my last season, however, my mind filled with thoughts of the thick, dark oil traveling down hundreds of miles of pipeline and how much of it would eventually end up as exhaust, spiraling into the air.

We returned to the AMF camp. The hum of the generator continued to drone outside the window of my quarters. I had the room to myself, and once the surveyors left, the camp would be down to five men awaiting the bay to freeze solid. I opened my journal and a piece of paper fell out. Before he left, Swan had given me a section of prose he had written when he was captaining the *Prudhoe* during the spring ice breakup.

> *in the bright deathly silence and neglect of the arctic night, a statue turned its head ... and the ice went away ... just like that ... no fanfare no goodbye ... so no more belligerent 'berop watching our every move w/their beady little pebble eyes ... now little wavelets are breaking pie-crustwise on our manmade shore ...*

END OF THE LONGEST DAY

AFTER A LATE SEPTEMBER workday, I walked into the comm shack to check the latest temperature reading. At -5°F and a five-mile-per-hour wind, it equaled -16°F with the wind chill factor. When I went back outside into the arctic breeze, something else had changed, besides the increasingly frigid weather. The sky had dimmed, and a soft pinkish glow enveloped the camp. Each evening had gotten a little darker, but nothing prepared me for that first arctic sunset. I grabbed my camera from my quarters and made my way to the bow of *Barge 212*, joining The Bear and three other remaining crew-members, as the sun continued to dip below the horizon for the first time since I had been at camp.

A person witnesses many sunsets over the course of their life, and each is unique. The one I experienced that day at the end of a barge, in one of the farthest northern locations on the continent, remains forever engraved in my mind. It was a moment in my life where I felt one of the strongest sensations of spirituality and fulfillment. The spectacular scene lasted for well over fifteen minutes; a feeling of awe and wonder overwhelmed us as we watched without saying a word to one another.

A yellow streak stretched low across the horizon, reflecting across the sea like a knife's edge. The colors in the sky melded into one another like a vibrant watercolor painting, with broad brushstrokes of varying shades of purple and pink blending into one another. Each minute we stared into the seascape, it continued to evolve and become more brilliant. In the foreground, the black form of the *Prudhoe* provided a stark silhouette.

"That'll make a hell of a picture," The Bear said, breaking the silence. I noticed the usual growl spoken out of the side of his mouth sounded softer. As the seasons went by, he had treated me well, assigning me to many of the better projects, and I had stepped up to the challenges. Although our conversations were brief and mostly pertained to the work at hand, I felt as though he provided me the ability to grow, both as a laborer and a person—I never let him down. For those opportunities, I would be forever grateful.

I walked reverently to the edge of the barge. The camera shutter opened and closed, capturing an image I would look back on for many years, remembering how I felt that day.

THE TEMPERATURE DROPPED to -22°F with the wind chill factor. Thick, white-fringed waves rolled in more slowly to camp, making a heavy sloshing sound as they broke against the hulls of the barges. I stood near the bow of *Barge 212* with Ward, a coworker. Icicles hung from the ship lines, dripping down like stalactites.

"I saw a bird flying south today." Ward looked into the gloomy gray sky. "As I watched it disappear, I thought—that bird only has a brain about this big…" He held up his hand, his index and thumb about a half-inch apart. The next day, he was on an airplane home. The crew had dwindled down to The Bear, a company assistant manager named Ted, the remaining cook, and me.

A few days later, a white edge of ice ringed the bay and causeway. It continued to get wider with every hour. The waves, thicker and slushier as the temperature dropped, piled against the growing ice. Each morning I awoke, the white border stretched farther out, smothering the expanse of water. Down to the last days and the fleet slowly freezing in, we spent most of the time inside, doing whatever we could to keep busy and prevent our minds from wandering into the white abyss.

"BRUCE—YOU AWAKE?"

I opened my eyes. "I am now."

"Sorry," Ted said through the partially open door. "You asked me to wake you up if I saw the Northern lights. They're out." He turned and shut the door.

I rolled out of my rack and pulled on a pair of jeans, slipped on my boots, grabbed a coat, and stepped out onto the catwalk. The arctic wind blasted my face as I climbed the stairs to the comm shack, still half asleep. Ted served as the night dispatcher, a shift that could have been the most difficult to pull. He sat on a stool by the radio controls when I entered the comm shack. Next to the handset was a book and a cup of fresh coffee.

"Sorry to wake you, but you said you wanted to see them." Ted pointed to the north.

"Whoa." My eyes adjusted to what hovered in the sky. I had to assure myself that I wasn't still sleeping, and that the patterns slowly swirling across sparkling stars like a curtain caught in a breeze, were real. As though looking through a prism, rainbow-like colors continued to oscillate in slow rhythm, an eerily surreal juxtaposition against a black canvass. Once again, like the first sunset, a sense of peace filled me. All the questions and uncertainties ricocheting in my head felt less critical, and their weight diminished into the myriad of colors in the northern sky.

It was the calm before the storm.

THE WIND PICKED up to over twenty miles per hour, dropping the temperature to -33°. I finished my breakfast as The Bear peered out at the whiteness.

"How good did you guys seal up those exhaust stacks?" he asked.

"Really well." I poured myself another cup of coffee. "We used about a half roll of duct tape on each boat." Before Ward left, we spent several days completing final winterization of all the boats. As per The Bear's instructions, we had stuffed rags down the exhaust stacks of every single boat, then tightly covered the top of each stack with duct tape to prevent drifting snow from entering and traveling down into the engine cylinders.

"The wind might blow that tape off if it gets much stronger." The Bear rubbed at the underside of his beard. "I don't want any snow to get down those stacks over the winter."

I didn't like where the conversation was going.

"How many of those plastic buckets are in the supply shack?" he asked.

"There're a couple stacks of them." I knew I had dictated the next course of action with this answer, because he was well aware we had an ample supply.

"Put a bucket on each of the stacks."

The logistics of this endeavor made absolutely no sense to me. Minus 40° with twenty-mile-per-hour winds did not make for optimum working conditions. To add to the challenge, I needed to set a ladder on the ice-covered decks under each stack. A brief image shot through my head—a bucket catching a gust of wind, and in my attempt to hold on to it, pulling me into the arctic airstream, never to be seen again.

"How do I fasten them down?"

"Use *wire*," he said out of the corner of his mouth, with an extra emphasis on *wire*. "Make at least three wraps around each stack, then more duct tape."

That meant I better take five wraps in order to assure I had adequately fulfilled the mission.

"All right." I looked down into the black circle of coffee. "I'll get to it."

I went to the warm-up shack and pulled on my worn Carhartt coveralls. The season had worn them into nearly unusable condition. The worn and torn fabric represented a history of the season—spots of red deck paint, black hull paint, white and buff for the wheelhouse, and Crowley red for the stacks. Both leg zippers had blown out, so I spent a couple of minutes wrapping them with duct tape to seal up gaps that could fill up with wind and send me airborne above Prudhoe Bay like a giant kite.

I never enjoyed wearing face protection. This venture, however, required it. I pulled a ski mask over my face, then covered my ears with the warmers strapped to the top of my winter hat all season. My bitterness toward the task at hand grew. *To hell with a hard hat— when I get blown off the ladder, bounce off of the bulwark, then tumble onto the ice, it'll only be one more thing that they'll have to gather up.*

I pulled on my gloves and headed to the supply van. By the time I got there, the freezing temperature had already chilled my body. I had to pull hard on the metal handle to get the door open—it felt like the very camp itself was freezing and shutting down with every hour that passed.

Okay, I'll start with two plastic buckets and do one boat at a time. I pointed to one of the stacks in the corner and walked over to it. *Let's see—there are fifteen boats in the fleet, two stacks per boat, but the triple screw has three stacks—and there are four of them. That makes thirty-four.* I made three stacks of ten, and one stack of four, counting as I went along—*one, two, three… thirty-two, thirty-three, thirty-four. Need a reel of wire from the shelf next to the tool bench. And a roll of duct tape. Put it all in one of the buckets to carry it out there.* I took my time as I looked around the shack. *Okay, will I need anything else?*

It was then when I noticed exactly how loud my internal voice echoed, debating my actions.

"How long has that been going on?" I asked out loud. *I don't know. I can't remember when it began—minutes, hours, days, or maybe months.*

"Crap!"

I opened the door and made my way to the first boat and set the bucket near the bulwark, away from the direction of the wind, and grabbed a ladder from the 212. Climbing onto the *Kavik River*, the cuff of my coveralls caught the edge of the railing and I almost tumbled overboard.

If it can, it will… I heard Lee say. Apparently, other voices had joined in the conversation.

I looked up at the comm shack. The Bear had made his way up to it, and looked down at me with binoculars. I propped the ladder against the stack, and it slipped a couple of inches on the deck before wedging itself against the bulwark. *Oh yeah, this is going to be fun.*

I climbed the ladder one-handed, carrying a bucket filled with wire and duct tape in my other hand. Once on top, I wedged the wire between a rung of the ladder and the stack, then stuck the tape in my coverall pocket. I quickly pulled the bucket over the top of the exhaust stack.

Hey Lee, tell us an industrial accident story... I heard Mike say.

Shut the fuck up, Mike, I'm trying to work here. I pushed the bucket around to test its stability. *The wind seems to push the bucket down, and not pull it up. Maybe this will work.* The wire was a different story, and the freezing temperature made it stiffer than I ever thought possible. Wrapping it with covered hands was near impossible, so I stashed my gloves in my pocket and continued without them, pulling the wire through a hole in the bucket where the bail handle connected, before my fingers became numb.

I invented the plastic rollers on paint can handles... said the man I had met on the Seattle bus before my first season at the North Slope. *Had I really met that guy?*

Are you sure you want to spend five months up there without a break? That's a long time to be away... Chris said.

Yes. Yes it is.

I wrapped the wire four times around the stack, the cold air making it more and more difficult as I continued. With the final wrap completed, I threaded the wire back through the opposite hole in the bucket, then did my best to tie it all tight and cover it completely with duct tape. *One down.*

Every day's a holiday, every meal's a banquet... Bourke said. *What a racket!* Angelo, the cook, chimed in.

I squinted my eyes and peered into the whiteness due north. The bay had disappeared—only a flat tabletop of nothingness. I wondered if Panuk had hunkered down in the warmth of his home back at Kaktovic. I thought of Lee, and whether he was still alive. *He's already gone—or wandering somewhere out in the arctic void, trying to find his way home.*

I completed the second stack, then moved on to the next boat, the *Meridian*. Other workers had re-painted it three times after the first season I had painted it. I thought my paint job would last forever, or at least hold up for a few years. *Nothing is permanent, nothing is long-lasting—everything is ever-changing.*

The cold continued to seep through layers of clothing—coveralls, jeans, thermal underwear, long-sleeved work shirt, hooded sweatshirt, and headgear. It numbed my mind, reminding me of a prior experience. I had tried to bury the memory. After a late work night at the German bar in Denver, Chris and I had been on our way back home to Boulder. My truck stalled on the highway. A load of bad gas required me to periodically replace the fuel filter, so I crawled under the truck with a screwdriver and vice-grips. The temperature was below freezing. Gas dripped down my arms as the traffic rushed by, the sound of rubber tires across a frozen highway. After replacing the filter, we made it home. I curled up on the bathroom floor. Maybe because of the cold, pressure from school, or a panic attack, I had experienced total mental detachment—a dark, cold void that could easily have pulled me under if I allowed it to. I remained on the floor for almost an hour as Chris lay asleep in bed, unaware of my spiraling state of mind. Forcing myself to stand, I finally made it to bed. For many days later, unyielding cold, and the smell of gasoline, invaded my senses. I told no one of the experience.

I completed wrapping the stacks on the last boat. It had taken me a full day to secure all the buckets and darkness had set in. I shuffled into the galley—cold, tired, and ready for dinner.

"All done?" The Bear asked.

"Yep, finished all of them."

"Think they'll hold for the winter?"

"I think so." I poured myself a hot cup of coffee and sat down. "The wire cinched down tighter than I thought it would." I could see the long season etched in The Bear's eyes. He spent more than a normal amount of time looking at me, and I could tell he saw what I was feeling. I wanted to be the last one out of camp—the guy who shut the door and turned off the generator—but I had completed everything I needed to do.

"We're only going to be here another couple of days," The Bear said. "Ted'll be on his way to the airstrip tomorrow—you should ship out with him."

"Yeah," I said. "Guess it's time to leave."

THE TEMPERATURE hovered at -44°F when I walked down the gangplank of *Barge 213* for the last time. I took one last look at the camp before getting into the same truck I arrived in four years earlier. The fleet of tugboats sat on top of the barges with buckets on each of their stacks, the crane booms were lowered, and everything had been lashed tight to the decks. Long, icicle-laden mooring chains stretched from each of the barges to the side of West Dock. The fleet and all the equipment, void of color and frozen solid into the arctic landscape, resembled a large panorama of white-washed fossils.

We pulled onto the causeway leading to the mainland and Deadhorse, the sound of the generator fading into an increasing wind.

CABIN FEVER

WALKING DOWNSTAIRS, I open the window shades and make my way to the kitchen. Each window frames a landscape of snowflakes descending against a backdrop of pine trees. The heavy winter has temporarily ended another California drought.

Hot coffee releases its rich aroma as it brews in our kitchen, ready for Robbin when she wakes up and comes downstairs. I spent the larger part of the weekend organizing photography from Alaska—artifacts from my early twenties.

To shake a case of cabin fever, I slip on a pair of cross-country skis and head outside. The fresh snow squeaks under my weight as I slide into the forest, thoughts still focused on the photo negatives sitting on my light table. Swirling flakes float in the wind as a neighbor's snowblower drones in the distance, reminding me of the generator back at the Arctic Marine Freighters camp in Prudhoe Bay.

It's amazing how projects get delayed over the years. After returning home from Prudhoe for the last time in 1985, I moved seven times before finally settling into our present home. We've lived here for over twenty-three years and raised a family. I've managed a local business for over thirty-two years. The Alaska photo album and boxes of film moved from place to place, and it wasn't until this last year that I began organizing and scanning the film negatives and slides. I've heard that certain things come along in your life not when you plan for them, but when you are ready for them—and they find you. I find consolation in this thought.

Capturing images of the sprawling Prudhoe Bay oil field and the fragile surrounding area, I often wondered how long it would take for a change in direction—for less destructive and wasteful forms of energy to be developed. Over thirty years later, oil still powers and controls the world. There are over 65,000 oil and gas fields of all sizes worldwide; however, ninety-four percent of known oil is concentrated in fewer than 1,500 major fields. Most of the world's largest fields are in the Middle East, but there are also supergiant oilfields in India, Brazil, Mexico, Venezuela, Kazakhstan, and Russia. Exxon has major leases in the Russian Arctic, and production in that area could be huge. Nigeria, where I once sailed as a merchant marine, is in a state of turmoil. Oil revenue now accounts for two-thirds of their government's funding, and corruption is rampant.

When I worked for a company contracted by the oil companies, it was easy to ignore the consequences of their endeavors. Over thirty years later, I feel as though it's time to confront the storm.

Two of my favorite quotes regarding our dependence on oil are by American astrophysicist Neil deGrasse Tyson: "If aliens did visit us, I'd be embarrassed to tell them we still dig up fossil fuels from the ground as a source of energy," and, "Aliens might be surprised to learn that in a cosmos with limitless starlight, humans kill for energy sources buried in the sand."

As growing snowdrifts surround me, I'm thankful that Tahoe has finally had an above-average winter. Will it last, or will these wild swings of radical weather continue to oscillate out of control? While snow blankets the surrounding mountains, the Standing Rock Sioux Tribe of North Dakota are still fighting the completion of the Dakota Access Pipeline (DAPL). Their goal is to stand for their rights, for water protection, and for future generations of all people. They are fighting against the strongest power in the world—a power that has fueled countless wars between nations.

The Cold War was still in full swing when I sailed to several

Alaskan radar outposts, and the Distant Early Warning Line (DEW Line). I didn't understand how my interest in both big oil and nuclear proliferation were related—why had I always been obsessed with connecting the dots? Today, I realize that both human endeavors offer the greatest threat to the world.

I recently attended a conference in the Marshall Islands in early summer. Lee's story of witnessing the atomic tests at Bikini Atoll always fascinated me. The United States detonated a series of twenty-three nuclear devices between 1946 and 1958 at seven test sites on the reef itself, on the sea, in the air, and underwater. The impact devastated the health and culture of the surrounding island people.

Talking with some of the Marshall Islands people during my visit, I gathered personal accounts of how their lives drastically changed after the testing. I also witnessed firsthand the effects of global warming on the islands, caused by fossil fuel consumption. As if atomic testing wasn't bad enough for the Islanders, rising seas now devour their homes. This small chain of islands in the Pacific Ocean exemplifies my interest and fears of both atomic proliferation and the damages produced by big oil and climate change.

Sheltering ourselves from certain realities is no longer possible. Can we correct our present path, or are we destined to follow it to the end? Natural selection always wins out, and maybe mankind will be responsible for its own demise. But the earth will go on. Time. It's the great equalizer.

While working up north, I gained some of my most long-lasting memories and life lessons. Development of a strong work ethic, coming to terms with life and death situations, and experiencing the strength of camaraderie, all came into play. But most of all, I'm grateful for all the questions my northern sojourn offered. I still grapple over larger issues—the journey continues.

I come to an icy stretch meandering through a grove of pine trees and notice a fresh path recently formed, embedded in the crusty snow. A row of bear prints disappears into the forest. Bears—they remain a common theme in my life.

THE RIVER

I WAKE UP, trying to piece together another dream. Although my home is over 6,000 feet in elevation, and over one-hundred and fifty miles from the ocean, the sea often remains a backdrop to the stories that play in my head as I sleep.

It's now springtime, and the trail in our back forest leading to the Upper Truckee River is clear of snow. An early morning walk will help clear my head. I head out the back door and down the trail, thinking of the crews I once worked with at Arctic Marine Freighters, and the shipmates I sailed with on various tugboats.

I can still hear the distinct tone of each of my crewmates' voices, the way they uniquely tied sentences together, and how some of them colorfully butchered the English language, making it their own. Words said in seriousness, words said in jest, words muttered in frustration, and words cussed in vehement fury. I can still hear Lee's simple words of wisdom, including *Sometimes, you just have to work with what you got.* And I will always remember the laughter and smiles.

Our situation wasn't nearly as dire as fighting in a war or serving in the armed forces. The struggles we overcame were mostly psychological: isolation, loneliness, and fatigue were our enemies. But together, not individually, we all came out the other side feeling as though we had accomplished something important. And like a band of brothers, loyalties to each other grew stronger because of the extreme living conditions.

The past defines a person's direction in life, much like charting a path across a vast ocean. The decisions made along the way, the calculations, the relationships, and the amount of effort put into the endeavor all influence how a sailor feels when they see land on the horizon and put a foot on dock. I considered the four years of working in Prudhoe Bay an adventure—an opportunity to work in a remote location under extreme conditions. Looking back, it was more than that. The time up north helped establish values, create new thoughts, form attitudes, and both strengthen and shatter prior beliefs.

I arrive at an overlook to the Truckee River and sit down at the base of a pine tree. The snowmelt cascades from towering granite peaks, flows across a broad river, under a bridge near town, then into Lake Tahoe. Sun glitters across its surface, an endless dance, and a trout rises near a bend upriver.

A few nights back, Google Earth provided me the opportunity to zoom in on Prudhoe Bay and the end of West Dock where the camp had been located. They had moved most all the equipment down the causeway and the camp, as I remembered it, was long gone. The barges that had carried all the equipment, and the seagoing tugboats that transported them, headed south like everything else. Tugboats are unique, in that they maneuver other vessels by pushing or towing, such as ships in a crowded harbor or narrow canal, or those that cannot move by themselves, like barges, disabled ships, rafts, or oil platforms. They're powerful for their size and strongly built. I always admired these features, and the gritty image they exude.

In a couple of conversations with my old crewmates, we've discussed a road trip to Prudhoe Bay. You can now drive the Haul Road that follows the same general direction of the pipeline. The thought of traveling to Prudhoe creates mixed feelings. It's not the same place, and I'm no longer the same person.

A pine cone falling from a tree causes me to turn around. The path I took to the river is well-worn, and I've walked it seemingly countless times with, and without, Robbin and my family. A few years prior, my son and one of my daughters made their way along the same path under a late afternoon summer sun. My son offered my daughter advice about moving out of the house and how to approach her entrance into college. In the middle of listing recommendations, he abruptly stopped himself and flatly said, "Why am I telling you all this—make your own morals."

I remember the dream.

In past dream sequences, I often board a tugboat bound for places never seen. It's most always present day, and I'm leaving my family, but I know I will see them again. Last night's tugboat dream was different. Once again, I stood on a dock lined with a fleet of boats ready to depart. Daylight had not yet broken, and the engines roared in the early morning twilight, smoke billowing out of their stacks. As I turn to say goodbye, I realize I'm not the one leaving this time. It's my children who each board a different boat, joining other crews, bound for the open sea. Deckhands cast lines from the pier, and I watched each vessel debark for their own destinations. I closed my eyes. The smell of diesel exhaust, rusting metal, and the ocean hung in the air.

The sound of the river reverberates across my overlook perch. I stand to stretch my legs. Bodies of water, no matter how large or small, always draw me close. They provide comfort when it's most needed. Across the meadow several miles away stands Mount Tallac—*Tahlac*, the Washoe Tribe's word for "great mountain." A breeze sweeps across the tops of wild grass in the meadow, and it bends toward Tallac as if in reverence.

Near the top of the world, several hundred miles past towering mountain ranges, wide expanses of tundra end at the edge of the Arctic Ocean. Bowhead whales, walrus, ringed seal, and eider ducks survive in a sea patterned by angular ice. Underneath the surface, fish, zooplankton, and phytoplankton float along currents in a fragile never-ending cycle of survival, as they have for thousands of years.

On the shoreline, a lone polar bear stares into the distance, a wall of ice appearing to hover in the sky.

AUTHOR'S NOTE

In early 2021, Crowley Maritime Corporation formed its New Energy division, strategically focused on diverse services supporting the emerging energy sectors in the United States and adjacent regions. With over fifty years of providing support to the offshore oil and gas industry, the company planned to provide services to the U.S. offshore wind farm industry. Crowley had entered an agreement with Massachusetts' Vineyard Wind I, the first utility-scale offshore wind farm in the nation, scheduled to go online by the end of 2023.

Crowley also announced plans to build and operate a fully electric U.S. tugboat, or eTug. It would be the first all-electric powered harbor tugboat operating without the use of fossil fuel and featured artificial intelligence technology (AI) to increase mariner safety and efficiency. Scheduled to operate at the Port of San Diego's Tenth Avenue Marine Terminal and operational by mid-2023, eTugs would replace ones that consumed over 30,000 gallons of diesel per year and help the company increase efforts toward sustainability and decarbonization.

Crowley Maritime Corporation continues to navigate new waters.

ACKNOWLEDGMENTS

IT'S SEEMINGLY IMPOSSIBLE to mention all the people responsible for the completion of this book. I mostly want to recognize my uncle, Jim Rettig, who had the confidence that I would be a capable worker for Crowley Maritime, and my boss, Bill Payne (The Bear) of Arctic Marine Freighters, who taught me the power of determination and leadership. My gratitude to those mentioned in this book, including Derald Anderson, Christine Blackmon, Jim Bowman, Jim Clark, Dazzlin'D, Kevin Homan, Steve Marinkovich, David Masiel, Tim Payne, Jeff Salenjus, Bill Swan, Mike Thompkins, and Ken Townshend, as well as those not mentioned or whose names were changed, but are all a part of the story.

Thank you to Michael O'Laughlin, my creative writing instructor, whose comments and critical insight made me a better writer and definitely a stronger reader. Thank you, Kim Wyatt, who always supported my writing and recommended I submit to *Cold Flashes: Literary Snapshots of Alaska*, a collection of flash fiction and nonfiction stories and photography published by the University of Alaska Press. My published 433-word piece eventually grew into a 333-page memoir. Two workshops, the Community of Writers, and the Mendocino Writers Conference, both helped me hone this manuscript and I am grateful for all the help and support from both. A huge thank you to Tahoe Writers Works, my fellow writers and workshop family who meets every two weeks, and graciously read every chapter of my manuscript and kept me on task during its writing—I am forever grateful.

A very few of the collection of books that inspired my work include *Breaking Ice for Arctic Oil,* Ross Coen, *Heart of Darkness,* Joseph Conrad, *Rogue River Journal,* John Daniel, *Two Men at the Helm: The First 100 Years of Crowley Maritime Corporation 1892–1992,* Jean Gilbertson, *500 Nations,* Alvin M. Josephy, *Into the Wild,* Jon Krakauer, *2182 Kilohertz,* David Masiel, *Coming into the Country,* John McPhee, *Firecracker Boys,* Dan O'Neill, *The Eskimo and the Oil Man,* Bob Reiss, *Wild,* Cheryl Strayed, *Discovery at Prudhoe Bay,* John M. Sweet, and *Jarhead: A Marine's Chronicle of the Gulf War and Other Battles,* Anthony Swofford.

The deepest thanks to my publisher, Leslie M. Browning, and Homebound Publications. The value of independent publishers and bookstores cannot be underestimated. I am fortunate to be a part of the Homebound writing community and its continued support.

Most of all, thank you to my wife Robbin, who is the most supportive person I have ever known, and Conner, Brianna, and Riley, who were always patient and understanding when it was "dad's writing time." And to my father, mother, brother, sister, entire family, and friends who lent an ear to hear, or time to read my stories.

AUTHOR PHOTOGRAPHS